Conrad's Politics

Conrad's Politics

Community and Anarchy in the Fiction of Joseph Conrad

by Avrom Fleishman

The Johns Hopkins Press, Baltimore

For Sophia

A great man works with the ideas of his age, and regenerates them.... But his own mind has its ordinary side, the regeneration of ideas is not complete, and the notions of the day not only limit the range of his achievement ... but float about unassimilated within his living stream of thought. And thus he will seem to have preached the very superstitions which he combated.

—Bernard Bosanquet

Preface

Conrad has been freed of his reputation as a writer of sea-tales and boys' books,[1] he has been accorded a place in the Great Tradition of English fiction, but he is in danger of acquiring a new mythos that will make that place a straitened one. It is fashionable today to claim for him a tutelary role in the political awakening of the West to the Cold War—to make him into a prophet of Communist tyranny and revolutionary brutality, and his novels into *romans à clef* of the political struggles of our own day. The portrait of Conrad has come to resemble that of an unabashed propagandist—an unironic ironist denouncing radical causes—while his novels have been read as parables of the evils of "statist" societies and the foolishness of the humanitarian sentiments which give rise to them.[2]

These notions of Conrad's political beliefs are summarily stated by Leo Gurko in a recent study; his is the portrait of an old-fashioned conservative (or, as Gurko says, of an ultra-modern conservative):

> He was acutely distrustful of democracy in an age when the egalitarian spirit continued to flourish. His temper was rooted in the traditions of a landed gentry. . . . He took a dim view of revolutions and radical movements—just before they spread through the world and became respectable. He did not believe in the reform of institutions as long as the human heart remained unaltered, a doctrine which ran counter to the theory of the welfare state. And though he was a lifelong critic of imperialism and colonialism . . . it was not out of special feeling for the native populations. . . . [3]

Such judgments receive their boldest statement in the impressions of Conrad's early collaborator, Ford Madox Ford: "Conrad was, at heart, an aristo-royalist apologist; the whole Left in politics was forever temperamentally

---

[1] Nonetheless, the fever of curiosity about Conrad's romantic career, which has plagued criticism since the earliest reviews, shows no signs of abatement. Two recently published books based on the "biographical fallacy" of identifying an author's imaginative re-creation with his actual experience are Jerry Allen, *The Sea Years of Joseph Conrad* (Garden City, N.Y., 1965), and Norman Sherry, *Conrad's Eastern World* (Cambridge, 1966). In this sort of enterprise, it becomes possible for an enthusiastic journalist's book to be more rewarding than a competent literary scholar's, a sure sign that the talents of the latter are being misused. Miss Allen's book is a valuable quarry of non-biographical data for Conrad's treatment of political history, not only in her sections on *Nostromo* (p. 22 ff.) and *The Arrow of Gold* (p. 63 ff.) but also in her account of Berau, in Borneo, during the period of Conrad's visits (pp. 231–32 *et passim*).

[2] E.g., Robert Haugh, *Joseph Conrad: Discovery in Design* (Norman, Okla., 1957), p. 146 *et passim*.

[3] *Joseph Conrad: Giant in Exile* (New York, 1962), p. 1.

suspect for him, and, at the bottom of his heart, all his writing wistfully tended towards the restoration of the Kingdom of Poland, with its irresponsible hierarchy of reckless and hypersophistically civilized nobility."[4] These formulas for Conrad will, in the following pages, be found irrelevant to a sustained view of Conrad's fiction and the political sentiments from which it derived. Neither "conservative" nor "liberal" properly identifies his politics, and I shall seek terms closer to the philosophical and literary sources of his imagination.

From another political standpoint, there have been attempts—ever since the highly original and provocative study, *The Polish Heritage of Joseph Conrad*, by Gustav Morf—to see Conrad as an incipient or repressed revolutionary and to read his fiction as the record of his struggle with these latent tendencies. More recently, Irving Howe has restated the "Morf thesis," holding Conrad's writings to be an allegory of his desertion of the Polish independence movement. Howe explains Conrad's subsequent rejection of his father's revolutionary activities by the dictum, "When the children of revolutionaries revolt, it is against revolution. . . ."[5] The virtue of this approach is to link Conrad's more conservative statements to the doctrines of the anarchists who populate several of his tales: "Conservatism is the anarchism of the fortunate, anarchism the conservatism of the deprived. Against the omnivorous state, conservatism and anarchism equally urge resistance by the individual."[6] Yet Howe, together with Conrad's less politically sophisticated critics, assumes that the author was as conservative as he seems superficially to be. There is no doubt that Conrad made himself out at times to be a perfect British gentleman, with the proper political attitudes to suit, but an examination of his political essays and an unprejudiced reading of his novels reveals that the posture could not be long maintained.[7]

---

[4] Ford Madox Ford [Hueffer], *Portraits from Life* (Boston and New York, 1937), p. 65. The novelist will be referred to as Hueffer in this study, as that is the name used in most references to his relationship to Conrad.

[5] *Politics and the Novel* (orig. pub., 1957; New York, 1960), p. 78.

[6] *Ibid.*, p. 84.

[7] Edward W. Said, in *Joseph Conrad and the Fiction of Autobiography* (Cambridge, Mass., 1966), develops the view that Conrad's status as Englishman and author—after his identities of Pole and seaman were discarded—was a major tension in his mind and art until that tension was somewhat assuaged by his univocal response to World War I. I have not been able to respond to the many insights into Conrad's career in this book, published after my own study was completed. Said offers a complementary reading of little-considered letters and stories which I have examined for their political import. In particular, I must acknowledge his

A notable advance on the problem—at least in thoroughness of presenta-
tion—has been made in the only book-length study of Conrad's politics, by
Eloise Knapp Hay.[8] Mrs. Hay's great merit is to instill in the reader a sense
of Conrad's positive ideals of social cohesion—though she makes only
a passing effort to define them. She does, indeed, mention Burke, Hegel,
and Rousseau, but does not go on to link them with the novelist in the
tradition of organicist thought on the social community. When the conclusions of her study have been extracted from her commentary, they do not
sharpen the blurred image of Conrad that has come down to us from his less
exhaustive critics. The standard impression of him as an irascible anti-
revolutionist, lifelong Polish nationalist, and skeptical Tory is allowed to
stand, with minor modifications. A fresh approach to Conrad's political
background, opinions, and fiction reveals the growth in depth and flexibility
of his thought on the leading ideologies of his time, his winning free of the
prejudices with which he began, and his achievement of a grand vision of
social community—maintained with an ironic perception of the forces on
the present political scene that inhibit its realization.

A full accounting of Conrad's political views makes it difficult to categorize
him in any of the readily available rubrics, and the political implications of
his fiction are sufficiently subtle to leave any interpretation of them as doctri-
nal statements adrift in the wake of his art. The present study maintains that
the novels must be read as dramatic expressions of a complex political imagination, and are therefore not reducible to political ideology. It attempts
to show, moreover, that Conrad was open to the prevailing political ideas
of his time, those which it inherited from a century-old debate on the bases of
social philosophy, and that the fiction which derived from his speculations
was more complicated than received opinion would have it—indeed, was
much the better art because of its rich intellectual tradition.

It will be necessary to set the fiction aside for a time to review Conrad's
political essays and his letters on political subjects. It will also at times be
tempting to speak of works of art as though they were mere bearers of
political or other ideas. This procedure will be justified in the degree to which
it eventually adumbrates the artistic embodiment of those ideas. It is, more-

---

antecedence in publishing on two important points: the similarity of Conrad's
thought to that of F. H. Bradley (pp. 103, 108–9), and the relevance to Conrad of
the distinction between "community" and "individuality" (p. 196 *et passim*);
Said also suggests but discounts the influence of Rousseau (p. 53).

[8] *The Political Novels of Joseph Conrad* (Chicago and London, 1963).

over, not only necessary but desirable to take this course, since cursory judgments of Conrad's political writings have led to mistaken notions not only of his ideas but of his art.

It need hardly be said that this account of Conrad will not please every reader. This is to be expected by the nature of the subject—both because of the political commitments it is likely to engage and because of the long-standing tradition of seeing Conrad in a certain light. Beyond the usual appeal for the reader's indulgence, I must add an appeal to his self-critical objectivity.

Acknowledgments

I wish to thank Earl R. Wasserman, David Spring, and Robert M. Slusser of The Johns Hopkins University for their advice on special aspects of my research. My greatest debt is to J. Hillis Miller, of Johns Hopkins, who guided and encouraged me throughout my research and writing.

The librarians of The Johns Hopkins University, Columbia University, the University of Minnesota, the New York Public Library (including the Berg Collection), the Université Catholique de Louvain, the Bibliothèque Nationale de Belgique, the Universiteit van Amsterdam, and the Instituut voor Sociale Geschiedenis of Amsterdam have all been most helpful. My gratitude goes also to the Belgian-American Educational Foundation, for the fellowship under which I did preliminary research for this book, and to the University of Minnesota, for a Faculty Research Grant which aided in the preparation of the manuscript.

My thanks go to J. M. Dent & Sons, representing the Trustees of the Joseph Conrad Estate, for permission to quote from the collected edition of Conrad's works; to the Henry W. and Albert A. Berg Collection of The New York Public Library, Astor, Lenox, and Tilden Foundations, for permission to quote from the manuscript letter to Ramsay MacDonald; to Frederick R. Karl, for advising me on some of the material in his projected edition of Conrad's letters; to *ELH—A Journal of English Literary History*, in which my article on *The Secret Agent*, which forms the bulk of Chapter VII of this book, originally appeared; and to *Victorian Studies*, for allowing me to use material which originally appeared in my review of Eloise Knapp Hay's *The Political Novels of Joseph Conrad*.

I wish also to thank Mrs. Jean Owen, of The Johns Hopkins Press, for many saving graces, and my typist, Miss Delphine Swanson.

My wife took little interest in my work, did no typing, and failed to insulate me from our children. She helped immeasurably simply by being there.

Contents

Abbreviations

References to Conrad's works are to the edition published by Dent from 1946 forward. Pagination and, apparently, text are similar to those of earlier editions published by Dent. Reference style here is that of parenthetical incorporations in the text. The titles of certain works have been abbreviated as follows (for the reader's convenience, the date of first publication is included):

AF   *Almayer's Folly: A Story of an Eastern River*   1895
AG   *The Arrow of Gold: A Story Between Two Notes*   1919
Inheritors   *The Inheritors: An Extravagant Story** 1901
LE   *Last Essays*   1926
LJ   *Lord Jim*   1900
MS   *The Mirror of the Sea: Memories and Impressions*   1906
NLL   *Notes on Life and Letters*   1921
NN   *The Nigger of the "Narcissus": A Tale of the Forecastle*   1898
OI   *An Outcast of the Islands*   1896
PR   *A Personal Record: Some Reminiscences*   1912
Rescue   *The Rescue: A Romance of the Shallows*   1920
Rover   *The Rover*   1923
SA   *The Secret Agent: A Simple Tale*   1907
SS   *A Set of Six*   1908
Suspense   *Suspense: A Napoleonic Novel*   1925
TH   *Tales of Hearsay*   1925
TLS   *'Twixt Land and Sea*   1912
TU   *Tales of Unrest*   1898
UWE   *Under Western Eyes*   1911
WT   *Within the Tides*   1915
Youth   *Youth, and Two Other Stories*   1902

Other abbreviations, mainly to editions of Conrad's letters, are introduced with full bibliographical information in the notes.

*Not included in the Dent edition.

Chapter I

THE POLISH MYTH

Joseph Conrad. Courtesy of the Beinecke Library of Yale University

For the only sound ground of democracy is ... unselfish toil in a common cause.

—Conrad to the Polish
National Committee in America

The widely accepted account of Conrad's national origins and their shaping of his career—an account fostered by his Polish critics and in some measure by Conrad himself—cannot be maintained after close examination. The myth of Conrad's Polish background runs somewhat as follows: his nationality, it is never doubted, was Polish. His father was a well-born aristocrat, an other-worldly romantic, a cosmopolitan *littérateur*, yet had enough political dynamism to become a nationalist leader and national hero. His mother was an angelic figure who died young, in voluntary exile with her husband, a victim of the so-called barbarism of Russia. Conrad's uncle and guardian, Tadeusz Bobrowski, was a complacent bourgeois, practical to the point of pedantry—the chafing harness from which the high-spirited colt had to break away. Conrad's youthful plan of emigration was imperative in order that he escape the civil disqualifications of a rebel's son and avoid conscription in the Russian army—in short, it was an escape from tyranny. His literary career was a ceaseless effort to apologize for—or, through allegory, to relive—the original sin of deserting his country in the time of its prostration. Finally, he made his return to the fold during World War I by political and propaganda activity for a resurgent Poland.

The definitive account of Conrad's Polish origins remains to be written by a critic of English literature who can read Polish. In the present state of our knowledge, English and American critics cannot even agree on the proper translation of a letter in which Conrad is alternately said to have attempted suicide or to have been wounded in a duel. More important, though less sensational, matters remain to be resolved, matters of Polish history, on which Poles are strongly partisan and on which a foreign commentator is likely to be accused of naïveté. Such risks must be taken, however, if we are to determine the influences of Conrad's youth which most deeply touched his later career.

It should be noted at the outset that the definition of Conrad's original nationality requires qualification. Conrad's sense of being Polish was based not on political or legal circumstances but on cultural and familial heritage. He was born in an area of the Ukraine, in the neighborhood of Berdichev, which has at best only a marginal claim to being considered Polish. Historically, it was a conquest of the Kingdom of Poland that was held for four centuries preceding the First Partition of Poland in 1793; by a similar exercise of power, it was made over to Russia and during the nineteenth century became an integral part of the Russian state, although the native population was no more Russian than it had been Polish; in the Treaty of Brest-Litovsk establishing Polish independence, it was well within the Russian side of the British-proposed Curzon Line, drawn on the basis of population and history; *pace* the intransigent *émigrés* in the West, it is not claimed by Poland today.

The population statistics and the social structure of Conrad's native region partly account for the anomalies of its history and of his national status. Only 3 per cent of the population was Polish, and this small minority constituted the landowning class—which had seized control during Polish suzerainty—while the native Ukrainians were serfs. Needless to say, these latter, the overwhelming majority of the people, had no interest in the political restoration of their Polish overlords.

One of the foremost authorities on eastern European history sums up the consequences of this demographic imbalance:

> In the nineteenth century, when nationalism and democracy destroyed the foundations of the old Polish commonwealth, when the Lithuanian and Ruthenian [Ukrainian] peasants awakened, like the Poles themselves, to national consciousness, the Poles, similar therein to the German nationalists, continued to regard themselves as mandated by history with a civilizing mission in the vast expanses of the East. They insisted on the restoration of the historical boundaries of the pre-nationalist commonwealth as a Polish national state in the age of nationalism. This romantic nationalism based on the veneration of a past without foundation in the present . . . prepared the soil for the Polish messianic Slavism with its metaphysical dreamlands, its poetical grandiloquence, and its noble delusions.[1]

Considered in the light of his social origins in the landholding gentry—separated from the mass of people around him by culture, religion, language, and class—Conrad's Polishness can account for many of the peculiarities of his political attitudes, not only his occasionally rabid nationalism but also his more subtle feelings about imperialism. The analogy between Polish landlords and British, Dutch, or Belgian colonists might well have been repressed in later years, but there must have been an insidious sense of alienation in early childhood, a sense of living among strangers, surrounded by darkness.

Conrad's awareness of his alien status in his own homeland was renewed at the moment when he came to write his closest approach to an autobiography, *A Personal Record*. He recalled the destruction of his uncle

---

[1] Hans Kohn, *Pan-Slavism: Its History and Ideology* (rev. ed., orig. pub., 1953; New York, 1960), p. 30.

Nicholas' estate by serfs in 1863, when they were given carte blanche by Russian troops tracking down Polish insurrectionists (*PR*, pp. 57–63). Conrad put the blame on the Russians, of course, but the precarious status of the Poles amid an indifferent or hostile peasantry is implicit in this narrative. It is not lost on the reader that the Russians' role is simply to unleash the resentments held in check beneath a thin veneer of Polish authority.

A similar covert meaning of the facts is to be found in Conrad's accounts of his father's revolutionary activity. Conrad made every effort to deny the implications of that well-known patrimony; he was incensed at every suggestion that his father's extremism was in any way related to that of the left-wing revolutionaries about whom he wrote so disparagingly. Yet he always acknowledged that his father's revolutionary approach to political change was doomed to fail; if its motives were better than those of the socialist revolutionaries, the enterprise was equally futile and inept.

What Conrad failed to acknowledge, though he may have known it, is that in practice, and even by alliance, both nationalists and socialists in Poland were terrorist in method. Indeed, Apollo Korzeniowski himself changed from a mystical program of national redemption to the more aggressive forms of social action. The standard history describes his development in this way:

> At Kiev . . . there arose soon after the death of Nicholas a Polish society, called the Trinity. Its moving spirit was Apollo Korzeniowski, the father of Joseph Conrad. At first its objective was purely spiritual: to nourish resistance to the idea then insinuating itself into the class from which most of the students came that national emancipation could be achieved through political co-operation with Russia or with the Tsar. . . .
> Slowly and imperceptibly but inevitably "The Trinity" became political. By 1858 its members had established contact with Polish students in all parts of the Russian Empire as well as with General Mieroslawski in Paris who allied himself with the anarchist Bakunin.[2]

Thus the visionary artist found himself compromised by association with the most violent of anarchic forces, for one of the charges which exiled him named him as founder of a group known as "Mieroslawski's Reds."

Korzeniowski's career was, in fact, vigorous, headlong, and brief. In the

[2] W. F. Reddaway *et al.*, *The Cambridge History of Poland* (orig. pub., 1941; London, 1950–51), II, 369–70.

grand division within Polish political circles between Whites (adherents of cooperation with the new and conciliatory Czar Alexander II) and Reds (uncompromising in their territorial demands and activist in their methods), Conrad's father was a mainstay of the Reds. Paying no heed to his brother-in-law Tadeusz Bobrowski's perceptive indications of the need for a promise of land reform before the peasantry could be expected to support any movement for Polish independence, Korzeniowski rushed off to try to give a Polish cast to a Ukrainian peasant revolt, but the revolt was suppressed with the support of the Polish gentry, who were more interested in protecting their property than in Polish independence.

In addition to some posturing in peasant dress on the streets of Warsaw and a campaign to encourage the idea of Poland's historical claim to Lithuania (whose own national self-consciousness was beginning to assert itself), Korzeniowski's major achievement was his initiative in founding the so-called City Committee, from which emerged the Central National Committee that gave direction to the Revolution of 1863. But Korzeniowski was active two years before the great event, and four days after his group was established he was arrested and his political career terminated.

In his attempts to exculpate or ignore his father's extremism, Conrad fell victim to a related error of omission: it was his uncle, Stefan Bobrowski, rather than his father, who was the guiding spirit of the 1863 revolution. In *The Cambridge History of Poland*, the younger Bobrowski is mentioned throughout the account of the revolution. It was he who in 1858–59 enlisted the support of Russian officers in St. Petersburg; he, together with his friend Zygmunt Padlewski, drew up the Central National Committee's proclamation of itself as the provisional government, on the basis of "unconditional and permanent emancipation and the complete enfranchisement of every person in the Polish realm without regard to race, religion or previous condition of bondage"[3] (a position far in advance of the program of Korzeniowski's or of any other group); it was he who initiated the reconciliation of the Reds and Whites, which brought the revolt financial support from the bourgeoisie and aristocracy. Bobrowski was killed in a mysterious duel in 1862, before the revolt broke out,[4] but the political acumen with which he turned the rev-

---

[3] *Ibid.*, p. 376.

[4] Zdzisław Najder, in the Introduction to his edition, *Conrad's Polish Background: Letters to and from Polish Friends* (trans. Halina Carroll [London, New York, and Toronto, 1964], p. 7), states that Bobrowski "was murdered by his right-wing political opponents in a staged duel," but does not indicate his evidence for the statement.

olutionary organization into a popular front on the basis of an incisive interpretation of the economic and social needs of his country went far toward
making the Revolution of 1863 an impressive revelation of continuing
Polish nationalism.

It has been mentioned that Korzeniowski's student organization made
contact with General Mieroslawski's supporters and, through them, with
Bakunin. The subsequent development of this anarchist link reveals the
difference between Bobrowski and Korzeniowski in fundamental political
beliefs and practical ability. Acting outside Bobrowski's command, Korzeniowski's organization followed its own devices:

> Two complete "governments" . . . were set up in Warsaw: the Central
> National Committee, which considered itself an outpost of the universal
> liberal movement and counted for moral support on general European
> pionion; and the Revolutionary Committee, the organ of General Miero-
> slawski, which counted for moral support on its affiliations in the House
> of Bonaparte and for military success on the realization of some ancient
> prophecy of the sage Wernhora that the outcome of Poland's long struggle
> with Muscovy would be decided in "Rus" by a spontaneous rising for
> Poland of the peasantry of the steppe.[5]

Stefan Bobrowski's politics, therefore, stood in the tradition of Western
liberalism, the main stream of the nationalist independence movement not
only in Poland but throughout Europe. Korzeniowski, by his alliance with
Mieroslawski, reveals himself as a Pan-Slavist mystic, believing in the re-
generative power of the (non-Polish) peasantry. Korzeniowski's allies were
unwilling to commit themselves to real political action; as the *Cambridge
History* puts it, "when the test came the old general [Mieroslawski] proved
impotent. Bobrowski and Padlewski wielded the actual power."[6]

It is, then, on the Bobrowski side of Conrad's heritage that we must look
to find the Western, democratic-nationalist tradition which Conrad in his
later years claimed for himself. It is another Bobrowski, Tadeusz—although
his intellectual influence has rarely been taken seriously—who emerges as
the political, as well as moral and practical, mentor by whom Conrad's
mind was shaped. Tadeusz Bobrowski opposed Korzeniowski's "radicalism"
because it was not truly radical: it left the fundamental economic and social
problem, the ownership of the land by the Polish gentry rather than by the
peasants who worked it, unresolved and scarcely considered. Korzeniowski

---

[5] *Cambridge History of Poland*, II, 377.
[6] *Ibid.*, p. 378.

stood on a platform derived from the constitution of 1793, proclaimed under the aegis of the Prussian and Russian autocracies during their partition of Poland, which provided for a continuation of the *ancien régime*, retained serfdom, lacked wide (not to speak of universal) suffrage, and placed almost exclusive power in the hands of the aristocracy. Bobrowski's view of Korzeniowski's politics is a pointed one:

> Though he considered himself a sincere democrat and others even considered him "extremist" and "red" he had a hundredfold more traits of the gentry in him (as I often told him) than I had in myself, though I was not suspected, either by him or by others, of being a democrat. In point of fact, he had an exceedingly tender and soft heart—hence his great sympathy for the poor and oppressed; and this was why he and others thought he was a democrat. But these were only impulses of the heart and mind inherent in a member of a good family of the gentry; they were not truly democratic convictions. I could never establish the real composition of his political and social ideas, apart from a hazy inclination towards a republican form of state incorporating some equally hazy agglomeration of human rights as set out by the Constitution of May the Third—which for our times was not far-reaching enough.[7]

Under Bobrowski's tutelage, Conrad was subjected to a program of minimizing the romantic ne'er-do-well Korzeniowski side of his nature in favor of the mature and enlightened Bobrowski heritage. He learned to recognize the obsoleteness of his father's theories, both in method and aim. Conrad's subsequent political principles and aversion to radical violence were shaped by his uncle's mentorship, not by his father's example. Despite much chafing at the bit, Conrad retained his lessons in the very process of revolt against them. "I cannot write about Tadeusz Bobrowski, my Uncle, guardian and benefactor without emotion. Even now, after ten years, I still feel his loss. He was a man of great character and unusual qualities of mind. . . . I attribute to his devotion, care, and influence, whatever good qualities I may possess."[8] So wrote the mature Conrad in an autobiographical account to a Polish historian, and it behooves us to take seriously the intellectual and moral influence of this father-figure.

The most comprehensive exposition of Bobrowski's politics and their underlying philosophy is his letter of October 28 (November 9), 1891, in the year of Conrad's emotional crisis after returning from the Congo.

---

[7] *Pamiętniki* (Lwów, 1900), I, 362; quoted in Jocelyn Baines, *Joseph Conrad: A Critical Biography* (London, 1960), p. 8.

[8] Najder (ed.), *Conrad's Polish Background*, p. 239, letter of December 5, 1903.

Bobrowski's consolatory and pedagogical letter must be quoted at length for its detailed anticipation of Conradian themes and attitudes:

My dear lad, whatever you were to say about a good or bad balance of the forces of nature, about good or bad social relationships, about right or wrong social systems, about the boundless stupidity of crowds fighting for a crust of bread—and ending up in nothingness—none of this will be new!! You will never control the forces of nature, for whether blind or governed by Providence, in each case they have their own pre-ordained paths; and you will also never change the roads along which humanity goes, for there exists in social development an historical evolutionary compulsion which is slow but sure, and which is governed by the laws of cause and effect derived from the past and affecting the future. If, on this road, the will and work of man mean anything—if in this field all the endeavours of man and their chosen individuals—the geniuses—are effective—everyone may and even ought to contribute to it his hand or head, according to his strength and talents—but not himself dreaming of being the chosen Apostle of the people—for that way he may only meet with bitter disappointment—but rather thinking of himself as a modest tiny ant which by its insignificant toil in fulfilling its modest duty secures the life and existence of the whole nest! . . . Our nation unfortunately, as Słowacki so truly remarked—although he himself was not immune from the accusation—is a "peacock among nations," which in simple prose means that we are a collection of proclaimed and generally unrecognized celebrities—whom no one knows, no one acknowledges, and no one ever will! So that if both Individuals and Nations were to make "duty" their aim, instead of the ideal of greatness, the world would certainly be a better place than it is! And those crowds "aiming instinctively at securing only bread," so detestable to all visionaries, have their raison d'être: to fulfill the material needs of life; and they no longer seem detestable when, as often happens, a more thorough evaluation reveals that they embellish their existence, their work, and often even their short-comings, by some higher moral idea of a duty accomplished, of a love for their family or country to whom they leave the fruit of their endeavours and labours in the form of sacrifices or bequests.[9]

In this letter (which goes on at some length with the same burden), Bobrowski expresses a mixture of moral idealism and worldly-wise pragmatism reminiscent of Stein, who plays a similar role *in loco parentis* with the hero of *Lord Jim*—and who is given a characteristic homiletic phrase which appears in this same letter, "*usque ad finem.*" The influence of Bobrowski's letter may be seen even more clearly in "Heart of Darkness," where Conrad dealt with

[9] *Ibid.*, pp. 153–54.

the experience which had caused his depression, and with a "genius" who "dreams of being the chosen Apostle of the people." While the Bobrowski letter anticipates these and other Conradian themes, its direct reference is to the frivolous career of Apollo Korzeniowski and the nationalistic messianism of his successors. In place of their wish fulfillments, Bobrowski advocates stoic patience, hard work, and the renunciation of egotism. These values, designed to correct his Polish tradition, are the source of Conrad's own guiding principles, of what we shall have occasion to describe as the doctrine of organic community, the work ethic, and the critique of individualism.

.Bobrowski's letters sowed the seeds of change in Conrad's political attitudes. In answer to the despairing remarks condemning the crowds "aiming instinctively at securing only bread," Bobrowski proposes the ethical value of fulfilling familial and national duties by material means. To this recommendation of temperance and compassion in judging the working classes may be traced the later political sophistication with which Conrad replaced his early scorn of the proletariat. Finally, the letter contains anticipations of Conrad's agnostic position in the late nineteenth-century debate on evolution and its social and religious consequences: Bobrowski here, as Conrad would do later, assumes a physical and historical determinism, moots the question of theist design ("whether blind or governed by Providence"), and rests his faith on the human capacity to modify an alien universe by dint of free will and dedicated effort.

Most critics have assumed—partly because of Conrad's ambiguity on the subject—that his emigration from Poland was an escape from the limitations placed on a young man's career by the partitioning powers because of his revolutionary ancestry. A closer look at his words indicates that he might well have stayed in Poland, particularly in the city of Cracow in Austrian-held Galicia, where he was brought up by his father after their return from exile. Indeed, with his Bobrowski connections, and despite his Korzeniowski name, he could have enjoyed a successful career in government service. It would even have been possible to satisfy his wish to become a seaman and in the same motion avoid entirely the service of the hated Prussia and Russia. "The feeling against the Austrian service was not so strong, and I dare say there would have been no difficulty in finding my way into the Naval School of Pola. . . . the truth is that what I had in view was not a naval career, but the sea" (PR, p. 121).

To ask why Conrad left Poland is to ask what the sea could have meant to a Polish youth of his time. His biographer, Jocelyn Baines, probably comes closest to suggesting an answer when he remarks that the sea was the one thing in the world for which it was then absolutely necessary to leave land-locked Poland.[10] To desire the sea was, then, equivalent to an absolute rejection of Poland. How could so intense a desire to separate himself from a nation to which his forebears had been so deeply attached have arisen in Conrad?

For one thing, there was the contempt he felt for all things Germanic. His education in the Austrian zone was stiflingly pedantic (*LE*, p. 12).[11] For another, at the age of fourteen he made a thoroughgoing disavowal of the Catholic faith in which he had been raised.[12] But basically the lack of Polish self-government made Poland unbearable, and the Poles themselves, with the special psychology of defeated and occupied nations, also contributed their mite. Conrad was not alone in his desire to escape. Polish intellectuals of the older generation, like the poet Kraszewski, felt obliged to make passionate exhortations to Polish youth from their own places of exile: "Endure, do not run away, do not emigrate, for that is always a cowardly thing to do . . . and above all, be done with insurrections."[13]

Conrad's restlessness was a widespread feeling in a defeated and dis-membered nation, whose youth inevitably looked abroad for its culture. J. H. Retinger, Conrad's collaborator in propaganda work in behalf of Polish independence during World War I, has written of their generation's experience in the Poland of the postrevolutionary era:

> We, Polish youngsters of the latter part of the nineteenth century, felt like hopeless automatons, moving blindly in mansions of many rooms, which once were painted with glory and splendor, but now were tarnished, because untouched by the brush of new accomplishments. The history of Poland had been at a standstill for over a century. Dust of many sorrowful years covered the multi-coloured traditions of the past; windows were barred with grilles of inept impossibilities, doors were closing on them-

[10] Baines, *Joseph Conrad*, p. 32.

[11] Paul Wohlfarth, in "Joseph Conrad and Germany" (*German Life and Letters*, XVI, n.s. [1963], 81–88), calls attention to the life-long prejudice against Germany which Conrad developed from his first schooling, but the article does not, unfortunately, describe the curriculum at that time, which may have formed his attitude.

[12] *Letters from Joseph Conrad, 1895–1924*, ed. Edward Garnett (London, 1928), p. 185, letter of December 22, 1902 (hereafter cited as "Garnett Letters").

[13] Quoted in *Cambridge History of Poland*, II, 386.

selves, giving way only to those who had the impudence or the indignity to abandon the past. . . . [14]

Despite his errors of diction, Retinger conveys the feeling of cultural suffocation and of political impotence that Conrad must have experienced.

It was natural that among the reactions of the younger generation there should be a fad of oriental exoticism, of whatever was most remote and apparently unattainable; this was the gambit of the literary movement known as "Young Poland." In the last decades of the nineteenth century, this taste became linked to a predilection for French Symbolism, Satanism, and other forms of neo-Romanticism from Hugo and Baudelaire to Mallarmé and Huysmans.[15] To poets who found themselves in a disaffected mood, recalling that of Rimbaud, the sea was the route to the remote, open, and unexplored.

As the well-known story has it, Conrad pointed to the white (unexplored) portion of a map of Africa and intuitively predicted, "I shall go *there*." It is no accident that the largest part of his subsequent merchant marine service —as well as most of his early fiction—took place in Africa and the Orient. Nor is it necessary to seek far to explain his absorption in French *fin-de-siècle* literature and his sharing of its subjectivity and pessimism.

To feel to the full the tragic character of Conrad's emigration—tragic not only because he was caught between mutually exclusive imperatives but also because he embodied the social problem of his generation—one has only to examine the language in which he described his choice: "He [i.e., Conrad himself] had not known how to preserve against his impulses the order and continuity of his life—so that at times it presented itself to his conscience as a series of betrayals" (*NLL*, p. 149); "I had to justify my existence to myself, to redeem a tacit moral pledge" (*NLL*, p. 151); "I verily believe mine was the only case of a boy of my nationality and antecedents taking a, so to speak, standing jump out of his racial surroundings and associations" (*PR*, p. 121). "I have the conviction that there are men of unstained rectitude who are ready to murmur scornfully the word desertion" (*PR*, p. 35), he feared. Nor was he wrong in this expectation.

[14] *Conrad and His Contemporaries: Souvenirs* (London, 1941), p. 13.
[15] See Maxime Herman, *Histoire de la Littérature Polonaise (dès Origines à 1961)* (Paris, 1963), pp. 359 ff. The group flowered in Cracow after Conrad had left it, but its roots must have been already planted in his student days there.

In 1899, the year in which Conrad was writing *Lord Jim*, the first of his parables of men who "jumped" their social or political attachments, there opened a debate within the Polish intelligentsia which took its name from an article by Wincenty Lutosławski, "The Emigration of the Talents," in the magazine *Kraj (Homeland)*. The author's points are temperate and re-signed: Poland loses nothing by the emigration of its talented men, since if they were to remain they could not develop their talents. Lutosławski retains a hope that the "talents" will return after making their success abroad, or that their achievement will reflect credit on Poland. He concludes shrewdly, "Those who stay at home are not necessarily the ablest but the most patient and enduring." How accurate Lutosławski was is borne out by the subsequent attack on Conrad by the novelist Eliza Orzeszkowa, which must be cited at some length so that the author's tone and its effect on Conrad may be appre-ciated:

> the gentleman who in English is writing novels which are widely read and bring good profit almost caused me a nervous attack. When reading about him, I felt something slippery and unpleasant, something mounting to my throat. . . . Creative ability is the very crown of the plant, the very top of the tower, the very heart of the heart of the nation. And to take away from one's nation this flower, this top, this heart and to give it to the Anglo-Saxons who are not even lacking in bird's milk, for the only reason that they pay better for it—one cannot even think of it without shame. And what is still worse, this gentleman bears the name of his perhaps very near relative, Joseph Korzeniowski over whose novels I shed as a young girl the first tears of sympathy and felt the first ardors of noble enthusiasms and decisions. Over the novels of Mr. Conrad Korzeniowski no Polish girl will shed an altruistic tear or take a noble decision.[16]

Mme Orzeszkowa betrays in her prose style a hysterical streak which should have been apparent to Conrad, but given his normally high-strung pride and his special vulnerability on the point of her attack, it is not surprising that her subsequent letter to him struck a nerve.[17] There was, however, beyond the psychological disturbance created by such accusations, a deeper in-fluence of literary nationalism on Conrad's career.

It is apparent from the quoted passage that Mme Orzeszkowa's literary

[16] Both Lutosławski and Mme Orzeszkowa are quoted in Ludwik Krzyżanowski (ed.), *Joseph Conrad: Centennial Essays* (New York, 1960), pp. 113–14.

[17] Despite his statement that she had written him, it has been suggested that Conrad's memory failed him here, and that he knew of her only through her article; see Najder (ed.), *Conrad's Polish Background*, p. 23.

values were far from Conrad's own. Hers are the canons of moral, nationalistic, and sentimental uplift, and his the canons of artistic impartiality and moral discovery. We can now see in Conrad's expatriation a movement away from a culture which would require of its artists an exclusive and militant engagement. Such a cultural movement was active in the Poland of Conrad's youth. Eliza Orzeszkowa was one of the foremost of a group of writers known as Positivists because of their commitment to the use of fiction not only for realistic social analysis but for disseminating the doctrines of Polish nationalism and the moral values held to be appropriate to it.[18] It was the Orzeszkowas dominant in Polish culture whom Conrad may have been seeking to escape when he left his country. He typified in his expatriation the reaction of the Young Poland movement to the dominant Positivist school.

Conrad's *Papierkrieg* with Mme Orzeszkowa does not, however, exhaust his relations with Polish Positivism. This literary and scholarly movement was begun in the disillusionment following the defeat of the Revolution of 1863, i.e., in the same crucible in which Conrad himself was tempered. Although influenced by Comte, Polish Positivism was less scientific than anti-romantic. Its chief antagonist was the naïve mystical nationalism which had undermined the revolution. In place of the grand illusions, the Positivists preached realism: realism in life—evolutionary rather than revolutionary social change through hard work—and realism in art, in place of the afflatus of Polish Romanticism.[19]

Eliza Orzeszkowa was temperamentally uncharacteristic of the Positivists: in her inspirational demands upon art she was as idealistic as the Romantics whom they had succeeded. (Similarly, she was one of the least positivistic of her school in her dedicated refusal to condemn the Revolution of 1863, in which she had participated.) If Conrad received from her the demand for sentimental engagement, he received from the Positivists at large an orientation toward work, realism, and political evolution which was to remain his hallmark.

The point of contact is not far to seek: it was Conrad's uncle whose maxims echo the mood of the Positivists. The education Conrad received from his guardian, Tadeusz Bobrowski, has been described by a recent Polish critic as having been conducted according to the "principles of the

[18] See Edward H. Lewinski-Corwin, *The Political History of Poland* (New York, 1917), p. 507.

[19] See Manfred Kridl (ed.), *An Anthology of Polish Literature* (orig. pub., 1957; New York and London, 1964), pp. 358–59, 399.

Polish era of positivism."[20] In the language of his uncle's letters, the Positivist influence is unambiguous. The difference between Conrad and the literary Positivists like Mme Orzeszkowa remains, however; he refused to employ his fiction for ethical uplift or political propaganda—though its subject matter is consistently ethical and political.

Even in the first years of his self-imposed exile, Conrad continued to indulge himself in certain of the mystical theories of Polish national revival, namely those which go under the general heading of "Pan-Slavism." In the later nineteenth century, this fantasy of the union of all the Slavic peoples was fostered by Russia in the hope of extending its influence farther into eastern Europe. Yet some of the smaller nations, or independence movements desiring to become nations, were deluded enough to discount Russia's preponderance in such a coalition of forces. With this in mind, Bobrowski wrote to Conrad another of the sobering letters that were eventually to sophisticate his nephew's political views:

> What you write of our hopes based on Panslavism is in theory both splendid and feasible, but it meets great difficulties in practice. You don't take into account the significance which actual numbers have in the affairs of this world. Each of the more influential nations starts by relying apparently on the Panslavic ideal and by forgetting about its own interests—but secretly and almost unconsciously relies on some aspect of its existence which will ensure its leadership. You yourself have fallen into the same error, attributing to our country certain positive qualities, which are partly but not wholly true. And so Russia does not interpret Panslavism otherwise than as a means of russifying all other nations. . . . And to our claim that we have a higher culture and a longer history they reply: this was only the life and culture of one class which claimed to be a nation (this contains a grain of truth) and that only she, Russia, will develop the real elements of the people. . . . since like pariahs we are deprived of our own political and national rights, we, more than the others, have to preserve our individuality and our own standpoint, till the time comes when Nemesis, as a result of our own efforts, spins out some situation which will give us the right to have a real national existence— and possibly something more.[21]

[20] Stanisław Helztynski, "Joseph Conrad—Człowiek i Twórca," in *Joseph Conrad Korzeniowski: Essays and Studies* (*The Neophilological Quarterly*, Special Number; Warsaw, 1958), p. 60.

[21] Najder (ed.), *Conrad's Polish Background*, pp. 79–80, letter of September 11/ 23, 1881. Conrad was then twenty-three and was about to sail on his first voyage to the Far East.

The effect of such counsel was to emphasize the distance Poland would have to travel to become a modern nation, and must have served only to further disillusion Conrad. His break with Polish nationalist dreams—and with Polish claims upon his art—was not, however, made with impunity. He lost the friendship of the Kliszczewskis, who were among his first friends in England (and with whose son, Spiridion, he exchanged youthfully extremist reactionary sentiments—see below, Chapter II), apparently because of his refusal to work in behalf of Polish independence. Throughout the years of his literary apprenticeship, he had few contacts with Poles, and these were usually as furtive and disturbing as that with one visitor whose apparently needless request for secrecy as he departed upset the calm of the Conrad household.[22] It was only with the approach of the world war, at a time when Conrad found himself growing old and his sons growing up as Englishmen, that he felt the need to revisit his home in Cracow and made his near-disastrous trip.

The most important consequence of that visit, however, seems to have been Conrad's contact with Poles who pressed him to join in a campaign to influence British government policy and public opinion in behalf of Polish independence. At the outset of the war, Conrad advocated what has come to be called the Austrian solution to the Polish question: it called for the reconstruction of Poland as a semi-autonomous state of the Austro-Hungarian Empire.[23] This program must have been proposed to him in the café debates that flourished in Cracow at the time of his visit; he made contact there with a Dr. Theodore Kosch, who sent one Marjan Bilinski to visit him in Vienna; Bilinski induced him to make direct approaches to the British Foreign Office upon his return to England. Their plan called for the re-establishment of Poland as a monarchial state within the Austro-Hungarian Empire, and not

[22] Jessie Conrad, *Joseph Conrad and His Circle* (London, 1935), pp. 53–55. The most incisive statement of Conrad's relations with Poles in England is in Jerzy Peterkiewicz, "Patriotic Irritability: Conrad and Poland: For the Centenary," *Twentieth Century*, CLXII (1957), 547: "Joseph Conrad, with the help of his perfect manners, kept at a distance from those who tried to attach labels to him, from well-wishers who were eager to tell him what sort of oddity he really was. Early in his career he sensed around him the romantic bias, the sea dreamer's myth, the Slav *idée fixe*, and, of course, the Polish innuendoes dipped in blood sacrifices and smelling of betrayal."

[23] See Krzyżanowski (ed.), *Joseph Conrad*, p. 123 ff., for relevant documents of the campaign. The text of a "Political Memorandum," written by Conrad and apparently based on the plans of J. H. Retinger, is given in Najder (ed.), *Conrad's Polish Background*, pp. 303–4; see also p. 260n.

as a modern democracy. It was thus doomed to irrelevance, for the war said "goodbye to all that," dismantling the Austro-Hungarian and Prussian empires and their aristocracy. What was most unfortunate for Conrad, however, aside from the failure of his proposals, was that his loyalty as a British subject was called into question by his advocacy of a special relationship with Austria. The plan provided an Austrian alliance with the Western powers against their ally, Russia, with an ultimate view toward prying Polish territory loose from the latter. Thus Conrad's long-cherished claim to being an Englishman with only sentimental ties to his homeland was jeopardized, in the eyes of such staunch patriots as Arnold Bennett.

Meeting with public indifference and an icy reception at the Foreign Office, Conrad changed his Polish views in 1916, about midway through the war, after Russia proclaimed its intention of reconstituting a semi-autonomous Poland within the Russian Empire at the end of the war, and after Germany and Austria signed an agreement to create a Polish kingdom as their protectorate in the event of their victory. (Though the pact was secret, it may have been made known to Polish circles, for it was manifestly designed to curry their favor.) Conrad's new program was based on the realization that there might be something worse than *not getting* what he wanted (Polish independence): *getting it* under Russia or Prussia, depending upon which won the war. Faced with these prospects, he made a remarkable proposal in his "Note on the Polish Problem" (*NLL*, pp. 134–40), delivered as a letter to the Foreign Office and published in *The Times* in 1916: England and France, Poland's cultural models and natural allies, should guarantee a Polish state with a semi-colonial status—a new "overseas" territory for the Western imperialist nations. His letter is aimed at dissociating Poland from its Slavic neighbors and identifying it with the West in political ideals, religion, and cultural tradition. For all its impracticality, Conrad's mid-war politics can be considered a step forward. The character of the new state he envisioned was necessarily democratic—he spoke of its institutions of representative government—and thus marks an advance over the royalism of his initial solution.

Conrad's final Polish proposal came at the war's end, at the time of the Peace Conference, and it can be understood only by considering it in terms of that historical moment. The tone as well as the proposals of his 1919 essay, "The Crime of Partition" (*NLL*, pp. 115–33), point to a new attitude toward France and England. He distrusted their intentions for Poland as he viewed the spectacle of their callous power politics at Versailles. Undiplomatically,

Conrad makes every effort in this essay to point out to his British audience
that Poland owes nothing to the Western powers for its re-emergence (which
he grandiosely claims was won by the Polish Legion under Pilsudski). In
general, he takes an intransigent nationalist position, denouncing the in-
clusion of the Soviet Union in the conference to determine Poland's frontiers,
insulting the Western powers for their pusillanimity in acceding to Russian
territorial claims by their drawing of the Curzon Line, and insisting on the
most extreme Polish claims to territory (including the incorporation of the
equally self-conscious nation of Lithuania, which had been joined with
Poland, then absorbed by Russia, and was pursuing its own fight for independence at the Peace Conference). One Polish critic (who is, doubtless, unim-
peachable, as he held high office in the interregnum Polish government),
has declared of this essay: "On peut céder à l'illusion que nous lisons ici,
dans une traduction en anglais, de la prose d'émigration du romantisme
polonais après 1831," and adds that the essay expresses itself with a "violence
qui n'avait rien d'anglais.[24]

How are we to account for this abandonment by Conrad of his mature
political views and his usually tactful expression of them? The answer is
implicit in the remarks of Ujejski quoted above: Conrad seems to have
reverted from his acquired English nationality—and the manners and loyalties
he acquired with it—to his father's political heritage and to the extremist
rhetoric which surrounded him in his youth. The resurgence of an aggressive
attitude on the part of Polish nationalists toward other national claims that
conflicted with theirs—which D. W. Brogan has called an instance of the
"perpetuity of *any* national claim"[25]—was an atavistic tendency, on a grand
scale, of the sort that Conrad seems to have experienced in his own person.

As a result of Conrad's fusion of an early nationalistic dedication, an almost
lifelong separation from the homeland, and a compensatory extremism
in his ultimate return to the fold, Polish critics have been able to maintain
a wide variety of attitudes toward him as a national author. There are those
who consider his Polish heritage to be so alive in his work as to make him
accessible only to Polish readers: "*we* alone are in a position to understand
him entirely and to feel what he expresses and what he suppresses, what he

[24] Józef Ujejski, *Joseph Conrad*, trans. Pierre Duméril (Paris, 1939), pp. 37, 55.
[25] *The Price of Revolution* (London, 1951), p. 125.

conceals and what he obscures with symbols."[26] At the opposite pole are those critics who face up to the fact of his alienation from Polish life: "If Conrad was a true Polish patriot, as so many Polish critics claimed him to be, his was indeed a strange kind of nationalism, for, 'he could not be held within his own nationality; he adopted another one, and considered "national egoism" repulsive.' "[27]

A similar dichotomy exists among Polish critics on the subject of Conrad's revolutionary heritage, especially as it affected his writings:

> Few of the great writers of this age are so free from, and so opposed to, anything revolutionary in the accepted "bourgeois" sense of the word, and yet Conrad . . . analyzes and decomposes until the conventional reality, the reality of people accustomed to mental and physical comfort and to certitude seems altogether an absurdity. What bond could there be between his enthusiastic public and the revolutionary visionary he is himself?[28]

Yet critics in present-day Poland have been hard-pressed to adapt Conrad to their literary politics, although his works were defrosted in the "thaw" of 1955, and even his father's plays have come to be performed, "finding favor with Marxist critics because of their violent diatribes against the propertied classes."[29] The competition for the prestige and authority of Conrad's name has recently proceeded along the lines of the Cold War. In the one camp, a Conrad Centennial Celebration was held in Warsaw in 1957, and the proceedings were published as a special number of *The Neophilological Quarterly* the following year. In the other, Polish exiles in the United States have published frequent Conradian articles and documents in their journal, *The Polish Review* (a group of these have been reprinted in the Krzyżanowski volume cited above).

With all this activity it is surprising that so little has been made of Conrad's own statements on the strand of his Polish experience that was most influential in forming his political attitudes. He was frequently offended by references—such as H. L. Mencken's—to his Slavic origins, with the implied mysticism, orientalism, or even barbarism that the term connotes to critics

---

[26] Stefan Żeromski, quoted in Gustav Morf, *The Polish Heritage of Joseph Conrad* (London, n.d. [1930]), p. 232.

[27] Maria Dąbrowska, quoted in Krzyżanowski (ed.), *Joseph Conrad*, p. 157.

[28] Stefan Napierski, quoted in Morf, *Polish Heritage*, pp. 237–38.

[29] Czesław Miłosz, "Joseph Conrad in Polish Eyes," in R. W. Stallman (ed.), *The Art of Joseph Conrad: A Critical Symposium* (East Lansing, Mich., 1960), pp. 44, 36.

who take racial explanations seriously. Conrad's usual defense was to dissociate himself from Slavic clichés (although he elsewhere acknowledged
his "ultra-Slav nature"), while asserting the long-established cultural ties of
Poland to western Europe. The personal form of these ties was the intimacy
with French and English literature which his father had initiated in his youth.
It is, moreover, in the liberal politics of western Europe during the nineteenth century that Conrad sees the source of Poland's—and his own—
link to the West:

> the whole Polish mentality, Western in complexion, had received its
> training from Italy and France and, historically, had always remained,
> even in religious matters, in sympathy with the most liberal currents of
> European thought. An impartial view of humanity in all its degrees of
> splendour and misery together with a special regard for the rights of the
> unprivileged of this earth, not on any mystic ground but on the ground
> of simple fellowship and honourable reciprocity of services, was the
> dominant characteristic of the mental and moral atmosphere of the houses
> which sheltered my hazardous childhood. . . . (*PR*, p. vii)

It is the democratic-liberal element which Conrad ranks uppermost in the
Polish tradition, and whether or not that element actually commands an
important place there, it is significant that he valued so highly this, his
Bobrowski heritage. In going out of his way to insist upon his early education
in respect and concern for the lower classes, Conrad indicates the source of
an awareness of the social problems which form the dramatic situations of
his political novels. These elements of his Polish heritage in part account for
the development of Conrad's opinions on contemporary political affairs,
which will be traced in the following chapter.

Chapter II

THE MAKING OF A
POLITICAL IMAGINATION

George Bernard Shaw

H. G. Wells. Courtesy of Wide World Photos

..if way to the Better there be, it exacts a full look at the Worst.

—Hardy

The record of Conrad's political opinions is a record of growth. It shows no consistent application of first principles, nor systematic doctrine, nor even a sustained temperamental attitude. As in natural growth, there is an interplay of inner and outer forces which generates unlooked-for excrescences, and there is also an expanded comprehension—an ability to take in more of the world. Above all, this is the growth of an imagination: it is the mind of an artist with which we are concerned, not that of a philosopher or politician. The opinions are limited by naïveté, shaped by circumstance, charged with passion. They make up a set of ways of looking at the world, ways of seeing the impersonal forces of history to be instinct with human tragedy. With this somewhat vague but steadily growing imaginative comprehension, Conrad fashioned the personal dramas of his political novels as parables of man's life in history.

The first substantial expression of Conrad's political opinions that has come down to us is a long letter to Spiridion Kliszczewski, his first Polish friend in England. Conrad was twenty-eight when they corresponded during his absences at sea. Despite the relative immaturity of the writer and the patently unstable tone in which he expresses himself, this early letter has been taken by most Conrad critics as a summary statement of his later political mentality.

He addresses himself to the 1885 general election, in which a large new segment of the public (mainly agricultural laborers) exercised the franchise for the first time. Conrad assumes that "the International Socialist Association are triumphant, and every disreputable ragamuffin in Europe feels that the day of universal brotherhood, dispoilation and disorder is coming apace, and nurses day-dreams of well-plenished pockets amongst the ruin of all that is respectable, venerable and holy. . . ." Further, he expresses an astonishing pessimism whose rhetoric can be accounted for only by his youth:

> Where's the man to stop the rush of social-democratic ideas? The opportunity and the day have come and are gone! . . . The destiny of this nation and of all nations is to be accomplished in darkness amidst much weeping and gnashing of teeth, to pass through robbery, equality, anarchy and misery under the iron rule of a military despotism! Such is the lesson of common sense logic.
>
> Socialism must inevitably end in Caesarism. . . . Disestablishment, Land Reform, Universal Brotherhood are but like milestones on the road to ruin. . . . Still, there is no earthly remedy for these earthly misfortunes, and from above, I fear, we may obtain consolation, but no remedy. "All is vanity."[1]

[1] Gérard Jean-Aubry (ed.), *Joseph Conrad: Life and Letters* (London, 1927), I, 84–85, letter of December 19, 1885. Subsequent references to this collection will be made parenthetically in the text and abbreviated *LL*.

The stimulus to Conrad's hostility should not be sought in the defeat of Tory conservatism and the victory of Liberal progress, even though he condemns specific Liberal reform measures. The Liberals actually lost ground in the 1885 election, and their majority gave way to a division in which the Parnellite Irish members held the balance of power. Conrad's contempt for the "newly enfranchised idiots" is not, moreover, to be taken as a condemnation of the working class's voting in this election. The agricultural laborers, who voted for the first time, did respond to the Radicals' promise of limited land reform—"three acres and a cow," as it was phrased—but the Tories did well in the boroughs, where the urban workers sensed an advantage in their program of tariff reform.

To consider the letter against the facts of the case is, however, to miss its curious tone and unique character. Conrad reveals here no inclination to discriminate political issues or to evaluate historical events; he is given rather to mouthing the clichés of nineteenth-century anti-revolutionary hysteria—clichés which have new but reminiscent counterparts today. The most peculiar element of this youthful outburst is its religious piety, coming as it does between his schoolboy disavowal of Catholicism and his mature agnosticism. His opposition to Disestablishment may be explained on political grounds as truculence toward any Liberal reform, but his references to "all that is holy" and heavenly consolation tempt one to judge them as cant. Yet the animus that runs through both the political and the religious sentiments, uncharacteristic of the later Conrad as it is, does represent a stage of his intellectual development.

That stage may be located quite precisely in time and place—Marseilles, 1874–78—because Conrad himself fixed it there in his semi-autobiographical novel, *The Arrow of Gold*. The hero, M. George, is exposed to the same ultramontane politics (absolutist royalism with a strong mystical Catholic cast) that Conrad evinces in this letter; and although the mature novelist insists that the impressionable youth did not believe a word of it even then, there can be no question but that the young Conrad himself did. *The Arrow of Gold* will be treated below, in its place in the Conrad canon; suffice it to say here that the Kliszczewski letter reveals that Conrad brought Bourbonist politics with him to England after his escapades in the Second Carlist War, and that these sentiments of a Continental aristocratic tradition were progressively modified during his acclimatization in England.

Ten years intervene before Conrad's next surviving statement on politics. These were the years in which he left the sea and turned to writing, and in which his political imagination was broadened by his Congo voyage. "Before the Congo," he later said of this time, "I was just a mere animal" (*LL*, I, 141). The growth of his mind is expressed in a series of letters to R. B. Cunninghame Graham, one of the most prominent socialists in England at the time. How much Conrad had changed since the vituperations of the Kliszczewski letter is suggested by his defense of this damaging personal association before his staid publisher: "I do not dedicate to C. Graham the socialist or to C. Graham the aristocrat (he is both—you know) but to one of the few men I *know*—in the full sense of the word—and knowing cannot but appreciate and respect—abstractedly [sic] as human beings. I do not share his political convictions or even all his ideas of art, but we have enough ideas in common to base a strong friendship upon."[2]

Following Conrad's lead, critics like Baines[3] have tried to minimize the importance of Cunninghame Graham's politics and to describe him in the aura of his romantic career as an adventurer, horseman, and eccentric. However, an awareness of the politics of the period will not allow the daring of Conrad's friendship with Graham to recede into the background, as it did not for his publisher. R. B. Cunninghame Graham was one of the founders of the modern socialist movement in Great Britain—in particular, of the Scottish Land and Labour League—the first president of the Scottish Labour Party, a Radical member of Parliament from 1886 to 1892 (just after the elections that had so disturbed Conrad), and one of the most successful of his group in bringing to wide public notice the land nationalization and social welfare programs which Conrad had anathematized.[4] The fact that Conrad could entertain such a friendship indicates that he was no longer the youth he had been, and his dialectic with Cunninghame Graham should be considered one of the chief experiences that brought him to maturity.

Their correspondence began with an appreciative letter from Cunninghame Graham on *The Nigger of the "Narcissus,"* and it was on the political implications of this sea tale that their first significant exchange of views centered. The immediate subject of the letters is the character of Singleton, the stoical helmsman who is venerated in the novel but who, Cunninghame Graham

---

[2] *Joseph Conrad: Letters to William Blackwood and David S. Meldrum*, ed. William Blackburn (Durham, N.C., and Cambridge, 1958), p. 51, letter of February 12, 1899. The dedication in question is to *Typhoon and Other Stories.*

[3] *Joseph Conrad*, p. 198.

[4] See G. D. H. Cole, *A History of Socialist Thought*, II: *Marxism and Anarchism, 1850–1890* (New York and London, 1954), 384; III: *Second International* (1956), Pt. I, 148.

claimed, could serve as an ideal man only if modified by education. Conrad replied that "Singleton with an education is impossible." Pursuing the definition of education in a direction most reformers had not considered, he claimed that Singleton was already educated, since he "was in perfect accord with his life. . . ." But his subsequent defense of the uncultivated man is less positive:

> Would you seriously, of malice prepense, cultivate in that unconscious man the power to think? Then he would become conscious,—and much smaller,—and very unhappy. Now he is simple and great like an elemental force. Nothing can touch him but the curse of decay. . . .
>
> Would you seriously wish to tell such a man "Know thyself! Understand that you are nothing, less than a shadow, more insignificant than a drop of water in the ocean, more fleeting than the illusion of a dream?" Would you? (LL, I, 214–15, December 14, 1897)

Why does Conrad denigrate intelligence as an ideal of life in favor of un-conscious assimilation to the environment? If this "noble savage" is placed within the tradition from Wordsworth's leech gatherer to Faulkner's Dilsey, he may be seen to bear an irony that is implicit in much primitivistic thought. Wordsworth's and Faulkner's heroes endure by drawing in upon themselves from the destructiveness of life. Conrad's hero is, similarly, a rock amid the fluid upheavals of the natural universe (the storm) and of the social order on the "Narcissus." The very terms in which Conrad chooses to defend his hero reveal his view of the threatening nature of that universe: consciousness of the world would make Singleton unhappy because that world is one of inevitable decay. It is this attitude toward life that is the source of Conrad's response to Cunninghame Graham's political program. This response is made not in political terms but in large philosophical ones. He resisted Cunninghame Graham's socialist ideals from a pessimistic notion of the impossibility of moral change, social advance, or general happiness.

This pessimism lies deep in Conrad's temperament, rather than being adduced *ad hoc* for political discussion. It may not, however, have been simply a defense mechanism against his personal despair, as some have described it. Conrad represents one of the most outspoken of *fin-de-siècle* English agnostics, in an era when Darwinism and other events had made such a position widespread. His explicit statements to this effect are frequent. He early avowed his dislike of the Christian religion, as he learned it in Catholic schools in Poland; he wanted—and found it impossible—to believe in "an intelligent, benevolent Supreme Being";[5] and he rejected the doctrine of expiation through suffering as "an infamous abomination" which "on the one hand, leads straight to the Inquisition and, on the other, discloses the possibilities of bargaining with the Eternal."[6] This skepticism in religious matters is closely associated with Conrad's political pessimism in his early years of authorship.

Less than a week after the Singleton letter, Conrad wrote Cunninghame Graham again to declare that their goals were the same, but that he lacked faith in their possibility of attainment. He employs the fatalism of the modern age to counteract the Victorian optimism implicit in utopian socialism. Conrad proposes the metaphor of the universe as a knitting machine—one which has evolved itself without purpose or even consciousness—much like Hardy's conception of Immanent Will. But Conrad turns the vision of a meaningless universe into a political parable:

> I am horrified at the horrible work and stand appalled. I feel it ought to embroider,—but it goes on knitting. You come and say: "This is all right: it's only a question of the right kind of oil. Let us use this,—for instance,— celestial oil and the machine will embroider a most beautiful design in purple and gold." Will it? Alas no! You cannot by any special lubrication make embroidery with a knitting machine. . . . It knits us in and it knits us out. It has knitted time, space, pain, death, corruption, despair and all the illusions,—and nothing matters. I'll admit however that to look at the remorseless process is sometimes amusing. (*LL*, I, 216, December 20, 1897)

The sources of this compelling image—the universe as a knitting machine— may account for some of its power as a metaphor of a mechanical and indifferent universe. Conrad's use of it goes beyond its origin in the traditional iconography of the Fates. The knitting machine, as one of the bases of the British economy in the nineteenth century, would, for a mind like Conrad's, be a natural symbol of the modern industrial world. Seen in this light the argument against socialist progressivism cuts a wider swath: it takes in the widespread Victorian (and modern) faith in progress through industry. But the danger of this mechanical metaphor is its suggestion of a mechanistic view of the universe—a danger because it leads to a kind of quietism which

[5] Garnett Letters, p. 226, letter of August 28, 1908.
[6] *Letters of Joseph Conrad to Marguerite Poradowska, 1890–1920*, trans. and ed. J. A. Gee and P. J. Sturm (New Haven and London, 1940), p. 36, letter of September 15, 1891.

rejects all ameliorative action in favor of a passive spectatorship. All effort—
economic or political, conservative or revolutionary—is greeted with a sullen
irony.

In the next month, February, 1898 (*LL*, I, 229), Conrad bolstered his
skeptical view of all political progress by the traditional conservative belief
in human fallibility. If man, he wrote, is not inherently evil, he is at best
"silly and cowardly." In the entire body of Conrad's work, in fact, the only
examples of radical evil are Gentleman Brown in *Lord Jim* and the weird trio
of *Victory*. These are grotesques imported for the denouement of these novels,
and are given no symbolic reference to man in general. Why, then, does
Conrad employ the historical theory of "crimes and follies" as a disclaimer
of political aspirations for human betterment? The answer lies in his attack
on "material preoccupations," which he will soon after, in *Nostromo*, call
"material interests":

> What does it bring? What's the profit? What do we get by it? These
> questions are the root of every moral, intellectual or political movement.
> . . . Every cause is tainted: and you reject this one, espouse that other one
> as if one were evil and the other good, while the same evil you hate is in
> both, but disguised in different words. I am more in sympathy with you
> than words can express, yet if I had a grain of belief left in me I would
> believe you misguided. (*LL*, I, 229)

Conrad here sees all political systems as caught in the web of human selfishness. He seems to have been so repelled by the mercenariness of capitalist
society as to believe a pure socialism impossible, while conceding his sympathy for its unselfish protagonists like Cunninghame Graham.

The next extended entry in the Conrad-Cunninghame Graham correspondence occurs after the lapse of a year, when the latter invited Conrad to
participate in a peace rally whose platform was to include a broad range of
figures united only by their opposition to the impending Boer War. As will
be seen below, Conrad's position was equivocal; although he wanted England
to win, he opposed the British conduct of the war. He declined the invitation,
declaring himself out of sympathy with the platform, first, because he was
neither "peaceman" nor "democrat," and second, because he could not
appear with the Russians who would be participating—not because of their
political complexion but because they were Russians. He goes on to challenge
the internationalist slogan of "fraternity," holding that he cannot admit the
idea of "fraternity" because it "tends to weaken the national sentiment,

the preservation of which is my concern." He next turns, characteristically, to French to express his nationalist sentiments:

> Il faut un principe défini. Si l'idée nationale apporte la souffrance et son service donne la mort, ça vaut toujours mieux que de servir les ombres d'une éloquence qui est morte, justement parce qu'elle n'a pas de corps. . . . Moi, je regarde l'avenir du fond d'un passé très noir et je trouve que rien ne m'est permis hormis la fidélité à une cause absolument perdue, à une idée sans avenir. (*LL*, I, 269, February 8, 1899)

The nationalist tendency is valued as an integrative one, and the fraternal relation, with its internationalist implications, is scorned as disintegrative. Yet nationalism is based on divisive exclusions (such as Conrad's prejudice against Russians, which made it impossible for him to join them, irrespective of their politics), while fraternity is presumably necessary *within* a nation if it it is to survive. The contradictions of this distinction seem not to have occurred to Conrad because he was not employing it as a political concept but rather as a personal projection. Nationalism remained attractive to him, despite the gathering storm of imperialism and war, largely because he conceived it as an individual course of action. The concluding account in the letter of the lonely fighter in a doomed cause, in which Conrad characteristically turns to French, is a version of the heroic mythos which he inherited from his father's romanticism. He outgrew it in his later fiction, where the egoistic nationalism of Decoud and Razumov is modified by their need for fraternity.

Toward the end of the same year, 1899, Conrad placed himself on the same side as Cunninghame Graham on a major political issue, expressing in detail his opposition to the Boer War (*LL*, I, 284, October 14, 1899). He called it "idiotic," for the Boers were the intransigent opponents of a superior force, and consequently the war must be a prolonged agony leading to their extermination. In his moral evaluation of the struggle, Conrad was unhesitatingly "pro-Boer" (to use the term applied to the anti-war minority of the Liberal Party). He scoffed at Kipling's jingoistic pride in the war as a democratic one, and hoped the "torture" of the "victims" would end soon. Conrad's war stand, although it is congruous with his anti-imperialist attitudes, nevertheless runs counter to several of his other convictions and led to more complex statements in his other letters of this period. He repeats much the same pro-Boer line in a letter to E.L. Sanderson of October 26, 1899 (*LL*, I, 285), but within two months, writing to Angèle Zagórska, he sharply criticizes the Boers (*LL*, I, 288, December 25, 1899). He finds them to be fighting for independence in good faith, but the political content of their nationalism was antithetical to his own. He sees them as lacking the idea of liberty—an idea possessed, in his view, by the British alone. Moreover, he see the Boers as essentially despotic, due to the influence of Germanic traditions in their (Dutch!) ancestry. In another letter, to William Blackwood, on the following day, his attitude is pro-British:

> The war disturbed me not a little. I do not share the slightly frantic state of the press. They write as if they had expected the soldiers to run and the Empire to collapse and can't possess their souls for joy that these things did not happen. To me, seeing the initial non-success the develop-ment of the National Will on the lines of unflinching resolution seemed from the first as inevitable as the preordained motions of the stars.[7]

In these letters Conrad's political thinking shows itself in process of growth as he took a wider view of the issues involved in the war. His first reaction against an empire's suppression of a national group's right to self-determination must have been made on the pattern of his lifelong hatred of the imperial partition of Poland. With his growing awareness of the Boers' lack of democratic traditions, the question of their right to self-determination came to the surface. Finally, the British position could be regarded not simply as an imperial one but equally well as a "National Will" striving for expression—a doctrine related to Conrad's developing notion of the organic state.

In passing, it should be noted that Conrad's shift of judgment is not based simply on a prejudice against Germanic peoples; considered within the contemporary atmosphere of racist mythologies, Conrad is relatively un-prejudiced. A veneration of the Germanic "race" was an element of the imperialist mystique of such writers as Benjamin Kidd and H. S. Chamber-lain, and of such political figures as Cecil Rhodes and Joseph Chamberlain— who pursued the Boer War against that very race. With equal inconsistency, leading pro-Boers like Arthur Conan Doyle defended the Boers while evincing deep hostility to Germanic aggressiveness. Compared with such an irrational interplay of opinions, Conrad understates the element of race both in his defense of the Boers and in his support of England.

After his first period of correspondence with Cunninghame Graham,

[7] Blackburn (ed.), *Letters to Blackwood and Meldrum*, p. 80, letter of December 26, 1899.

Conrad wrote him infrequently but always with an assumption of underlying sympathy in their political attitudes. His next letter dates from 1905, after he had encountered Shaw, Wells, and other politically engaged writers in the Kentish literary community around the turn of the century. It was, significantly, to his old socialist friend that Conrad expressed his distance from the liberal political milieu with which he was then in contact. Instead of his early apocalyptic vision of universal doom through industrial progress and his subsequent despair of all political effort, however desirable its ends, Conrad now presented a bemused acceptance of the fact of social progress. He now rejected progress per se as unappealing to the individual temperament:

> *Vous—vous êtes né trop tard.* The stodgy sun of the future—our early Victorian future—lingers on the horizon, but all the same it will rise— it will indeed—to throw its sanitary light upon a dull world of perfected municipalities and W.C.s *sans peur et sans reproche.* The grave of individual temperaments is being dug by G.B.S. and H.G.W. with hopeful industry. (*LL*, II, 12, February 16, 1905)

His mocking of the technocratic optimism—faith in the application of social science to government and of physical science to the economy—of his acquaintances Wells and Shaw suggests that Conrad was over-reacting to the principle of progress because of the personalities that surrounded him. What offended Conrad in the progressives, whether Fabian or Wellsian, was their rationalistic self-assurance—a personality trait outstanding in his two fellow-artists.

It is curious, therefore, that he praised Wells two months later, on the publication of *A Modern Utopia*, for "intellectual kindliness characterizing your development of your ideal" (*LL*, II, 15, April 25, 1905). Conrad continued: "No civilized man, in his infinite variety, need, when reading that book, feel 'left' for a single moment." If we discount his habitual tendency to flatter his acquaintances, Conrad's praise of Wells's utopia shows that it was signs of humanity he sought in the reform programs of the day, and that when he found them he was willing to grant the desirability of the proposed improvements.[8]

[8] "A modern utopia differs from all the other Utopias in its recognition of the need of poetic activities," Wells himself claimed (*A Modern Utopia* [London, n.d. (1905)], p. 189). He also makes room in this collectivist state for individualism, personal freedom, privacy, competition, the home, and alcoholic beverages. Throughout the work there is an attempt to retain the flesh-and-blood man

Conrad's essays on political subjects, collected largely in Part II ("Life") of *Notes on Life and Letters*, have been subjected to remarkably little detailed analysis—I say remarkably in view of the laborious scrutiny to which much of his fiction has recently been subjected. The political essays, together with the letters which adumbrate them, cannot be said to command a prominent place in the literature of England or in the history of political thought, but they represent a more sustained effort to deal with subjects of contemporary political interest than that of any other artist of rank in England (with the possible exceptions of Shaw and Wells).

The Russo-Japanese War of 1905 is distinguished in history less for shifting the balance of power in the Far East than for damaging Russia's reputation in Europe, thereby creating a new estimation of the pre-World War I balance of power. It was this cultural-psychological change that Conrad wished to impress on the English public when he wrote his first lengthy political essay (in the *Fortnightly Review* for July, 1905), "Autocracy and War." The writing of this essay was the first political act in Conrad's career, and his renunciation of his studied distance from politics marked a major change in temperament (although his disdain of political concerns appears even in this essay, in a stray remark about "something subtly noxious to the human brain in the composition of newspaper ink" [*NLL*, p. 90]). The essay seizes the opportunity to exult in the exposure of Russia as an ineffectual, as well as a brutal, reactionary force. But Conrad widens its scope to include the whole range of European politics, examined in the light of nineteenth-century history. As a result, "Autocracy and War" emerges as one of the most acute predictions of the aggressive tendencies and vacuums of power that produced the world wars. It also ranks as one of the first expressions of internationalist ideals that only after the wars began to be popular. Conrad was one of the few men in his adopted country who were able to take a broad, European perspective on the forces of nationalism, imperialism, and monarchism. Consequently, "Autocracy and War" reads like a message to England: not simply an exposure of Russia but an introduction to the debacle on the horizon.

---

rather than to substitute an ideal abstraction. Further, Wells's elitist notion of a "Samurai"-like ruling class of "voluntary nobility" accords with Conrad's inherited ideal of aristocratic noblesse (see below, Chapter V). Despite Wells's suspicion of the Rousseauistic natural man, Conrad would have stopped short of even his qualified belief in man's essential goodness (though he would have agreed with Wells's rejection of the doctrine of original sin); see *A Modern Utopia*, pp. 119, 205.

The thesis of the essay is difficult to abstract from its welter of perceptions on current affairs, and it is necessary to arrange its assumptions more clearly than Conrad himself does in the course of his sometimes meandering thought. Conrad's commitment to the ideal of European unity is the development of a more balanced nationalism than he had earlier entertained. On the one hand, he declares, "the solidarity of Europeanism . . . must be the next step towards the advent of Concord and Justice; an advent that, however delayed by the fatal worship of force and the errors of national selfishness, has been, and remains, the only possible goal of our progress" (*NLL*, p. 97). On the other hand, "instead of the doctrines of solidarity it was the doctrine of nationalities much more favourable to spoliations that came to the front, and since its greatest triumphs at Sadowa and Sedan there is no Europe" (*NLL*, p. 103). He looks forward to a time when "there will be no frontiers" as the only alternative to the current unstable system of European alliances (*NLL*, p. 103). Further on in the essay he declares his contempt for the Hague tribunal as "that solemnly official recognition of the Earth as a House of Strife" (*NLL*, p. 108), but this statement is based on distrust of the pacific declarations of the participating powers, not on opposition to international organizations.

Conrad's new internationalism, it may be noted here, continued in his later writings. In a 1912 letter to *The Times* on "The Future of Constantinople" (*LE*, pp. 149–54), he proposed an international solution, in the form of an internationally guaranteed free city, as a compromise of the strident nationalist claims of the emergent Balkan states. In his writings on the Polish question during World War I, however, he returned to the tone of aggressive Polish nationalism. In his last essay on the subject, written in 1919 ("The Crime of Partition"), he added a note of scorn of internationalists who, in regard to Poland's negotiations on the disputed eastern lands, wished to support the self-determination of peoples (Ukranians and Lithuanians, in this case) at the expense of Polish historical claims (*NLL*, p. 121). It seems that for Conrad, as for the new nationalists of our own day, international unity and compromise are solutions for the conflicts of every nation but their own.

Conrad's internationalism is founded on his nationalist ideals, and in "Autocracy and War" they become explicit: "The true greatness of a State . . . is a matter of logical growth, of faith and courage. Its inspiration springs from the constructive instinct of the people, governed by the strong hand of a collective conscience . . ." (*NLL*, p. 91). This collective spirit of national will had been fostered by the old monarchies, according to Conrad (who curiously neglects to mention the bourgeois nationalist revolutions against imperial monarchies):

> In Europe the old monarchical principle stands justified in its historical struggle with the growth of political liberty by the evolution of the idea of nationality. . . . This service of unification, creating close-knit communities possessing the ability, the will, and the power to pursue a common ideal, has prepared the ground for the advent of a still larger understanding: for the solidarity of Europeanism. . . . (*NLL*, pp. 96–97)

Here Conrad acknowledges the end of monarchism, but sees its historical value in its furtherance of nationalism. Yet he envisions their achievement of a grander destiny in an evolution toward international cooperation and European unity.

Conrad carefully distinguished the organic nationalism that strives to express the popular will from the aggressive nationalism based on military force and economic competition. "The idea of ceasing to grow in territory, in strength, in wealth, in influence—in anything but wisdom and self-knowledge is odious to them as the omen of the end" (*NLL*, p. 109). To stop this nihilistic aggressiveness, the only solution is to fill the void with organic values: "The trouble of the civilised world is the want of a common conservative principle abstract enough to give the impulse, practical enough to form the rallying point of international action tending towards the restraint of particular ambitions. Peace tribunals instituted for the greater glory of war will not replace it" (*NLL*, p. 111). What this "common conservative principle" was, Conrad never made explicit, but it may be deduced from the similarly operating "idea" that is said to redeem imperialism in "Heart of Darkness." It is a set of cultural values that could provide the basis for widespread public belief in international institutions (rather than in the organs of peace-making which are used by aggressive states as instruments of power politics). This "common conservative principle" looks to the preservation of Europe through independent states linked together by historical traditions and cultural ideals.

Given the contemporary anarchy of international affairs, the immediate purport of "Autocracy and War" is to warn against the expansionism of the Continental imperial powers, Prussia in particular, and against the economic competition that motivates them. It is noteworthy that Conrad's warnings do not extend to another of the disturbing trends in modern times: socialism is not among the destructive forces that Conrad sees threatening Europe. He welcomes, moreover, "the real progress of humanitarian ideas" (*NLL*, p. 84)—

presumably the British (and German) advances in enfranchisement and social legislation. A major portion of the essay is, however, devoted to the subject of revolution *in Russia*, and it is possible to draw from this passage some of Conrad's ideas on revolution generally, but only if the local circumstances are carefully considered.

The lesson of the Russo-Japanese War was, for Conrad, not simply the ineffectuality of Russia as a military force but, more broadly, the stagnancy of its autocratic regime, "the black abyss which separates a soulless autocracy . . . from the benighted, starved souls of its people" (*NLL*, p. 89). Under these circumstances, revolution is inevitable in Russia: "Russian autocracy succeeded to nothing; it had no historical past, and it cannot hope for a historical future. It can only end" (*NLL*, p. 97). But there can be no peaceful progress in the absence of a tradition of political maturity: "There can be no evolution out of a grave" (*NLL*, p. 99). The coming revolution is, therefore, not to be greeted as a desirable development, for the Westerner's expectations of seeing a people free itself from servitude will be disappointed: "In whatever form of upheaval Autocratic Russia is to find her end, it can never be a revolution fruitful of moral consequences to mankind. It cannot be anything else but a rising of slaves" (*NLL*, p. 102). (In a letter to Ada Galsworthy later that year [*LL*, II, 28, November 2, 1905], however, Conrad declared himself "moved" by the Revolution of 1905, finding the results beyond his hopes.)

The implication of Conrad's scant expectations of the Russian revolution is that revolutions in more organic nations might be productive of greater progress. Earlier in the essay, Conrad suggests that revolution tends by its own nature to degenerate: "it is the bitter fate of any idea to lose its royal form and power, to lose its 'virtue' the moment it descends from its solitary throne to work its will among the people" (*NLL*, p. 86). But the old order, too, is burdened by a degenerative tendency: "The sin of the old European monarchies was not the absolutism inherent in every form of government; it was the inability to alter the forms of their legality, grown narrow and oppressive with the march of time" (*NLL*, p. 101). Between these two trends, the stagnation of the monarchies and the degeneration of all revolutions, Conrad chooses to take his chances with a revolution, *provided that it is the expression of the national will*: "A revolution is a short cut in the rational development of national needs in response to the growth of world-wide ideals. It is conceivably possible for a monarch of genius to put himself at the head of a revolution without ceasing to be the king of his people" (*NLL*, p. 101).

The consequences of this position for Conrad's view of the organic state will be discussed in the next chapter, while the importance of this image of the revolutionary king will be taken up in terms of a persistent hero type in Conrad's colonial fiction—in what I shall call the Brooke myth. We may conclude here that while Conrad was skeptical of a Russian revolution as a means of progress he was fully aware of the need for, indeed of the inevitability of, some forms of revolution. Characteristically, he saw such a necessary revolution as the act of an individual who caught up in himself the popular will, a concept strikingly similar to that of the Hegelian world-historical hero.

There is revealed, in the closing passages of "Autocracy and War" some of the profound distrust of industrial civilization which Conrad shared with many participants in an intellectual tradition that goes back to Carlyle and Ruskin and to their predecessors, the Romantic poets:

> the short era of national wars seems about to close. No war will be waged for an idea. The "noxious idle aristocracies" of yesterday fought without malice for an occupation, for the honour, for the fun of the thing. The virtuous, industrious democratic States of to-morrow may yet be reduced to fighting for a crust of dry bread, with all the hate, ferocity, and fury that must attach to the vital importance of such an issue. (*NLL*, p. 106)

The Romantic distaste for the profit motive is here mingled with disdain for inherently unheroic middle-class society. Conrad further echoes Ruskin and Morris when he described modern industrial products as "that variegated rubbish which it seems to be the bizarre fate of humanity to produce for the benefit of a few employers of labour" (*NLL*, p. 106); what seems to rankle is both the shoddiness of the merchandise and the irrationality of the distribution of wealth.

When speaking of the close ties between industrialism, commercialism, and *Weltpolitik* (Conrad's terms), he adds an ambiguous reference to democracy, "which has elected to pin its faith to the supremacy of material interests, [and] will have to fight their battles to the bitter end, on a mere pittance" (*NLL*, p. 107). The irony that is leveled at democracy throughout this and other Conrad essays is always a reflection of his scorn of the bourgeoisie; it apparently did not conflict in his mind with his fundamental commitment to democratic values. Conrad's view of democratic governments focuses on their reflection of capitalist interests and their inability to resist the will of the middle classes, which dominate the body politic. His faith in democracy is based on its breaking with capitalism: "The true peace of the world," he concludes, in terms that show how closely this essay followed the writing of *Nostromo*, "will be built on less perishable foundations than those of material interests" (*NLL*, p. 107). "Autocracy and War," in the final analysis, is a bitter commentary on modern capitalism, on the "swift disenchantment" which "overtook the incredible infatuation which could put its trust in the peaceful nature of industrial and commercial competition" (*NLL*, p. 106). It has, therefore, a place in the history of ideas in England as a reflection of the change from laissez-faire optimism to a new awareness of the dangers of economic competition among the imperial nations of Europe. Since in Conrad's view, as in that of the Marxists, capitalism leads straight to war, the solution must be a radical one. For Conrad it meant the evolution (perhaps hastened by revolution) of independent nations toward an international union devoted to the historical ideals of their peoples.

What is, perhaps, most remarkable about Conrad's next political essay, "The Censor of Plays," is its emotional intensity, expressed in a tone whose bitterness is exceeded only in *The Secret Agent*. That the essay is closely related to that novel is not surprising, since it appeared in the same year, 1907. Not only in tone but in imagery, the two are kindred expressions of Conrad's alienation from modern political institutions.

If we seek the source of Conrad's antipathy toward any kind of censorship, there are four intellectual traditions on individual liberties to be considered. These include the dominant culture of British Liberalism, as it was broadened by John Stuart Mill to encompass cultural as well as economic freedom; the broad trend of left-wing humanitarianism that has come to be called liberalism today; the aristocratic heritage of Poland, with its code of individualism and its scorn of bureaucracy; and the French literary tradition, from Gautier down, with its scorn of the public, especially that of a bourgeois society, as the natural enemy of the free artist. To discover the relative importance of these intellectual currents in "The Censor of Plays" goes far toward explaining not only the bitterness of this essay but also the sources of Conrad's political imagination.

From the onset, it should be clear that Conrad's resentment against governmental interference with civil liberties has little to do with the classical Liberal position, which linked restraint of expression to restraint of trade. He lacked Mill's faith in the eventual victory of the truest and best ideas in a free marketplace. He does, however, share Mill's skepticism of any person's capacity to judge the admissibility of another's opinions, and makes this one of his chief weapons of ironic attack on the Censor. Again with Mill, and here with the Liberal tradition at its best, Conrad approves, and portrays in *The Secret Agent*, the principle of permitting, even harboring, political heterodoxy, no matter how repugnant the belief, in the faith that any circumscription of belief is worse than the most odious belief itself.

This faith seems drived from the second of the above-mentioned traditions. Conrad has been taken to be far from modern liberalism, and he never failed to speak of humanitarianism with irony, but in the essay on the Censor he not only moves in its main stream but goes farther than one of its typical proponents. Conrad was invited to write the essay by Edward Garnett as part of a concerted propaganda attack on the institution by dramatic writers. Garnett's approach was circumspect; he wished to enlist public support without frightening the public with radical criticism, but Conrad took an uncompromising stand:

> You say: *The Censor should be a policeman etc.* But my conviction is that the Censor should *not be at all.* . . . He can't be a policeman he must be a magistrate, a high functionary—the supreme judge of form in art, the arbiter of moral intention. No. That function is impossible. The pretence to exercise it is shameful as all disguised tyranny is shameful. That's how I feel about it. The institution should be attacked on moral grounds as a cowardly expedient.[9]

The outcome of their differences is characteristic of the history of liberal politics: Garnett placed Conrad's essay with the *Daily Mail* for October 12, 1907, but modified several passages in order to lighten the blow to its respectable readers. Conrad later complained of this, as he never had of Garnett's extensive revisions and excisions in the manuscripts of his fiction.

We can begin to reach the personal roots of Conrad's stand against the Censor of Plays by remembering that it was not the content censored that was in question. (The Censor's interest has, down to the present, been largely in the areas of pruriency and libel, matters in which Conrad could have felt no personal stake.) Rather, it is the form, the manners, of governmental interference with personal expression that is the conscious antagonist in the essay. So irritable is Conrad made by being told what to do by a governmental authority that we must ask whether his personality generated egoistic hostility to government per se.

Irving Howe has suggested that even in Conrad's attack on anarchism in *The Secret Agent* there is an unconscious commitment to anarchist sentiments

[9] Garnett Letters, pp. 214-15, letter of October, 1907.

against society and officialdom. Howe connects this anarchic sensibility to Conrad's Polish origins and the aristocratic preference for the individual vis-à-vis the mass. Yet in "The Censor of Plays," despite a passing reference to the Censor's "anxious grandmother—the State," there is no animus against authority generally but rather against allowing *an individual* to sit in judgment:

> Its holder need not have either brain or heart, no sight, no taste, no imagination, not even bowels of compassion. He needs not these things. He has power. He can kill thought, and incidentally truth, and incidentally beauty, providing they seek to live in a dramatic form. He can do it, without seeing, without understanding, without feeling anything; out of mere stupid suspicion, as an irresponsible Roman Caesar could kill a senator. He can do that and there is no one to say him nay. (*NLL*, pp. 78–79)

What is denigrated here is not government but absolutism. The imagery with which Conrad pursues his ironic characterization of the Censor links this essay with the targets of "Autocracy and War": he is developed as a Chinese puppet, a symbol of the Chinese intellectual bureaucracy, with its connotations of oriental despotism and hidebound traditionalism. It is this orientalism that marks czarism in the above-mentioned essay, as it marks the representative of what is presumed to be the Russian embassy, Mr. Vladimir, in *The Secret Agent*. Conrad makes this political reference of the image explicit: "Hatched in Pekin (I should say) by some Board of Respectable Rites, the little caravan monster has come to us by way of Moscow—I suppose" (*NLL*, p. 80). The association of the Censor, then, with imperial despotism is the crucial point of Conrad's attack; censorship has no place in Western civilization.

If Conrad's extreme position with regard to civil liberties is to be distinguished from the compromising approach of humanitarian liberals, if his presumed aristocratic "anarchism" does not attack collective authority but its abuse by individuals, to what degree does his French aesthetic heritage—with its code of the artist's inevitable war against bourgeois society—stand behind his hostility to the Censor? While he does denounce the office as designed to "bring out the greatness of a Philistine's conceit and his moral cowardice" (*NLL*, p. 79), he does not deny the authority of the public as artistic judge. It is only the claim to represent public taste that Conrad attacks. He goes even further, maintaining the doctrine of the artist's social responsibility: "I was content to accept the verdict of a free and

independent public, judging after its conscience the work of its free, independent and conscientious servant—the artist" (*NLL*, p. 77). It is unlikely
that this is cant designed to appease his readers by deference towards them,
for Conrad's Author's Notes to the volumes of his *Collected Works* consistently
express his sense of a responsibility not only to tell the truth but to do so
without offense to the public and for its entertainment and benefit.

It will be seen in the following chapter that Conrad's attitude toward the
social role of the artist has its roots in his conception of the state as an
organic unity, so that the ideal status of the artist would be that of an acknowledged legislator of the spiritual life of the people. To account for
Conrad's attack on the Censor it is sufficient to see the latter as interfering in
the direct relationship of the artist and his audience, shattering the human
connection and the artistic communication that Conrad personally desired
and held to be necessary to the survival of the artist in society. The Censor is
denounced because he is artificial—an "expedient" which breaks the organic
ties of artist and audience.

Between 1907 and 1912 Conrad wrote nothing explicitly on politics,
although it was during this time that he wrote his third great political novel,
Under Western Eyes. In 1908–9 he was caught up in the publication of *The
English Review*, which Ford Madox Ford (then Hueffer) was editing. During
these relatively silent years, then, Conrad was in contact with a number of
politically liberal literary figures, and if any shift in his position took place
it is likely to have been to move further along the path he had already marked
out in "Autocracy and War" and "The Censor of Plays." It is not, of course,
true that Conrad shared the political views of all the writers who published
in the Review (they represented a wide variety of opinion), but the contents
of the first number provided an idea of the prevailing tenor of his milieu.
The issue includes an editorial, probably by Hueffer, on "The Unemployed,"
which laments the estrangement of the educated classes from the poor, who
"are breaking in on us everywhere";[10] an article by Cunninghame Graham,
"Aspects of the Social Question," which declares socialism to be the only
answer to the unemployment problem; an autobiographical piece by W. H.
Davies, "How It Feels To Be Out of Work," which proclaims the superiority
of the irresponsible life of the tramp over the mercenary activity of the

[10] *The English Review*, I (1908), 161 ff.

ruling classes; and a social insurance scheme by "A. M." (Arthur Marwood, who is held to be the model for Christopher Tietjens of *Parade's End*).

Conrad made no statements on the "condition-of-England" questions of the day, but when he took up a political issue once again—although it was an international rather than a social problem, to be sure—he reflected some of the prevailing sentiments of *The English Review*. In 1912, he published a letter to *The Times* which, with a subsequent rejoinder, was included in *Last Essays* as "The Future of Constantinople." The Constantinople letters were written in November of that year, at the close of the First Balkan War, in which Greece, Bulgaria, and Serbia secured their independence from Turkey. Conrad might have been expected to support the victorious nationalists' claims to Constantinople against those of an oppressive imperial power, but Greece and Bulgaria both claimed the city. Faced with this complication in nationalist doctrine—that emergent nations can compete as aggressively in their territorial claims as did the old imperialists—Conrad proposed a solution that was a pragmatic application of his nationalist and internationalist ideals: the establishment of a free city under international protection.

Conrad wrote his second letter to answer the charge that he had joined the "ideologues," presumably the class of internationalist reformers descended from the Enlightenment. There is, indeed, an element of utopianism in Conrad's outline of a system of checks and balances among the national groupings within his proposed free city (the Greeks to control the Senate by virtue of their population majority, the Slavs to nominate the administrative head, the Moslems to pass on the acts of government through their religious leader). To found his plan on *Realpolitik*, he made it dependent on the good will of the Triple Entente, but here again the limits of his political imagination are revealed. Russia, he thought, had abandoned its designs on the city and on an outlet to the Mediterranean (*LE*, p. 153), while England and France he assumed could be depended upon to guarantee the freedom of the port, the Dardanelles, and the Bosporus, irrespective of their western European orientation (*LE*, p. 150). The events, of course, proved Conrad's estimations of power politics to have been hopelessly optimistic, and his later essays during the war and postwar periods reveal a bitter distrust of the Entente's motives and intentions. Far from abandoning its desire to reach the sea, Russia backed the claims of Bulgaria (the weakest of the three) to Constantinople, and thereby precipitated the Second Balkan War. As for France and England, they were unwilling to alienate their ally, Russia, by backing

a solution inimical to its interests. As with Polish hopes for Western intervention in support of the Polish insurrections and, later, with Polish territorial
claims at the postwar partition conference, reliance on these nations resulted
in disappointment.

In what respect, then, does Conrad's Constantinople plan display his
developing political insight? Despite its historical shortcomings, the plan
reveals his deepest beliefs in political matters, beliefs based on the tradition
of English political thought that descends from Burke. It is present in this
essay in the use of such terms as "the historical sense," "the fitness of things,"
and "symbolic":

> The Constantinople of which I think . . . is the Imperial and symbolic
> city, one of the refuges of European civilization and the fit object of
> Europe's care. . . . I had meant my suggestion to be eminently practical.
> Practical—that is, strictly in accordance with the fitness of things.
>
> For to any one with a little historical sense it is not in the fitness of
> things that Constantinople should become the capital of a Bulgarian
> kingdom. I do not wish to hurt youthful susceptibilities but frankly the
> city of the Bosphorus is too great, too illustrious for that fate. (*LE*, pp.
> 149, 151)

Conrad's plan for Constantinople is an attempt to base politics on history,
to conceive political justice from the shape that history has taken in the
imagination of the Western nations.

However illusory it was to think that "a neutralized Bosphorus and a free
Constantinople would arouse no envy, no jealousies, and give no offence"
(*LE*, p. 153), there was yet a sane principle behind Conrad's thinking. In a
situation where nationalism might, and did, lead straight to war, he invoked
historical tradition in behalf of international cooperation: "Every Bulgarian,
Greek, Serb, or Montenegrin entering Constantinople should be able to say:
'I am at home here' " (*LE*, p. 154). Conrad thus, on the eve of world war,
had expanded his view of history to sanction not only national organisms
but also larger international unities. The great failure of his political imagination in this case lies in a direction in which he is at his strongest elsewhere:
the awareness of human irrationality and its destructive—even self-destructive—potentialities.

It is possible to account for the naïveté, as well as the strength, of Conrad's
prewar estimates of *Realpolitik*. It is more difficult to explain the apparent

foolhardiness of his trip to his childhood home of Cracow in Austrian Poland at a time when war was on the horizon and when he himself was more aware of its dangers than were many of his contemporaries. The trip, its perils for himself and his family, their hairsbreadth escapes and roundabout voyage home are too well known for detailed narration here. What is worthy of more attention than it has received is Conrad's explanation of his reckless decision, and its implications for his political imagination. The crucial note in his account of the affair, "Poland Revisited," is sounded almost at the outset: "My present, all that gave solidity and value to it, at any rate, would stand by me in this test of the reality of my past" (*NLL*, pp. 145–46). Conrad's attempt to establish for himself and for his sons the reality of their heritage, in the face of the coming upheaval, suggests that the trip was imperative at that precise time not only because the boys were growing up but also because the past was about to be erased by the war. It was necessary to "test . . . the reality of my past" before that reality was destroyed for good.

The succeeding pages of "Poland Revisited" are devoted to an account of the Conrads' voyage to and across Germany on their way to Cracow. In it Conrad reiterates his warning of the threat of Germany, as he had in "Autocracy and War." His hostility to Prussianism emerges in his fiction in repeated caricatures of Germanic selfishness and bullying, from the captain of the deserting crew in *Lord Jim* to the treacherous Schombrun of *Victory*. (Conrad points out in the Author's Note to the latter novel, which was published in the same year as "Poland Revisited," that he was not indulging in wartime hysteria in making his villain a German, for his anti-German sentiments were of long standing.) What is unique in the essay is an insight into the character of English and American admiration of Germany that is valuable as a document of the temper of the Anglo-Saxon world at the time of its entry into World War I. His description of Germany as "that race planted in the middle of Europe, assuming in grotesque vanity the attitude of Europeans amongst effete Asiatics or barbarous niggers; and, with a consciousness of superiority freeing their hands from all moral bonds" (*NLL*, p. 147), contrasts with the views of the American family which had raced across England as quickly as possible in order to see, with mixed awe and delight, the first German light. Conrad's explanation of this adulation was prophetic: "I had observed long before that German genius had a hypnotising power over half-baked souls and half-lighted minds. There is an immense force of suggestion in highly organized mediocrity" (*NLL*, p. 159).

What most concerns us here, however, is the startling fact that even without the good advice Conrad received against traveling to Poland on the eve of the war, he seems to have been fully aware of the source of the danger and of its potential destructiveness. Some of his compatriots were more sanguine, however. The basis of these counselors' view of international conflict was economic and rational: Conrad was told that the war ultimately would not occur because it was dangerous for the business interests that control modern states. Using the terms he had made central to his picture of capitalism in *Nostromo*, Conrad quoted a Polish interlocutor as saying, "War seems a material impossibility, precisely because it would mean the complete ruin of all material interests" (*NLL*, p. 174, in the complementary essay, "First News"). Conrad admitted that he had accepted this argument (as did many others, occupying political positions ranging from the far right to the far left), but his subsequent account of the nature of modern war indicates that he had become doubtful that reason would finally prevail: "Mankind has been demoralised . . . by its own mastery of mechanical appliances. Its spirit is apparently so weak now, and its flesh has grown so strong, that it will face any deadly horror of destruction and cannot resist the temptation to use any stealthy, murderous contrivance" (*NLL*, p. 163). Even the spirit of nationalism as a vital force in history had, according to Conrad, been warped by its confrontations with imperial power, as revealed in the anecdote of the Balkan waiter who corrected his customer's order for Turkish coffee by saying, "*Monsieur veut dire Café balkanique*" (*NLL*, p. 143).

Conrad's response to the war itself proceeded on two fronts, in parallel, if not causal, fashion. With the entry of his elder son, Boris, into the British army, Conrad assumed the attitudes appropriate to fatherhood and extended them to create a new self-image in his advancing age. Conrad became in 1917 the old salt reminiscing about his maritime adventures, reminding the new and weaker generation of the virtues of his own. He appears in his own vignettes as a Blimp-like figure being escorted (with what smiles behind his back one may imagine) on his first plane ride by the air force ("Flight," *NLL*, pp. 209–12), volunteering jingoistic articles on the navy ("The Dover Patrol," *LE*, pp. 58–65), and entering into strenuous debate on the precise measure of adulation to be accorded the merchant marine (" 'Well Done,' " *NLL*, pp. 179–93). In effect, Conrad in the later years of the war became a propagandist, a new role for a man who had disdained public postures all his life. The ironic attitude of Conrad the European was replaced by the bravado of a wartime Englishman.

At the same time, his heightened nationalism ran parallel to a solidifying of his views on class issues, reaching a climax in his response to the Russian Revolution. As early as May 18, 1917 (*LL*, II, p. 194), he wrote to Hugh Walpole with a skepticism about the new regime that matched his fatalism concerning the old. The "moral destruction" of czarism was unavoidable, but Western culture would henceforth vanish from Russia. (This was a departure from his original view of Russia as standing outside the pale of Western civilization.) His apocalyptic note swelled with the advent of the Bolsheviks; to the same correspondent he wrote of "great cataclysmic forces" on the loose, and invoked English intervention, appealing to the moral ideals of the English tradition (*LL*, II, 211, November 11, 1919).

Conrad's final utterance on the future of European politics is only apparently hopeful: "Europe collectively may be dead but the nations composing it don't give me that impression" (*LL*, II, 343, May 24, 1924). He went on to mention France, Germany, and Italy—speaking of the latter's "marvelous example of vitality." The reference to Italy, following as it does the advent of Mussolini, is disconcerting and suggests a slackening off in Conrad's critical abilities in his last days. The picture thus emerges of a successful man settling deeply into the conservatism of old age. His new skepticism about the West, his savage indignation before emergent Soviet power, his complacent acceptance of a Fascist regime, his disdain for popular politicians have been taken to be his typical habits of mind, but we can see them here to be quite out of keeping with his career. What was missing in his postwar temper was the application to politics of his artistic habits of subtle examination and ironic judgment.

Is it possible to form a general view of a mind so various, if not self-contradictory, so passionately committed to diverse ends, often so crotchety in its hold on fixed ideas? That there was a process of development (not necessarily of progress) at work in Conrad is attested to by the fact that changes in his political positions occur in close association with the phases of his artistic maturity. At first there was the no longer young novelist, emerging from his inherited orthodoxies, who focused on the imperialist cheat that had awakened him from his dogmatic slumber. There followed, at a time when Conrad found it necessary to maintain a double vision of socialism and socialists, stories that develop complex attitudes on European political movements. Later came the period of the great political novels at the precise time when Conrad was beginning to write essays on European politics and to take a stand on civil liberties in England. In the last phase of his art, the flabbiness of rhetoric and the weakening of artistry that have been widely noted occur simultaneously with his stiffening opinions on contemporary affairs and relaxing of his constitutional irony.

In this slow but transforming development a writer who began with a virulent anti-democratic bias came round to an extremist position against restrictive authority, not only in its blatant form in autocratic nations like Russia and Prussia but also in its relatively modest appearance in England, as we have observed. His early nationalistic sentiments have been seen to reappear throughout his career, yet to leave room for international solutions to national rivalries and for the ethos of European solidarity—this despite his continued doubts about international peace organizations and despite his insight into the decadence of European civilization.

The ambiguity of Conrad's thought on political questions is a necessary condition for the power of his political fiction. Nowhere did his complex political viewpoint enter into his fiction as fruitfully as on the subject of revolution. In order to gather the full measure of the art of Conrad's political novels, we need to be aware of how deeply he struggled with the issues of social change, how he remained committed to nationalist revolutions and declared social revolution a potential shortcut for the popular will, yet recoiled from the emergence of the anarchic forces which he knew to be latent and volatile in men. Not all his politics were ambiguous, however. Conrad retained throughout his career a straightforward attitude toward governmental abuse of power, particularly in the area in which such power was most flagrantly increasing human misery—imperialism. Imperialism became for him a consistent bête noire (although he mitigated his initial opposition to the English show of force in the Boer War), and a large part of his fiction is shaped by his outspoken, emotional response to it.

A letter from the close of his life may stand as typical of the complex play of feelings and values that marks Conrad's political opinions throughout his career. In May, 1924, under Britain's first Labour government, Conrad received one of the few official recognitions of his work, the offer of a knighthood. His letter to Ramsay MacDonald, the Prime Minister, declining the offer expresses several aspects of his political imagination:

It is with the deepest possible sense of the honour H.M. The King is graciously willing to confer on me on your recommendation, that I beg leave to decline the proferred Knighthood.

In conveying to you my sincere thanks I venture to add, that, as a man whose early years were closely associated in hard toil and unforgotten friendships with British working men, I am especially touched on this offer being made to me during your Premiership.[11]

Three aspects of this formal note deserve attention. First, it marks a symbolic act of renunciation of his own aristocratic tradition which, if not an operative political sentiment, was still an emotional influence on many of his political opinions. Second, the refusal to identify himself with the community by receiving a national title might suggest a departure from the idealization of the organic state which has been suggested above, but the second paragraph in the letter makes an effort to reaffirm his tie with the social community. It would seem that Conrad conceived of the community as the fellowship of all working men, rather than as an abstract political symbol, the Crown. Third, by the lines addressed specifically to MacDonald, Conrad anticipates the possible interpretation of his action as a snub of a Labour government. By identifying himself personally with the working class, Conrad indicates an aspect of his political sympathies that cannot be ignored when dealing either with his essays or with his fiction.

Lest it be considered that this expression of sympathy with the Labour Party reflects only Conrad's wish to flatter MacDonald, a passage from an earlier letter on the rise of the Party's power should be considered together with it:

I don't know that the advent of class-parties into politics is abstractly good in itself. Class for me is by definition a hateful thing. The only class really worth consideration is the class of honest and able men to whatever sphere of human activity they may belong—that is, the class of workers throughout the nation. . . . But if class-parties are to come into being (the very idea seems absurd), well then, I am glad that this one had a considerable success at the elections. It will give Englishmen who call themselves by that name (and amongst whom there is no lack of intelligence, ability and honesty) that experience of the rudiments of statesmanship which will enable them to use their undeniable gifts to the best practical effect. For the same reason I am glad that they have not got the majority. (*LL*, II, 285, November 20, 1922)

[11] MS, New York Public Library, Berg Collection.

Conrad's attitude toward the political left is complicated by his unwillingness to accept the fact of the class struggle and its expression in party politics,
but, given the manifest signs of growing class consciousness among the
workers, he takes a deftly balanced view of them: he knows and admires their
talents and welcomes them to government, but he also knows and fears their
weaknesses and wishes their power to be balanced by that of others. He
would very likely have said the same of the middle and upper classes as well;
indeed, the political faith that emerges in Conrad's writings is one skeptical
of the exclusive rightness of any ideology or class but unstinting in the hope
that they may complement each other in a unified whole—the organic
community of the nation.

Chapter III

CONRAD IN HIS TRADITION

Jean-Jacques Rousseau

Edmund Burke

But the greatest figure of the times through which we have lived was The People itself, la Nation. For 150 years the French people has been always greater (and better) than its leaders, masters and teachers. And the same can be said of the English....
—Conrad, letter of April 21, 1917

Conrad's fiction has rarely been read in the light of contemporary currents of thought, probably because he has not been considered the sort of author, like Hardy or Shaw, who catches up and transforms into art the central ideas of his time. The preceding examination of his letters and essays should dispel any lingering assumptions that his reflections on politics and society were random or superficial. Yet it remains to account for the peculiar form which his broad social views took. To do so it will be necessary to make a brief review of a widespread intellectual tradition that prevailed throughout the nineteenth century and to look, in particular, at the form it assumed at the turn of the century, when Conrad was beginning to write.

The dominant culture of nineteenth-century England has been called by various names, according to its manifestations: "Utilitarianism" in ethics, "Liberalism" in economics, "Radicalism" in politics, "individualism" in private life and business practice. Basic to its spirit was the tradition of empiricism in British philosophy and of pragmatism in the national temperament, especially since the ascendancy of the middle class. This culture of hard facts and unsentimental outlook had been under continuous attack by the Romantic poets and their Victorian successors, but the advance of industrialization, imperialism, and national wealth made it the moving spirit of the Victorian age. In the latter half of the century, what we shall henceforth call "individualism" received an enormous boost from the popularization of the theory of natural selection as "survival of the fittest," while attempts to prevent the degeneration of Darwinist theory into an apology for economic amorality and nationalist aggressiveness proved ineffectual.

The individual, in classical Liberal theory, was a rational being who could be depended upon to know his self-interest and to act on it in predictable ways. These acts would be aggressive and competitive, even vicious, but out of private vices emerged public virtues, as the aggregate of selfish actions tended to further the economic development of the nation as a whole. Each person was an atom without inherent connection with other atoms or with the mass of them, but the system if left undirected would act *as if* it had an inner direction, and this unplanned and uncoordinated activity would lead more dependably to the good of the whole than any attempt to adjust it or tamper with its free operation.

In the capitalist era, both on the international and national scenes, the reverse of these expectations appeared to be coming about. True, national wealth was increasing, the Empire was expanding and the system was relatively stable, but that wealth was not being distributed effectively to ensure social stability, and the future promised not peace but class conflict—

possibly revolution. Similarly, on the international scale, because of unrestrained economic and colonial competiton between nations, war was on the ascendant and was even deemed inevitable. Within the economy, instead of the celebrated free competition, government had taken an active role to support business enterprise by allowing it to utilize public resources to further private gain. Economists like J. A. Hobson questioned whether imperialism was a profitable venture for the national economy, in view of the public outlay required for military protection of private interests. Liberal theory had held that state to be best which governed least and made it serve the negative role of "hinderer of hindrances" to free competition; in practice, laissez-faire society gave the state a positive role—but only to serve class interests. To an increasing number of thinkers, then, social stability seemed to lie in giving the state a positive function in fostering the entire community's welfare.

Toward the close of the century, the shortcomings of individualism in its social application had been manifested clearly enough to give rise to a variety of opposition movements. The Marxist Social Democratic League under Hyndman, the gradualist Fabian Society of the Webbs, and the minority wing among the Liberals which was to become the Labour Party—these were signs of a trend that reached its peak in the wave of strikes of 1908–12. It was to this set of phenomena that Conrad was responding when he made revolution the theme of his political novels. The native left wing was not as dramatic a threat to English institutions as Conrad's anarchists might have seemed to be, yet his readers must have felt the subject was one that involved the fate of Britain.

As we have seen, Conrad was fully as dismayed by certain aspects of Victorian culture as were the most radical of its critics, but he was far from joining cause with them, due to a temperamental difference that extends to the deepest sources of his thought. His philosophical temper makes itself felt in the course of political arguments with his friends among the socialists. As we have seen in his letters to Cunninghame Graham, Garnett, and Wells, Conrad's politics were derived from a set of absolute presuppositions about the nature of reality, and he held that the politics with which he differed were equally tied to a metaphysics—one that he could not accept. In point of fact, the philosophical roots of the leftward movement of the British intelligentsia were not distinct from the rationalist-empiricist sources of the individualistic culture they were attempting to reform.

In contrast to the latter tradition, there had survived from the world picture of the Middle Ages and the Renaissance a set of ideas about the way the world is organized which can be called "organicism" in its Romantic and Victorian form. In place of the nominalist or atomist metaphysics implied by individualist theory, the varying forms of belief in a chain of being had emphasized the interconnection and unified direction of the myriad members of the universe. In the social sphere, the Medieval-Renaissance doctrine of the place of the state in a system of divine governance, and the related notion of the mutual responsibility of all members of the body politic, had survived in an altered form in the eighteenth-century version of the Great Chain of Being, and particularly in the ethics of sympathy. But within the Romantic movement, a social philosophy was erected to challenge the individualist ethos at its root: its conception of man as an isolated, rational, and scarcely responsible atom, and its conception of a society as a mere artifice designed to maximize individual freedom by keeping its functions negative. Although the socialists of Conrad's acquaintance went beyond this view of the negative state, they failed to develop a philosophy of man which would give the state more than the mechanical function of fostering material improvements. The idea of the brotherhood of men was certainly espoused at this time, but lacked a philosophical basis that could make it acceptable to a skeptic of Conrad's temper. Such a basis existed in organicism.

At first glance, it might seem unlikely that organicist philosophies could have had a direct impact on Conrad, an artist with little academic training or contact, with an ingrained suspicion of philosophical systems, and with a pessimistic bent that alienated him from most schemes of social improvement. But the philosophy of the organic state, as I shall attempt to demonstrate, has many points of correspondence with Conrad's thought. Like him, the British organicists, who base themselves on German idealism, sharply criticize laissez-faire society and its individualist ethic; they envision a social ideal of community, though they differ on the possibility of its attainment. Some of their views are akin to the Romantic theories of the *Volk* which informed Polish nationalism (among other nineteenth-century European independence movements), for Polish thought also had its origins in German idealist philosophy. It was in a Germanic intellectual milieu that Conrad was raised, especially after his father's death, and it is therefore possible to account for a German-idealist strain in his work even in the absence of direct contact with his philosophical contemporaries in England.

There were, moreover, two elements of his Polish heritage which were peculiarly well suited for preparing to conceive of society as other than an anarchic competition of independent individuals. The first of these was the keynote of nationalism itself: the doctrine that the real political entity is not the artificially constructed state (which may be arbitrarily imposed on a nation by an occupying power) but the historical community of the people, whose culture survives the vicissitudes of political power. It is unlikely that Conrad's preparatory education in German-speaking schools in Austrian-held Cracow would have made him aware of the sources of this doctrine in the works of Herder and Hegel. But political discussion in nineteenth-century Poland was charged with a variety of interpretations of the root ideas of German organicism, ranging from mystical notions of a spiritual community of the Slavic peoples (led by a resurgent Poland, of course) to Joachim Lelewel's sociological account of the deep ties of the peasant *Gemeinschaft* community.

The second cultural tendency at work in Conrad's Poland was the Romantic literary tradition in which he was steeped. Conrad's latest editor sums it up:

> Ideas of moral and national responsibility pervaded [Polish Romantic] literature: it would be difficult to find a major work in which the two types of duty were not closely linked. It meant that the moral problems of an individual were posed in terms of the social results of his actions; and ethical principles were based on the idea that an individual, however exceptional he might be, is always a member of a group, responsible for its welfare.[1]

In addition to this emphasis on the unity of the individual with his community, there are organicist historical theories at work in the literature of Conrad's youth. The influence of organicism can be traced even more directly: Conrad's father wrote in the train of Zygmunt Krasiński, a major poet whose social idealism was a Christainized version of the Hegelian progress toward a rational state.

Another work of the period stands in the Polish organicist tradition in a position equal to the central role of Scott in English organicism. The out-standing work of nineteenth-century Polish literature, Mickiewicz's *Pan Tadeusz*, is shot through with the same notion—that of the organic unity of

---

[1] Najder (ed.), *Conrad's Polish Background*, p. 15.

a nation created by its history and folk traditions—that is to be found in the novels of Scott. Just as Scott expresses in fiction the organicist doctrines of Burke, so Mickiewicz expresses the comparable doctrines of Germano-Polish nationalism.[2] Conrad's own fiction, especially his historically placed political fiction, is in the spirit of Scott and Mickiewicz, not only in historical form but in political content. Like them, he celebrates the values of the *Volk*, its traditional manners and moral ties, and suggests the weight of national history in shaping, almost determining, human action.

Apart from the Polish sources of his thought, Conrad was steeped in the literary culture of his adopted country and formed himself, consciously or unconsciously, in the "great tradition" of nineteenth-century British fiction. To a large extent, the tradition runs parallel to the organicist tradition, and Conrad could have gradually acquired his organicism through his reading of the Victorian novelists, poets, and "prophets."

This group of writers has also been called "the Burke tradition,"[3] but this puts too much emphasis on its political side, unless we remember, with Matthew Arnold, that Burke is "so great" because he "saturates politics with thought." The kind of thought to which Arnold points, in making Burke an example to mid-Victorian England in this well-known passage of "The Function of Criticism at the Present Time," is precisely the organicist thought he had himself inherited from Burke by way of his father. Seen in this light, the Burke tradition becomes a broader intellectual movement than can be circumscribed in such phrases as "political conservatism" or "the Old Tory orthodoxy." It is itself a prime example of its own intellectual ideal: a living current of ideas that branches into many streams and penetrates to unexpected regions. To list the main figures in this tradition is to name

[2] Cf. Donald Davie, *The Heyday of Sir Walter Scott* (London, 1961), pp. 19–20, 54–55. Passing references in this study are among the clearest statements of the relationship that I have seen, e.g., the mention of their

perception that the central fact of politics, and the guiding principle of all public and much private morality, is the fact of community considered as a state of being or a state of feeling. The name of Burke and the title of a work so strictly and deliberately parochial as "The Old Cumberland Beggar"—these may suffice to distinguish this wisdom from the nationalistic chauvinism which is its perversion. And this is a wisdom rediscovered by the Romantic movement, which both Pushkin and Mickiewicz appreciated in Scott. . . . (P. 19)

[3] Frederick Mulhauser, "The Tradition of Burke," in Joseph E. Baker (ed.), *The Reinterpretation of Victorian Literature* (Princeton, 1950), pp. 153 ff.

most of the major forces in nineteenth-century English literary culture: the Lake Poets, especially Coleridge; the Arnolds, father and son; the Christian Socialists; Disraeli's "Young England" movement; Carlyle and his heirs, Ruskin and Dickens; and one writer who represented a mixture of this and other intellectual currents, George Eliot. Their broad social views took final form in the systematic philosophical formulations of the Oxford group of neo-Hegelian idealists who loomed large in English academic life in the last third of the century.

No doubt the first thing to be said of this group of thinkers and artists is that it is, in a cultural sense, conservative. Its conservatism will be found to rest on values of a large-minded and life-enhancing kind: the values of historical tradition, human community, and natural vitality. As a result of these habits of mind—and quite apart from the affirmation of progressive political measures which such figures as Matthew Arnold and George Eliot make—this is a constitutionally cautious breed, willing to let little die that man has thought or made. Even Arnold and Eliot, who stand out from their largely Tory brotherhood, betray signs of profound agitation at the advent of the Second Reform Bill, which enfranchised a large part of the working class.[4] Although their critique of contemporary society led them to voice some doctrines similar to those of the developing socialist ideology of the nineteenth century—general notions which were only rarely translated into practical programs like those of Maurice and Morris—the root ideas of the organicist tradition, as well as the political programs drawn from it, are different from those of socialism. When once it is clear that the organicist tradition has little to do with socialism, that it is often politically conservative, and that its proponents are weighted down with anxieties about any radical transformation of the living tradition of the past, it becomes possible to see Conrad, standing at the end of the century, within this broad movement of social thought.

The prevailing approach to Conrad, emphasizing his interest in the isolated individual and the crucial need for social roots, can now be placed on a philosophical basis: the primacy of the community, which gives individual life its possibility and its value. It is his awareness of the priority of the social unit

[4] Cf. Raymond Williams, *Culture and Society: 1780–1950* (orig. pub., 1958; New York, 1960), pp. 115–16, on Eliot's "Address to Working Men, by Felix Holt," warning the workers against radically changing the nation before radically changing their own moral character; also pp. 134–36, on Arnold's fears after the pulling down of the Hyde Park railings—and the expression of those fears in the description of the "Populace" in *Culture and Anarchy.*

to the individual self which places Conrad squarely within the organicist tradition. To follow the development of this root idea we must go back to Burke.

The Burke tradition began as a "revolt against the eighteenth century," in Alfred Cobban's terms,[5] and particularly against the Enlightenment concept of society as a contract. The implication of the contract theory is that the state is a legal fiction whose real existence lies in its constituent elements, the individuals who will to become citizens or members in a kind of corporation. It was this atomistic conception of the individual—and the corresponding conception of society as an artificial, voluntary, legalistic arrangement—which extended into the theories of nineteenth-century individualism, and which Burke criticized by proposing another idea of society, that of organic unity.

Burke conceived society not as a businesslike contract but as a spiritual and cultural union: "Society is indeed a contract . . . but the state ought not to be considered as nothing better than a partnership agreement in a trade. . . . It is a partnership in all science; a partnership in all art; a partnership in every virtue, and in all perfection. . . . it becomes a partnership not only between those who are living, but between those who are living, those who are dead, and those who are to be born."[6] It becomes so through the historical process in which the people of a nation share common experiences and develop common values, bequeathing them to their children. The underlying metaphor here is of the family, rather than of the business, and Burke's thought tends toward the psychology of blood ties, race, and heredity, rather than toward individual psychology. Burke's conception of society is, then, a critique of his own age's assumption that individuals willed their relationship to society, and could reject their creation, the state, at will. It suggests a radically opposite theory, that society is an organism of which the individuals are the "members"—almost in the physiological sense of the term—and that the state is not merely the sum of their divisive interests but a source, perhaps the only source, of the values by and for which they live. It is to such values that Conrad's "common conservative principle" ultimately refers.

[5] *Edmund Burke and the Revolt against the Eighteenth Century* (2d ed., 1st ed., 1929; New York, 1960).

[6] *Reflections on the French Revolution* (orig. pub. as *Reflections on the Revolution in France*, 1790; London and New York, 1910), p. 93.

In close relation to the Burke tradition, another strand of Romantic
political thought lies behind Conrad's view of society. It centers on the
name of Rousseau. Again, there is no need to establish that Conrad read the
philosopher: his influence is so pervasive in nineteenth-century nationalistic
movements as to affect anyone who grew up in their shadow, as Conrad did.
It is Rousseau (and Herder) to whom modern historians ascribe a tutelary
role in the resurgence of most of the minority groups throughout Europe,[7]
but the influence of Rousseau on Poland is especially direct and striking.
It was the scandalous *philosophe* who was invited by a group of enlightened
Poles to draft a constitution for Poland in 1772, at a time when its national
survival was being threatened by the Partitions. Rousseau's *Considération sur
le Gouvernement de Pologne* is an outline of his theories of the organic state:
it calls for the development of institutions which will further the cohesive
tendencies of the people, and places heavy emphasis on the integrative use
of the arts, education, local customs, and direct stimulants to patriotism like
national honors and holidays. Today some of these proposals bear the stigma
of their later totalitarian perversions, but throughout the last century they
were progressive ideals cherished by European nationalists and, by the same
token, combated by those empires which sought to maintain their ascendancy over subject peoples.

On first consideration, it may appear absurd to place both Burke and
Rousseau at the roots of Conrad's intellectual tradition. These two names
stand as polar antagonists not only in the debate on the French Revolution
but in the continuation of that debate which absorbs most modern political
philosophers. It was Burke who was among the first to place Rousseau's
name at the head of the list of enemies of civilization, and the majority of
commentators after him have maintained the view that "despotism was in his
brain if not in his heart."[8] Another view of Rousseau, best represented by
Alfred Cobban—who is also one of the ablest interpreters of Burke—holds
that the two resemble each other more than they conflict, and suggests that
they have a common progeny in the line of the "Burke tradition." The state
for both these thinkers is the ultimate political norm and is conceived by
both as a *nation*, the community of people bound together by organic ties
derived from their historical tradition and sense of place, their continuity in

---

[7] E.g., Carlton J. H. Hayes, *The Historical Evolution of Modern Nationalism* (New
York, 1931), *passim*.

[8] Guido de Ruggiero, *The History of European Liberalism*, trans. R. G. Collingwood (London, 1927), p. 63.

time and space. From this common ground of Romantic nationalism are derived the numerous positions held in common by Burke and Rousseau: their opposition to revolution, which shatters the continuity of historical development; their affirmation of a national culture to express the unity of popular belief; their contempt for any cosmopolitanism which is not rooted in a deeper love of homeland; and their awareness of the need for an international federation of nations, retaining their independence but observing a pre-established rule of international law. As we have seen, Conrad stands in this tradition at most points.

Beyond the doctrines of the state and of the relations of states to each other, there is a strong current of influence stemming from Burke and Rousseau which colors much of nineteenth-century thought on the relation of the state to the individuals within it. Cobban sums the matter up: "according to Rousseau's way of looking at the question, the isolated individual in the state of nature is virtuous, society brings corruption, from which, since there is no returning to the state of nature, the only escape lies through the creation of political institutions, definitely planned to create an environment in which virtue becomes possible."[9] By another of the ironies which the reader of Rousseau learns to expect, the Romantic affirmation of the isolated individual in the state of nature turns into an ethic of sociability, in which the very notion of human values presupposes the rootedness of the individual in a community. This view of the moral value of social life is to be found not only in Burke but in a succession of organicist writers, to which Conrad is a major addition.

With Coleridge, the German sources of organicist thought were brought into English letters, but in a form which dissolved at least part of their abstractness. His effect was to cut through the German tendency to exalt the collectivity at the expense of the individual, and to establish a stronger emphasis on the full social development of the person. It is his membership in the community that allows the putative individual to develop: citizenship makes men human.[10]

Even before his political conversion, while still in his radical youth,

[9] *Rousseau and the Modern State* (2nd ed., 1st ed., 1934; Hamden, Conn., 1964), p. 135.
[10] See Robert Preyer, *Bentham, Coleridge, and the Science of History* ("*Beiträge zur Englischen Philologie*," Vol XII; Bochum-Langendreer, 1958).

Coleridge revealed a belief in the value to the individual of group loyalty that preceded his philosophical development. In "Religious Musings" (1794) he had written:

> 'Tis the sublime of man,
> Our noontide Majesty, to know ourselves
> Parts and proportions of one wondrous whole!
> This fraternises man, this constitutes
> Our charities and bearings. . . .

In the middle of his career, when he turned to political theory in *The Statesman's Manual* (1816), his organicism was directed against the atomistic theory that society is an aggregate of individuals. He addresses the "man of understanding" or lower reason:

> Canst thou persuade the living or the inanimate to stand separate even as thou hast separated them? . . . Do not all press and swell under one attraction, and live together in promiscuous harmony, each joyous in its own kind, and in the immediate neighbourhood of myriad others that in the system of thy understanding are distant as the poles?[11]

Coleridge's organicism took a practical turn in *A Lay Sermon* of the following year (1817). It is his clear statement of the positive ends of the state that gives a new note to organicist thought, a note that was to be sustained by the numerous Coleridgians of the Victorian age. His definition of these ends approximates later notions of the welfare state:

> We suppose the negative ends of a State already attained, viz. its own safety by means of its own strength, and the protection of person and property for all its members, there will then remain its positive ends: 1. To make the means of subsistence more easy to each individual. 2. To secure to each of its members the hope of bettering his own condition or that of his children. 3. The development of those faculties which are essential to his humanity, i.e. to his rational and moral being.

This conception of society holds that it is a positive force: that it is not only a hinderer of hindrances to individual freedom but that it can become an active agent of individual self-realization; that it is, ideally, a living culture which should lead men to moral and intellectual development and through which they might learn to govern their divisive individualist impulses; and that it is only in society that culture can accomplish its educative function.

---

[11] Appendix, sec. (A); quoted from *Political Tracts of Wordsworth, Coleridge and Shelley*, ed. R. J. White (Cambridge, 1953), p. 39. The quotation which follows is from pp. 108–9.

In defining the social formation of the individual, the organicism of Coleridge's political theory employs the synthetic logic of his literary criticism, as in the following example:

> Unlike a million of tigers, a million of men is very different from a million times one man. Each man in a numerous society is not only co-existent with, but virtually organized into, the multitude of which he is an integral part. His *idem* is modified by the *alter*. And there arise impulses and objects from this *synthesis* of the *alter et idem*, myself and my neighbour.[12]

Coleridge's organicist conception of human life amounts here to a new conception of the individual, much more relevant to a social conception of man like Conrad's than the notions of the individualist school. Coleridge conceives the individual as changing his nature in the community; indeeed, for him, man's nature is fulfilled only in social life. The true problem for the individual becomes, from this point of view, not the competition of his claims with those of the group, but the discovery or creation of the conditions that will allow him to fulfill himself within the social organism.

Coleridge's thinking on the idea of nationalism is the organicist principle closest to Conrad: "a People *derives* it's [sic] unity from the Government (or the State) & that unity is *real* only where each individual of the 3 or the 30 million yielding the same obedience to the State, all are capable of being contemplated as *one*, as *a* people, *this* or *that* People!"[13] National unity, then, presupposes a high moral level in the individuals who compose it; it is likely to be rare. It is his skeptical view of actual nations that saves Coleridge from

[12] "An Essay on Faith," *Aids to Reflection and the Confessions of an Inquiring Spirit* . . . (orig. pub., 1838–39; London and New York, 1893), p. 347. Although here the interaction of persons is shown to effect real changes in the nature of individuals, Coleridge was aware that organicism is ultimately metaphorical—that only biological life is truly organic, while society displays only some features of organic organization, but not the crucial feature of organic relationships: automatic activity. To put the matter in the words of a recent commentator:

> The members of a society are self-conscious; they know themselves to be members and fulfil their functions in the light of this knowledge. The organs in an organism are not self-conscious and do not know that they are organs. They fulfil their functions blindly and automatically. A society lives in the thought and volition of its members; the life of an organism is a complex process of natural events. (A. J. M. Milne, *The Social Philosophy of English Idealism* [London, 1962], p. 63)

[13] Marginalia to Sir John Walsh, *Popular Opinions on Parliamentary Reform Considered* (1831); quoted in Carl R. Woodring, *Politics in the Poetry of Coleridge* (Madison, Wisc., 1961), p. 41.

that worship of the *status quo* into which Burke fell. J. H. Muirhead enlarges on this point:

> while in [Burke's] mind the balance actually attained by the British Constitution dominated all his thinking, and the 'moral unit' was interpreted in terms of what he saw before him, Coleridge regarded all actual Constitutions, including that of his own country, as temporary and imperfect embodiments of an 'idea' that was slowly revealing itself on earth, if not as a city of God, at any rate as a society of seekers after Him.[14]

It is this strong skeptical note in Coleridge's idealism that clearly anticipates Conrad's view of society. The political condition of the West was to both minds by and large contemptible. Although Conrad lacked a City of God as a divine ideal to propose for the future, like Coleridge he saw the movement of "seekers" as a glimmering light in a darkening world, and the direction in which his seekers moved was toward an organic community. It is to Colderidge that we can trace the impetus of organicist social criticism that filters down through the major Victorian literary figures to such modern writers as Forster, Lawrence, and Conrad.

In the same decade in which Coleridge was applying his organicist theories to the condition of England, another wave of German thought, represented by Carlyle, began to appear in England. Carlyle's influence is too diffuse and fundamental for easy summary; it is also so widely acknowledged that a review may be superfluous here. The organic metaphors (such as the world-tree, Igdrasil) in which he set out his *Weltanschauung* and the medieval ideals of an integrated and responsible society which he recommended to his contemporaries are only the most prominent aspects of his organicism. Yet in Carlyle's career—beginning as it did in a clarion call for action against the decadent condition of England and ending in jingoism, power worship, and reactionary hysteria at the prospect of reform—the organicist tradition reaches a fork in the road. Carlyle took the path toward totalitarianism (whether he reached it is still open to debate), while the main stream of the tradition needed another "prophet" to direct it toward modern democratic society.

It remained for Matthew Arnold to make organicism a distinctively modern answer to individualism by developing Coleridge's organic society into a

---

[14] *Coleridge as Philosopher* (London and New York, 1930), p. 194.

concept of "culture."[15] Faced with the mid-Victorian "condition-of-England" question, Arnold was alarmed at the dangers entailed in the individualist norm of conduct—in economic activity, in personal relations, and in politics —based on constant competition, irresponsible subjectivity, and unlimited freedom. Hence the emergence in *Culture and Anarchy* of a positive conception of the state that implies the development of regulative laws and cultural institutions that would channel individual dissidence into national unity.[16] The state must be strong enough to control the individual's absolute claim to liberty of action, and the Protestant mind's "dissidence of dissent" must be replaced by the capacity to see the social structure steadily and whole, free of class bias and personal eccentricity. "Anarchy" (Arnold's term for unbridled individualism) acquires considerable amplification in the writings of Conrad, and we shall see that it is used to attack not only the radical left but, much as Arnold had done, individualistic society as well.

When Arnold emphasizes the values of cooperation and the spirit of unity in national life, he shows himself akin to Carlyle as a voluntarist rather than a determinist in ethics. The burden of creating social community is placed, ironically, upon the individual—upon the moral will—and the sum of these wills (together with their concrete actions) makes up the national life, its progress or its stagnation: "And because men are all members of one great whole, and the sympathy which is in human nature will not allow one member to be indifferent to the rest or to have a perfect welfare independent of the rest, the expansion of our humanity . . . must be a *general* expansion."[17] Arnold's alternating irritability with Carlyle and constant reversion to Carlylian formulas are the result of a fundamental affinity with Carlyle's philosophy which had been outraged by the ghastly forms it took in his politics. Indeed, Arnold's central effort in his political writings may be said to be an attempt to lead organicist thinking out of the desert of Carlylian authoritarianism and into harmony with progressive legislation. That he

[15] Arnold was, in political thinking as well as in personal temperament, the true son of his father. The elder Arnold's political theory has recently been termed the "Liberal Anglican idea of history," and that idea has been shown to be markedly organicist (see Duncan Forbes, *The Liberal Anglican Idea of History* [Cambridge, 1952], p. 1 *et passim*).

[16] Thomas Arnold, too, has been shown to uphold statist doctrines; cf. Lionel Trilling, *Matthew Arnold* (orig. pub., 1949; New York, 1955), p. 51. It was he, of course, who provided the point of contact with Coleridge's thought.

[17] *Culture and Anarchy* (orig. pub., 1869), ed. J. Dover Wilson (Cambridge, 1952), p. 45.

succeeded in doing so indicates the possibility of deriving a meliorist politics from organicist assumptions; it is a reassurance that organicism need not lead inevitably to the strident nationalism, hidebound conservatism, or absolute statism of its most notorious twentieth-century descendants. It will be seen that Conrad's politics stand in the Arnoldian rather than the Carlylian branch of the tradition.

The history of nineteenth-century English organicism might profitably be continued at greater length (a full-length study of this major theme remains to be made). If it is to be related to Conrad's mind, it should, however, emphasize the genre to which he was most deeply tied, the Victorian novel. From Disraeli on, Victorian novelists rest their social criticism on an organicist ideal of social community more or less directly received from Carlyle. The list might include Dickens, Kingsley, Mrs. Gaskell, Trollope, Meredith, and Hardy; the idea can be seen most clearly in George Eliot.

The organicism of George Eliot's fiction is implicit in her choice of subject matter: the ongoing life of the country folk, the village community, and the social structure of the town. It is also present in her literary style, as John Holloway has characterized it (speaking of her metaphors): "They all liken human life to those parts of nature that are gradual or complex or that take place unseen. The slowly growing tree is one of the commonest. . . . "[18] The sources of this language lie in the social philosophy by which Eliot's works are shaped.

Before embarking on her career in fiction, George Eliot had studied German philosophy (and much else), and in the summer of 1856, while planning her first novel, she set out an organicist view of society in a long review of two books by a contemporary German sociologist.[19] She seized this opportunity to dissociate her brand of organicism from Victorian medievalism, the post-Romantic nostalgia that idealized a feudal past without a realistic notion of poverty and other social conditions:

the aristocratic dilettantism which attempts to restore the "good old times" by a sort of idyllic masquerading, and to grow feudal fidelity and veneration

[18] *The Victorian Sage: Studies in Argument* (orig. pub., 1953; New York, 1965), p. 147.
[19] "The Natural History of German Life," review of W. H. von Riehl, *Die burgerliche Gesellschaft* and *Land und Leute*, in *Essays of George Eliot*, ed. Thomas Pinney (New York and London, 1963), pp. 266–99.

as we grow prize turnips, by an artificial system of culture—none of these diverging mistakes can co-exist with a real knowledge of the People, with a thorough study of their habits, their ideas, their motives. (P. 272)

Riehl, on the other hand, is erected into a type of those who, like George Eliot herself, do know the folk in the concrete process of their development:

> He sees in European society *incarnate history*. . . . The external conditions which society has inherited from the past are but the manifestation of inherited internal conditions in the human beings who compose it; the internal conditions and the external are related to each other as the organism and its medium, and development can take place only by the gradual consentaneous development of both. (P. 287)

Since society is an organism, the sociologist, the political theorist, and the novelist must have (to extend the term) organic knowledge, concrete and sympathetic, if they are to attain their object. But the novelist has a special responsibility, by his absorption in individual character, to know the organic ties of the individual to his society.

The passage continues by illustrating the relations of individual and society in the moral and political realms:

> As a necessary preliminary to a purely rational society, you must obtain purely rational men, free from the sweet and bitter prejudices of hereditary affection and antipathy; which is as easy as to get running streams without springs, or the leafy shade of the forest without the secular growth of trunk and branch.

This is a statement of George Eliot's political position—later to be adumbrated in her "Address to Working Men, by Felix Holt"—implying considerable skepticism of the reformist ideal of a rational society. Further, this sentence shows the difficult, even tragic, consequences of organicism disregarded by previous writers: since men are rooted in the past and bound by irrational ties of society and kinship, there is very little that can be done at the level of public policy to change their deepest values and habits. This is an attitude which Conrad considerably amplifies, and it is no accident that it was given to two novelists to maintain the organicist ideal in the face of a tragic insight into human limitations. It is their knowledge of the organic roots of human nature and its impermeability by changed social conditions, rather than a disavowal of those social changes themselves, that informs George Eliot's and Conrad's so-called conservatism. It is because it lacks moral efficacy, rather than for any immorality inherent in it, that both novelists stand off from revolutionary change. And it is their sense of the depth of people's inherited prejudices that makes them set down as a precondition of social progress the growth of the individual self, its purgation (or propitiation) of the irrational and egoistic forces that tend to destroy it—a process which George Eliot traces in the careers of reformers like Daniel Deronda and Will Ladislaw.

George Eliot's version of the organicist tradition does not have its main stem in the English, Burkian school; her initial inspiration is from the left-Hegelian Feuerbach, and she draws freely on other organicist thinkers, like Riehl, in the German tradition. Even more important, however, in her unique formation is her absorption in Comte's Positivism and closeness to its English descendants. In some members of this movement, particularly Lewes and Spencer, a rationalist dedication to modern science mixes curiously with the older organicist thinking: social institutions and personal behavior are to be described by scientific laws devoid of idealist metaphysics; but these laws are to be framed in such a way as to account for the complexity and evolutionary character of psychological and sociological phenomena.[20] There is, as a result of this relationship, an inveterate scientism in George Eliot's accounts of the individual's relation to society that is far from Conrad's studied belletristic tone. But he shares with her a firmly rooted distrust of abstract laws as applied to human things—shares, too, her avowed casuistry in morals and politics. And her tragic individuals sundered from their societies (Maggie Tulliver, Tito Melema, Gwendolen Harleth, and others) are closer to Conrad's isolated individuals than are those of any other of his predecessors.[21]

A further phase of English organicism was its reformulation by a school of systematic philosophers at Oxford in the 1860's and after. The Oxford "neo-Hegelian" group was centered at Balliol College around T. H. Green

[20] Lewes uses the term "super-organically evolved" to describe the social organism; how much of an innovation this term indicates in his Positivist version of organicism is not clear to me, but it implies an effort to put the originally idealist theory on a materialist basis. See, on George Eliot and Positivism, Bernard J. Paris, *Experiments in Life: George Eliot's Quest for Values* (Detroit, Mich., 1965), p. 25 ff.

[21] Of Tito it is said: "It seems to me that he is one of the *demoni*, who are of no particular country. . . . His mind is a little too nimble to be weighted with all the stuff we men carry about in our hearts" (*Romola*, Bk. I, Chap. 19). The language closely resembles the description of the rootless intellectual Decoud in *Nostromo*.

(its other major figure, F. H. Bradley, was at Merton). Green and most of his associates were products of the Rugby education established by Thomas Arnold. Their awareness of Coleridge, Carlyle, and the elder Arnold as seminal thinkers places this intellectual movement within the English tradition, for its studies in Hegel served to systematize a native tendency.[22]

It is not, however, to Green but to his successors in the neo-Hegelian group—Bradley and Bernard Bosanquet—that we must look for the final form of nineteenth-century English organicism. These two philosophers, whose impact began to be felt in the 1890's, when Conrad started to write, bear a remarkable number of similarities to the novelist on ethical and social issues. In developing this comparison, one cannot hope to demonstrate direct influence: although Bosanquet was a popular lecturer in London and Bradley was much discussed in literary circles (witness T. S. Eliot's interest in him shortly afterward), Conrad is notorious for his avoidance of London intellectual life and his preference for the society of a select number of his fellow novelists who had also settled in Kent. Although he was probably not directly exposed to the systematic theories of the neo-Hegelians, his explicit statements on politics and the dramatic structure of his novels both attest to the presence in his intellectual milieu of a living tradition of organicist thought. We have here to do with the same sort of relationship between the artist and the philosophy of his time as that described by the art historian Erwin Panofsky: neither a vague "parallelism" nor a direct personal "influence," but a widely diffused "mental habit."

To establish that Conrad shared the organicist's mental habits, it is necessary to compare in some detail his social and ethical notions with the formulations of Bosanquet and Bradley. Bosanquet's *Philosophical Theory of the State* is a careful restatement of the heritage of German and English organicism we have traced through the century:

> in its essence, the State is the indwelling and explicit end of these modes of living of the people, and is strong in its union of the universal purpose with the particular interests of mankind. . . . In the organism of the State, i.e., in so far as we feel and think as citizens, feeling becomes affectionate loyalty, and explicit consciousness becomes political insight. . . . This feeling and insight are the true essence of patriotism . . . the every-day habit of looking on the commonwealth as our substantive purpose and the foundation of our lives.[23]

[22] Cf. Melvin Richter, *The Politics of Conscience: T. H. Green and His Age* (London, 1964), pp. 46 ff., 95–96.

[23] (London and New York, 1899), pp. 281–82.

What Bosanquet has done is to psychologize the abstract notion of a community, to locate community in the sense of communion shared by the members of a society. In doing so, he might seem to have made modern community a remote ideal; in cold fact, however, he accounts for the emotions of nationalism which have toppled empires. In his interest in men's personal loyalty to and proud identification with the state, Bosanquet is akin to Conrad, for whom these emotions were objects of lifelong concern.

To measure Conrad's affinity with Bosanquet, we might examine a typical expression of his attitude toward the people, who by their sentiments constitute the nation:

> All passes, all changes: the animosity of peoples, the handling of fleets, the forms of ships; and even the sea itself seems to wear a different and diminished aspect from the sea of Lord Nelson's day. In this ceaseless rush of shadows and shades, that, like the fantastic forms of clouds cast darkly upon the waters on a windy day, fly past us to fall headlong below the hard edge of an implacable horizon, we must turn to the national spirit, which, superior in its force and continuity to good and evil fortune, can alone give us the feeling of an enduring existence and of an invincible power against the fates. (*MS*, p. 194)

Without attaching metaphysical weight to the notion, Conrad sees the "national spirit"—in this passage it is the national unity that lay behind Lord Nelson—as capable of giving us the "feeling" of having a place in the universe, however transitory that place may actually be. The community of men's historical consciousness is, then, the precondition for the individual's secure existence. It is only this secular-spiritual community that provides a bulwark against the forces of chaos in man's natural and social environment.

On the basis of this theory, we can better understand why Conrad's lifelong nationalist sentiments (both Polish and English) were maintained without a trace of his characteristic irony. His commitment to Polish independence was not always in the forefront of his mind, as has been seen, but its persistence in him must be attributed to the organicist doctrine of self-realization through identification with the community. To the last, he affirmed that "Polish loyalty will be rooted in something . . . which is, in fact, life-enduring. It will be rooted in the national temperament, which is about the only thing on earth that can be trusted" (*NLL*, p. 129). "National temperament" is Conrad's term for the popular sentiments, manners, and sense of identity which the organicist tradition made the basis of political organization.

In his most extensive political analysis, "Autocracy and War," Conrad places nationalism in its historical context and assigns it a role in the progress toward a higher community:

> In Europe the old monarchical principle stands justified in its historical struggle with the growth of political liberty by the evolution of the idea of nationality as we see it concreted at the present time; by the inception of that wider solidarity grouping together around the standard of monarchical power these larger agglomerations of mankind. This service of unification, creating close-knit communities possessing the ability, the will, and the power to pursue a common ideal, has prepared the ground for the advent of a still larger understanding: for the solidarity of Europeanism, which must be the next step towards the advent of Concord and Justice; an advent that, however delayed by the fatal worship of force and the errors of national selfishness, has been, and remains, the only possible goal of our progress. (*NLL*, pp. 96–97)

This vision of an international community of member nations represents the flower of the organicist tradition traced above. Just as monarchism is justified by stimulating national unity, so the nation is not an end in itself for Conrad, but is justified as a stage in the development of international peace. The true existence of a nation is in "close-knit communities," whose members give themselves to a "common ideal." The perversion of national unity occurs when the state develops a tendency to pursue power for its own sake: "the fatal worship of force and the errors of national selfishness." It can find its genuine realization only in quite other terms, idealistic ones:

> The true greatness of a State . . . is a matter of logical growth, of faith and courage. Its inspiration springs from the constructive instinct of the people, governed by the strong hand of a collective conscience and voiced in the wisdom and counsel of men who seldom reap the reward of gratitude. Many States have been powerful, but, perhaps, none have been truly great—as yet. (*NLL*, p. 91)

What this "constructive instinct" is to construct and what the "common ideal" of the preceding passage is to be, Conrad—like the organicist philosophers—does not specify. It remains throughout his work a beckoning but evasive realm of higher possibility.

The organicist ethic of allegiance to the concrete, popular community should be seen in contrast to the prevailing individualist ethic of self-direction, self-realization, and self-assertion. The neo-Hegelians, too, made self-realization an ultimate goal but found it to lie only in identifying oneself with a body larger than the self. Only by joining oneself to the social group—particularly the nation, which the organicist conceives as a living, real body of men, like a ship's crew—only by loyalty to such a body can the individual find himself.

With a common body of ideals and a similar fund of imagery, Bradley's *Ethical Studies* is close in tenor to the moral bearing of Conrad's fiction. Bradley writes:

> To know what a man is . . . you must not take him in isolation. He is one of a people, he was born in a family, he lives in a certain society, in a certain state. What he has to do depends on what his place is, what his function is, and that all comes from his station in the organism. . . . The mere individual is a delusion of theory; and the attempt to realize it in practice is the starvation and mutilation of human nature, with total sterility or the production of monstrosities.[24]

This position corrects the traditional individualist theories, which fail to account either for the brutality which the unfettered individual displays or for the achievement of altruistic self-transcendence in social existence.

If it is true that this view of the individual is close to Conrad's, what follows for the reading of his novels is an extensive re-evaluation of many conventional interpretations. If we re-examine the well-known language of the Preface to *The Nigger of the "Narcissus,"* it will be seen to express not only the aesthetic doctrine of impressionism, which has often been noted, but also an organicist ethical doctrine. If the artist is successful in his task, which is "to make you hear, to make you feel— . . . before all, to make you *see*," the vision "shall awaken in the hearts of the beholders that feeling of unavoidable solidarity; of the solidarity in mysterious origin, in toil, in joy, in hope, in uncertain fate, which binds men to each other and all mankind to the visible world" (*NN*, p. x). The artist's role, then, is to knit men together in a universal community based on their awareness of a common fate.

[24] *Ethical Studies* (2d ed. rev., 1st ed., 1876; Oxford, 1927), pp. 173–74. The first sentence seems to be at variance with one of Conrad's central tales; "Heart of Darkness" insists that a man cannot be known under the circumstances of civilized life, but shows himself only when released from the external restraints of police and public opinion. But the two viewpoints are mutually consistent, for what Bradley speaks of is the emergence of man's ideal nature in social rootedness, while Conrad refers to the revelation of his predatory nature outside society. "Heart of Darkness" may be read as a parable of the laissez-faire individualism of Kurtz, which literally produces the "mutilation" and "monstrosities" to which Bradley alludes.

In more explicitly psychological language, Conrad explains that this unification is due to

> the latent feeling of fellowship with all creation—and to the subtle but invincible conviction of solidarity that knits together the loneliness of innumerable hearts, to the solidarity in dreams, in joy, in sorrow, in aspirations, in illusions, in hope, in fear, which bind men to each other, which binds together all humanity—the dead to the living and the living to the unborn. (*NN*, p. viii)

Thus, early in his writing career, and in the course of the most systematic statement of his aesthetic aims, Conrad defines his highest ethical values with overtones of Burke (see the passage on the "national spirit" quoted above) and of the organicist tradition.

The ethics of organicism gives wider relevance to Conrad's fiction. The prevailing image of the typical Conrad hero is that of the lonely mariner facing the implacable sea, like Tom Lingard, or the "odd man out" who is destroyed by a corrupt society, like Nostromo, or the aristocratic man of honor who is an anachronism in the materialistic modern world, like Il Conde. When these heroes are considered as proponents of various forms of individualism, the sympathy with which they are endowed derives rather from their pathetic alienation than from their nobility. From Jim and Kurtz to Peyrol and Heyst, the alienated man is either redeemed or not only insofar as he is able to identify his personal career with the life of a community. The moral crises of Conrad's heroes are object lessons in the failure of individualism, and it is hard to believe that Conrad was unaware of the tendentious impact of his tales in the cultural climate of his time.

In Conrad's view of the great historical heroes—and, by implication, of his own fictional heroes—the popular notion of the isolated individual resisting the mass of men is ironically reversed. For Conrad, Lord Nelson is the social hero par excellence: "To be so great and to remain so accessible to the affection of one's fellow-men is the mark of exceptional humanity. Lord Nelson's greatness was very human. It had a moral basis; it needed to feel itself surrounded by the warm devotion of a band of brothers" (*MS*, p. 187). Similarly, in the novels, it will be seen that Jim achieves his recovery not through romantic estrangement from the world but through immersion in the political and social life of a native community. Another defiant individualist, Martin Decoud of *Nostromo*, overcomes his dilettantism by placing himself at the center of a social revolution; he provides it with its ideology of provincial separatism. By the same token, his suicide is motivated by his new horror of isolation, after he has achieved a measure of self-realiza-tion in his wholehearted identification with his society. To take a last case, Razumov, the hero of *Under Western Eyes*, has been read as a victim of the stifling effect of revolutionary politics on the free development of the individ-ual. It is much truer to the complexity of that novel to see him attempting to find a balance among various allegiances—to persons, to state, to humanity at large—conflicting claims which pull him apart and ultimately destroy him because he has been reluctant to realize and act on the fundamental fact that human life is social, that there is nowhere for the individual to retire in isolation.

The most important relationship of the neo-Hegelians to Conrad lies in his art, not in the realm of political or sociological theory but in that of ethics. The moral life tends to be seen increasingly by Conrad as possible only in the community of men, of which the ship's crew is a primary symbol. It is no accident that Conrad, the former seaman, should have chosen his heroes mainly from the mariner class; it is equally characteristic that Bradley chose the term "My Station and Its Duties" for the central chapter of his *Ethical Studies*. So germane is this metaphor to the subject matter of Conrad's tales that it suggests that they have a common source in the cultural imagina-tion of England. Since the dawn of Britain's maritime predominance, the imagery of the sea has been used to express the ideals of duty, loyalty, and hierarchy, but perhaps never as markedly as in Bradley and Conrad.

Beyond its evocation of these traditional values, organicist ethics provides a firm ground for any conventional moral obligation. It is a functional ethic that provides a norm of conduct. Bradley writes:

> if the self to be realized is not exclusive of other selves, but on the contrary is determined, characterized, made what it is by relation to others; if my self which I aim at is the realization in me of a moral world which is a system of selves, an organism in which I am a member, and in whose life I live— then I cannot aim at my own wellbeing without aiming at that of others.[25]

The question is raised, then, of what acts the self can perform and in what phases of personal life it can operate for the well-being of others.

The answer, occasionally explicit in the organicist tradition (especially in Carlyle) and consistently found in Conrad, lies in the sphere of work— in what we shall call the "work ethic." The practical doctrine of *Ethical Studies* often reads like a translation into philosophical language of Conrad's

[25] *Ethical Studies*, p. 116.

nautical pieties: subordination to authority, devotion to the given task, fidelity to comrades, identification with the mariner's tradition of service, acceptance of the difficulty of life within destructive nature, and the manifestation of effort and courage. In their narrower applications by Bradley or Conrad, these doctrines have the effect of rationalizing the *status quo* by extending the relationships of a work situation to political life generally. In their deepest sense, however, these values are the expression of a classically tragic sense of life.

"Work is the law": Conrad begins his essay "Tradition" with the Renaissance maxim of Leonardo. He goes on to develop it in terms not of Renaissance individualism but of organic community:

> From the hard work of men are born the sympathetic consciousness of a common destiny, the fidelity to right practice which makes great craftsmen, the sense of right conduct which we may call honour, the devotion to our calling and the idealism which is not a misty-winged angel without eyes, but a divine figure of terrestrial aspect with a clear glance and with its feet resting firmly on the earth on which it was born. (*NLL*, p. 194)

Work is thus not an end in itself, but a means to certain values: a shared cultural imagination, high aesthetic standards, the artistic strength gained from roots in the social organism, an unsentimental (and non-transcendental) spiritual life. The ideas are not original with Conrad but go back to Ruskin, who stands within the organicist tradition, deeply influenced by Carlyle. What is unusual is the application of aesthetic values to the homely subject of this essay, the merchant marine. Conrad has extended Ruskin's ideals of ethical craftsmanship from the realm of art to that of physical labor.

In Conrad's sea tales, the value of work lies not in itself but in the performance of a social obligation. With certain rare exceptions, work does not for Conrad exist in isolation, as an individual's act, but only as the combined effort of an organic group—the community of labor—the crew. Nostromo and Kurtz are defeated and destroyed largely because of their isolation in work: they fulfill the tasks of energetic labor but lack its ideal social form; usually they work alone. Nostromo's death is a perfect parable of this principle of social labor: he is killed by Viola in the midst of his secret activities, just because they are secret (Viola suspects him of being an unwelcome suitor for his daughter).

Further, the value of work is not found in the mere act of working, as it is for Carlyle, but rather in the commitment to and identification with a role, or "calling," in the terminology of the Protestant ethic. Conrad's account of the achievement of selfhood through work is related to the Goethian ideal traced by Carlyle in *Sartor Resartus*, but it has its classical formulation in a passage from Hegel quoted by Bosanquet:

> The individual's life is not predetermined by his birth, but he is thrown face to face with economic necessity. . . . He has to strip off his crudeness and vanity, and, of himself, mould himself into something which fulfills a want. This is a step without which there can be no true freedom—the giving one's self by one's own act a definite place in the region of external necessity, the "becoming *something*," or attaching oneself to a definite class of service renderers.[26]

In this light, we can understand the role of work in a type of tale frequently told by Conrad, of which the greatest examples are "Youth," *The Shadow Line*, and "The Secret Sharer." The problem of work is, in these tales, not one of overcoming laziness but of committing oneself to a role—of developing one's sense of self under a particular title, or officer's rank. Adopting this mask of authority commits one to responsibilities toward the crew and eventually leads one to identify with the social unit which they constitute: the ship.

Beyond the self-development process traced in Conrad's tales of young officers, the extreme of total absorption into the community is reached with Singleton. What distinguishes his labor is not simply his skill or his dependability but his unconsciousness; yet that quality is not a value in itself, as Conrad claimed in the heat of his correspondence with Cunninghame Graham. It represents a social value more characteristic of Conrad's thought: Singleton is in unconscious touch with the collective will of the ship's community, and predicts its temper and behavior. Whether Conrad believed literally in the psychic power to intuit the group will is less certain than that he believed in the existence of that will itself and in the existence of groups as real entities. This is the conclusion enforced by *The Nigger of the "Narcissus"*: throughout the novel, the narrator (who seems, as a former officer, to speak for the author) denigrates the cowardice, childishness, and mutinousness of the crew. Yet he closes his narrative with a paean to the class of mariners and the ideal of courageous service which they represent. As a collection of individuals they display all the vices of an individualistic society, but as a crew they acquire virtue through their common experience. Especially powerful as binding forces are the superstitions and illusions they have maintained as collective myths. It is the existence of these organic relations that led Conrad to deny Galsworthy's assumption that the organization of a ship is a

[26] *The Philosophical Theory of the State*, pp. 274–75.

democratic one. Conrad insisted that it is not constructed on the model of Liberal theory but according to an older pattern, requiring absolute allegiance in order to maintain its precarious unity. But this absolutism is the result of extreme conditions of the sea, and there is no sign in Conrad—and there were few signs in the English organicist tradition—of the belief in a military subordination of the individual in ordinary political life.

There was in Conrad, as in many of his organicist predecessors, a some-what amused contempt for the presumed laziness of the working class. Bosanquet quotes with approval a contemporary view on the welfare ques-tion: " 'The difficulty of living by regular work, and the ease of living with-out it . . . is the long and short of the matter.' "[27] In several tales, Conrad expresses much the same summary view of man's inveterate avoidance of struggle, effort, and endurance, but his depiction of the crew in *The Nigger of the "Narcissus"* is the most devastating. On the other hand, Conrad shares with Bosanquet and Green a generous respect for the working class, to the very degree that it is a *working* class. Bosanquet, for example, resents the reformers' excuses for the low moral condition of the poor on the grounds of environmental conditions. He holds instead that the poor are not as bad as their conditions might have made them: they have the same moral re-straints as the upper classes, the same sense of honor, devotion to home and country, and dedication to their work.[28] It is their sense of belonging to the social organism that accounts for this anomaly, according to Bosanquet; similarly, for Conrad, it is their sense of comradeship that does so.

The organicist theory also goes far toward refining other interpretations of Conrad's politics. He is taken to be an arch-foe of any and all revolution, but in the practice of his craft and in the expression of his opinions he was much more sophisticated on the subject than we have been given to believe. The anarchists are denigrated in *The Secret Agent, Under Western Eyes,* and other tales more for their threat to the cohesion of the social community than for their criticism of social corruption. In the Latin America of *Nostromo* and "Gaspar Ruiz," in the Poland of "Prince Roman," there are historical occasions on which revolution is justified. The principle by which Conrad distinguishes these cases is that which every organicist from Burke to Bosanquet employs: "we have to set the whole value of the existence of

[27] *Aspects of the Social Problem* (London and New York, 1895), p. 113.
[28] *The Philosophical Theory of the State*, p. 270 ff.

social order against the importance of the matter in which we think society defective."[29] This rule of thumb is not exclusive to organicists, of course, but in their hands it is founded on the criterion of an ongoing social community, the only source of permanence in a universe of flux.

It is not, however, the state that is the ultimate value for the organicists, although they speak most about that form of community, but community of any kind that can give the individual roots, duties, and sustenance. In Conrad as well, it is not only the nation from which his heroes are alienated, but all kinds of society: Almayer from The Netherlands, to which he aspires to return, and from Sambir, which he yearns to escape; Jim from the world-wide network of mariners and traders, in which he seeks the refuge of anonymity but which he finally flees; Nostromo from the social classes of Sulaco, which each in turn exploit him, to his growing embitterment; Heyst from all mankind, which he seeks to shun entirely. Almost *any* society would be sufficient to redeem the alienated: to Jim it offers itself in the form of a native town, to Heyst, in his personal attachment to Lena. The critical discussions of the isolated individuals in Conrad's fiction have neglected to make explicit the positive implications of their tragic separation. He dramatically affirms that an integrated community, in whatever form and of whatever magnitude, is the only viable framework of man's life.

To sum up the political views of the organicists in relation to those of Conrad; they have been taken to be much more conservative than they would have acknowledged themselves to be. There is, doubtless, ample latitude in organicist thought for a defense of the *status quo* based on the prior claims of civil authority. Indeed, Bradley was "deeply conservative or reactionary . . . he could not abide pacificism or generalized humanitarian sentiment, and any belief in the natural equality of man or in the inviolability of life (whether political or religious in inspiration) he regarded as 'sentimental,' 'degenerate,' and 'disgusting.' "[30] But, just as emphatically, T. H. Green wished to dissociate the intellectual movement which he founded from the political conservatism of much of the Burke tradition: "the view of the nature of human institutions associated in his spiritual predecessors with acquiescence, and even reaction, filled him with a divine discon-

---

[29] *The Philosophical Theory of the State*, p. 199; i.e., the social order is more important than most—not all—complaints, but certain improvements have to be made, sometimes by disturbing the order.

[30] Richard Wollheim, *F. H. Bradley* (Harmondsworth, England, 1959), p. 14.

tent. . . ."[31] Conrad shared some of the conservative temper exhibited in Bradley's impatience with humanitarianism, but he also relished, with Green, the heroic grandeur of certain historical revolutions—especially the Napoleonic, as we shall see—and the social progress which they effected.

Bosanquet probably represents the best balance of political sentiments within his school: he was a self-described "Radical" on such issues as Lloyd George's welfare state budget of 1909, but he held out against the humanitarian social reformers' underestimation of "character as a moral agent." He defined his politics as those of "State Socialism, which regulates the competitive struggle while enhancing the efficiency of competition."[32] What he shares most tellingly with Conrad is a consistent application to immediate social questions of the norm of human community as the guarantor of individual self-realization. This fundamental humanism—the sense of the *polis* as the ultimate human reality and the primary condition of being a man— also places Conrad, with the organicists, squarely within a tradition deriving from Aristotle and the Greek tragedians. It is this classical element in the Western imagination that accounts for the tragic power of Conrad's tales of lonely individuals separated from the human community.

[31] J. H. Muirhead, *The Service of the State: Four Lectures on the Political Teaching of T. H. Green* (London, 1908), p. 69.
[32] *Aspects of the Social Problem*, p. 291.

Chapter IV

COLONISTS AND
CONQUERORS

Sir James Brooke

"Your country is very powerful—we know," began again Hassim after a pause, *"but is it stronger than the country of the Dutch who steal our land?"*

"Stronger?" cried Lingard. He opened a broad palm. *"Stronger? We could take them in our hand like this—"* and he closed his fingers triumphantly.

"And do you make them pay tribute for their land?" enquired Hassim with eagerness.

"No," answered Lingard in a sobered tone; *"this, Tuan Hassim, you see, is not the custom of white men. We could, of course—but it is not the custom."*

"Is it not?" said the other with a sceptical smile. *"They are stronger then we are and they want tribute from us...."*

—The Rescue

In recent years—in the era of colonial independence—Conrad has often been cited in retrospect as a profound critic of imperialism and prophet of its decline. It is important to clarify the grounds of his anti-imperialism, for readers of the present day are tempted to assume that the turn-of-the-century writer's attitudes are the same as their own. If we can come to see Conrad in his contemporary perspective, we shall be in a position to learn something about his fiction, as well as something about imperialism, which we cannot know if we see him only as a reflection of ourselves.

The critics of imperialism, in the decades during which Conrad wrote most of his Asian and African tales, represented a spectrum of opinion about as broad as today's, but certain strains of opposition were especially prominent in Conrad's adopted land—the most successful and self-satisfied imperialist nation. Humanitarian critics there were in England, at least from the time of the abolitionist movement at the end of the eighteenth century on, but they did not focus their attack on African imperialism until the first decade of this century, when, after the appearance of a series of hair-raising exposés of Belgian rule in the Congo, the "pro-Boers" in the Liberal Party could charge Britain itself with "methods of barbarism" (in the famous phrase of the Liberal Prime Minister, Campbell-Bannerman). Besides the humanitarian outcry, another strain of resistance to imperialist ventures was based on inherited English distaste for entangling alliances, enlarged responsibilities, and increased public expenditure. Its proponents came to be disparagingly called "Little Englanders," for the basis of their program was resistance to the major effect of imperialism on the home country: the evolution of a powerful state with an expanded colonial bureaucracy, military establishment, and global policy, but without a developing sense of community. The rise of British nationalism to chauvinistic fervor at the end of the century distressed those who wanted England to be organically united, not merely powerful and proud.[1]

It is in relation to such views that Conrad's anti-imperialism should be considered, for his work is almost entirely free of the usual humanitarian sentiments of the time and even of the evidence on which they were based (with the exception, of course, of "Heart of Darkness," which employs

---

[1] The arguable premise of this view is that increased chauvinism, born of imperialist fervor, did not strengthen the sense of community. In practice, imperialist ventures substituted a tie between citizens through a common reaction to distant events—the fall of Khartoum, to cite one example—for a sharing of participation in tackling immediate social problems. That the substitution was psychologically effective is beyond doubt; whether jingoism is a genuine substitute for organic community is a matter to be decided on first principles.

other grounds of criticism as well). He is concerned instead with the social effects of imperialism on native communities and with its moral effects on European colonists. From the social and moral drama of Conrad's colonial tales derive their political implications.

To see Conrad's tales of imperialism in the light of his social values, it is necessary to summarize his account of native societies and the impact of Europeans upon them. He has little sympathy for the indigenous forms of social life: native rulers are predatory and rapacious (like the leaders of "civilized" states, he also suggests), and tribal history is an almost uninterrupted record of war and enslaving or enslavement. The coming of the whites, however, only makes things worse: the primitive social order is reduced to anarchy. This is Conrad's answer to the claims of literary and other propagandists that England had assumed the "white man's burden."

As for the moral effects of colonial rule on the Europeans, their participation in imperialist ventures tends to decivilize, dehumanize, and destroy them because of their severance from the organic ties of their own social community. Kurtz is merely the extreme example of a process to be observed in Almayer, Willems, and the maudlin adventurers of "An Outpost of Progress." Lingard and Jim, on the other hand, partly succeed in their attempts to establish sympathetic connections with the native communities they enter, thereby indicating the social ideal which would justify imperialism for Conrad but which, he knows, it characteristically fails to achieve.

Civilization and Barbarism

"The afterwards flourishing Sambir was born in a swamp and passed its youth in malodorous mud"—so begins the account of a native community's history, in *An Outcast of the Islands* (p. 65), with a reference to its emergence from the prehistoric slime. There is early "some semblance of organization amongst the settlers of various races who recognized the unobtrusive sway of old Patalolo" (p. 50), who holds it in fief from the Sultan of Koti. Lakamba arrives with two small trading vessels, claims to be an exiled prince (but he and his adviser Babalatchi were "Malay adventurers; ambitious men of that place and time; the Bohemians of their race" [p. 50]), and sets up camp fourteen miles down the Pantai River (seven miles, according to *Almayer's Folly*). Lakamba's attempted intrigue against Patalolo fails to gain sufficient support from the Sultan of Koti, and his subsequent attempt at an armed coup with the support of the migrant Bugis settlers is foiled by the appearance of

Lingard's brig and his backing of Patalolo, who guarantees the trader "his queer monopoly" (p. 202).

Babalatchi appears on the scene and proposes a scheme for Lakamba's accession to power through the entry of Arab traders into the port and the commercial displacement of Lingard and Almayer. Babalatchi is a follower of Omar el Badavi, the leader of a band of Brunei pirates which has been dispersed from the Philippines by the Spanish. In the romantic plot of the novel, Omar's daughter, Aissa, is used by Babalatchi as the temptation for which Willems betrays his boss, Lingard. Babalatchi brings Lakamba to power by having Willems pilot the Arab trading ship of Syed Abdullah into the harbor. The ship does not actively intervene in the coup but covers the town with its guns while Patalolo bows out (according to *Almayer's Folly* he continues to rule by sufferance for several years, until his death).

The coming of the Arabs is the climactic moment in Sambir's history: events are dated "before the Arabs," "after the Arabs." It changes not only Sambir's tribal chiefs but its colonial status. Sambir (whose original is Berau, as has recently been established in copious but idle detail—see Preface) lies near the northeast coast of Borneo, an area long disputed by the British and Dutch governments and traders. As long as Lingard's is the only European vessel to penetrate the Pantai estuary, the English flag is the only one to fly above Sambir, but when Willems brings in the Arabs, he hoists the Dutch flag, and Lakamba takes up local authority under it.[2] Through commercial rivalry, which preys upon the loose social organization of the natives, what was originally "some semblance of organization" breaks down into anarchy: "on that night there was no government in Sambir. Nothing to restrain those fellows" (p. 171). What emerges is a local tyranny under the flag of The Netherlands, ironically called "the flag under the shadow of which there is safety" (p. 179).

Although *An Outcast of the Islands* leaves the history of Sambir's economic and political competition at this point and turns to the destruction of Willems by his passion for Aissa, *Almayer's Folly*, written earlier, recounts the succeeding events in the history of Sambir. Almayer's failure in competition with the Arabs is, on the one hand, laid to a defect of character and, on the other,

[2] Ironically, Abdulla's ship, "Lord of the Isles," flies the British flag and Abdulla has British citizenship. The Dutch Almayer tries to protect his stores by flying the British flag, but a Chinese, Jim-Eng, who claims to be English, refuses to salute the Dutch tricolor and precipitates a row in which Almayer suffers as well. Conrad plays here on the meaninglessness of national identity and allegiance in colonial society, which has no genuinely national tradition.

explained by economic and political forces more powerful than he. Not only does Lingard's banker, Hudig, go bankrupt, but Lingard himself, in quest of a new monopoly, all but bankrupts the firm by his unsuccessful explorations for gold in the Borneo interior. Most important, the Dutch sanction of Lakamba's rule ensures the Arabs a virtual trade monopoly with the local producers: "Not that they loved Abdulla, but they dared not trade with the man whose star had set. Had they done so they knew there was no mercy to be expected from Arab or Rajah; no rice to be got on credit in times of scarcity from either; and Almayer could not help them, having at times hardly enough for himself" (*AF*, p. 28).

The only hope for Almayer's fortunes lies in a return to English domination, and this hope is briefly entertained: "The stir made in the whole of the island by the establishment of the British Borneo Company affected even the sluggish flow of the Pantai life. Great changes were expected; annexation was talked of; the Arabs grew civil" (p. 33). It is in preparation for the entry of the English that Almayer throws up the building that gives the novel its name. With the dashing of these hopes and the reassertion of The Netherlands' authority by the entry of a Dutch patrol boat, Sambir is secured for Lakamba and the Arabs, and Almayer is driven to his final acts of self-destruction.

At this point the full irony of Almayer's alienation from his own national community becomes clear: he is a Dutchman looking to the British to end the unfair competition of a British subject (Abdulla) sanctioned by the Dutch. When he first makes the claim of national ties to the visiting Dutch officer, he is rebuked for gunpowder smuggling—an unfair accusation inspired by his enemies. A further irony develops when Almayer comes to engage in this very activity in a last effort to gain a fortune. After his contraband is destroyed on Dain Maroola's ship, a further accusation by investigating Dutch officers carries the implication that he is responsible for the deaths of two Dutch sailors in the chase. He reaches the limit of isolation from his fellow countrymen in a drunken stupor, foreshadowing his ultimate removal from human society in the dream world of opium.

Meanwhile, Sambir goes on as a lawless trade concession, pursuing its traditional slavery ("the slaves were hurried out of sight into the forest and jungle . . . in expectation of a visit from Dutch man-of-war boats" [p. 34]) and its "desultory warfare carried on by the Arabs and the Rajah with the up-river Dyak tribes" (p. 48). A peaceful rudimentary society has been reduced to a condition of permanent warfare resembling barbarism. If we can hypothetically reconstruct Conrad's version of the social contract myth, the state of nature gives way to a village community which, though minimal, harmonizes the conflicting interests of the varied tribes; the appearance of a "higher" civilization has the effect of creating a more sophisticated anarchy, a legalized despotism which becomes the characteristic form of native society under imperialism.

Two further implications of Conrad's portrayal of imperialist civilization are suggested by the history of Sambir. Not only is Lakamba, like the Malays generally, engaged in traditional warfare with the inland Dyaks (p. 39), but Lingard is busy among the latter in order to penetrate their territory in quest of the legendary Gunong Mas, the mountain of gold. (It is to obtain Dain Maroola's promise of support in this venture, presumably in the form of a war party against the Dyaks, that Almayer engages to smuggle gunpowder for him.) The impression that readers are likely to receive from this account of the Dyaks, narrated from the point of view of the Malays and Europeans who are anxious to conquer them, is that they represent a barbarism that threatens civilization. Although famous for their intertribal headhunting practices, the Dyaks were in reality relatively innocent victims of the exploitation of the Malays, who are racially akin to them but different in religion (the name "Dyak" means "heathen" in Malay—they are animists). By engaging in further disturbance of the interior tribes, the Lingard-Almayer company represents the kind of adventurist intrusion into native societies which it was the policy of the more humane colonial administrators to suppress (see the Appendix).

The second point concerns the character of the Dutch administration. Almayer answers the charges of the Dutch gunboat officers with the question, "disloyalty and unscrupulousness! What have you ever done to make me loyal? You have no grip on this country" (p. 138). The Dutchmen are forced to admit privately, "That drunken madman was right; we haven't enough hold on this coast. They do what they like" (p. 145). The Dutch were active in Borneo, as the novel accurately shows, only to stop native traffic in gunpowder, and that only because they were themselves engaged in native wars; otherwise, they left Borneo to the tender mercies of the Lakambas. Indeed, so complete is their rejection of governmental responsibility that the Dutch commanding officer calls Lakamba's dictatorship a "model state" (p. 34), presumably because it does not give him any trouble, being effectively terrorized by its native ruler. This indifference results in Dain Maroola's voyage to Sambir to acquire gunpowder in his own war against the Dutch in

Bali, precisely because "there was no Dutch resident on the river, which would make things easier, no doubt" (p. 81).

What appears, therefore, as the most unsavory aspect of Dutch colonial administration is its cooperation with, use of, and even assistance to the most unscrupulous and predatory native rajahs. The major theme of Britain's proposed East Indies policy was the suppression of local autonomy to the extent that it was disruptive of good order; the Dutch, so Conrad insists, interfere only when their own authority is challenged, but leave the rajahs free to govern their own subjects with a heavy hand and even to pursue their private wars with the Dyak tribes. In practice, however, both nations used the native rulers to administer the collection of taxes and produce, and both stand responsible for the rajahs' brutal rule (on these points, see Appendix).

To put the matter in terms of organicist political theory, the charge against Dutch imperialism, as seen in tales based on Conrad's own experience in the Indies, is not what might have been expected from a former "English pedlar" (p. 7)—that it interferes with free trade. The trouble is rather that it does not have organic ties to local affairs. The infrequent visits of the Dutch gunboats are a mockery of government, and the governor in Batavia remains a shadowy and irrelevant figure in the lives of the people of Sambir. The town remains a loose collection of settlers from various islands, and is kept in a condition of fragmentation by the rivalries of British, Dutch, and Arab traders. Sambir, like other colonial societies, stands at the opposite pole from the ideal of an organic community.

It is little wonder, then, that Almayer's daughter, Nina, had, in her judgment of the men around her,

> lost the power to discriminate. It seemed to Nina that there was no change and no difference. Whether they traded in brick godowns or on the muddy river bank; whether they reached after much or little; whether they made love under the shadows of the great trees or in the shadow of the cathedral on the Singapore promenade; whether they plotted for their own ends under the protection of laws and according to the rules of Christian conduct, or whether they sought the gratification of their desires with the savage cunning and the unrestrained fierceness of natures as innocent of culture as their own immense and gloomy forests, Nina saw only the same manifestations of love and hate and of sordid greed chasing the uncertain dollar in all its multifarious and vanishing shapes. (*AF*, p. 43)

It is this judgment of the Europeans, English or Dutch, as all essentially alike—and akin to the most egregious of the natives—that leads Nina to leave the trappings of European civilization behind her and take a Malay as her lover, to the vast disappointment and eventual destruction of her father. It is this sweeping judgment of the Europeans that colors Conrad's depiction of imperialism in these early novels. With the qualified exception of Lingard, they are to a man moral desperados verging on criminality, and the only genuine attachment between people, Nina finds, is to be sought among the relatively uncorrupted natives.

A society similar to Sambir is presented in the Shore of Refuge, the setting of *The Rescue* (which was begun in the early period of Conrad's career, though completed much later). Although not as consistent in this novel as elsewhere in Conrad's work, navigational indications seem to place the Shore on the southwest coast of Borneo. Its name is given to it by virtue of its harboring of outcast and migratory native groups, which form a loose and unstable association rather than a community. To this agglomeration, just emerging from presocial life, without central authority or shared conventions, Lingard's alliance to support the legitimist claims of Hassim to the throne of Wajo gives temporary cohesion. Its ultimate effect is, however, to introduce unsettling temptations to intrigue and conflict, which lead to internecine warfare that explodes the society into fragments and alienates natives and Europeans alike. Lingard's arms cache is the center around which a semblance of community forms, but European intervention in native wars is an unstable element, like gunpowder, and the explosion of the cache marks the fragmentation of the group into its isolated members.

Lingard's involvement in Hassim's affairs is portrayed from his standpoint, as a desire to right a moral wrong. His idealism does not allow him to covet the offer of a trade monopoly at Wajo in the event of his successful prosecution of Hassim's campaign for reinstatement, "Wajo, on account of its chronic state of disturbance, being closed to the [other] white traders" (*Rescue*, p. 78). Yet the Wajo element at the Shore of Refuge distinctly suggests commercial activity. Not only were Wajo traders famous throughout the archipelago for their energy and aggressiveness, but their society strongly resembled that of the Europeans.[3] It is the Wajo—and the European—com-

---

[3] This fact caused Lingard's prototype, Rajah Brooke, who will be discussed below, to describe them with admiration: Wajo "bears a striking resemblance to the government of feudal times in Europe, or rather of that period in the history of the Low Countries when the rights of free citizens were acknowledged" (Rodney Mundy, *Narrative of Events in Borneo and Celebes, Down to the Occupation of Labuan: From the Journals of James Brooke, Esq.* [London, 1848], I, iv).

mercial and political aggressiveness and its volatile spirit that tear apart
the agglomeration of the Shore of Refuge.

A second, and probably the largest, element of this society is a band of
refugees led by Belarab, whose obscure history is sketched by the omniscient
Jörgenson:

> "I knew him, I knew his father . . . .Whom did I not know? I knew
> Sentot when he was King of the South Shore of Java and the Dutch offered
> a price for his head. . . . Belarab's father escaped with me . . . and joined
> the Padris in Sumatra. He rose to be a great leader. Belarab was a youth
> then. . . . " (P. 102)

Belarab himself picks up the story of how he and his father, Telal, came to
the Shore of Refuge and suffered starvation before clearing the land and
establishing the makings of a community. "I have given them homes and
quiet hearts and full bellies," he claims (p. 113), but they remain dissatisfied
and thirst for revenge. His reason for joining Lingard's war party indicates
the instability of his authority since the colonization: "He explained that
he wanted somebody at his back, somebody strong and whom he could
trust, some outside force that would awe the unruly, that would inspire their
ignorance with fear, and make his rule secure" (p. 113).

The forces arrayed against Belarab are indicated by Jörgenson in his letter
briefing Lingard: "Tengga always wanted to oust Belarab, and his chances
were getting pretty good before you turned up and armed Belarab's body-
guard with muskets" (p. 172). In addition, there is a priestly power in the
land, represented by Ningrat, who "after reading the prayers in the mosque
talked to the people outside" (p. 172). The final constituent of this *émigré*
society is the Illanun band under Sherif Daman. It is the unpredictable
factor in the plans of all parties, since the Illanuns are seafaring pirates who
do not seek political dominance but simply plunder. Their singleminded
desire is to loot the stranded Travers yacht; it is they who kidnap Travers and
d'Alcacer and precipitate the denouement, with its destruction of Lingard's
project. "They were the boldest and most courageous of the pirates" by all
accounts; "they would never give quarter, owing to a hatred, born of former
injustice and inhumanity, received at the hands of those whom they could
only have regarded as white barbarians."[4] Conrad puts it more dramatically:
" 'There is blood between me and the whites' [Daman] pronounced, violently.
The Illanun chiefs remained impassive. There was blood between them and

[4] S. Baring-Gould and C. A. Bampfylde, *A History of Sarawak under Its Two
White Rajahs: 1839–1908* (London, 1909), p. 93.

all mankind" (p. 222). The Illanuns represent the extreme of barbarism which is the enemy of *all* attempts to establish community.

The catalyst which separates this loose mixture of elements is the well-meaning and conscience-ridden white trader. Conrad's portrait of Lingard in *The Rescue* has been taken to show the failure of a typical idealist torn between the purest motives of love and duty. Read in this way, the story loses its special drama: the conflict of loyalties to political associates and to racial "equals." Lingard feels an inherited complex of ties to the Europeans, even before the added bond of his love for Mrs. Travers, and these prove stronger than his obligations to the natives. His choice shows the source of the inevitable failure of European intervention in native affairs. Despite Lingard's contempt for Mr. Travers, who is a parody of British snobbery toward the natives, the prior claims of his own "kind" prove strongest. The spokesman for this conviction in the novel is Jörgenson, who consistently warns against mixing in native politics, for it ultimately does the natives no good and undermines the morality of the whites, as it has done in him.

Despite some uncertainties in the execution of *The Rescue*, its view of imperialism emerges clearly: just as Dutch policy is inhuman because of its non-interference in onerous native rule, the British style of intervention in factional intrigues and of military action in native wars—the style practiced by Lingard—leads with equal inevitability to social disorder. By a strange fatality, *any* imperial relationship to native societies leads to a worsening of their condition. Conrad fully shared the suspicions of imperialism expressed by such contemporaries of his as Alfred Russel Wallace, the great naturalist who plotted the flora and fauna of the Indies and who commented on its human condition as well: "Will not evil passions be aroused by the spirit of competition, and crimes and vices, now unknown or dormant, be called into active existence?" Wallace hoped that "we may at length be able to point to one instance of an uncivilized people who have not become demoralized and finally exterminated, by contact with European civilisation."[5]

In Africa as well as in the Indies, the disruptive effects of imperialism on native society were clear to Conrad, and in "Heart of Darkness" he extended

[5] *The Malay Archipelago* (orig. pub., 1869; London and New York, 1894), pp. 70–71. Conrad refers to this work (in another context) in *The Secret Agent* (p. 118). For a discussion of other uses Conrad made of the book, see Sherry, *Conrad's Eastern World*, Chap. 7.

his range of perception of social and personal dissolution. The most prominent instance in Conrad's work of a white intruder inciting the natives to deeds
worse than those in their repertoire is, of course, Kurtz's provocation of a
tribe to organized warfare in order to obtain ivory for export. Contemporary
reports of the influence on the natives of the early Belgian traders in the
Congo bear out Conrad's account: "ils retomberont dans une barbarie pire
que celle où ils se trouvaient auparavant, une barbarie souillée par le passage
des barbares civilisés: la plus horrible."[6] Even the heads placed around
Kurtz's station are no exaggerated image: "twenty-one heads were brought
to Stanley Falls, and have been used by Captain Rom as a decoration round
a flower-bed in front of his house."[7]

It might still be possible for present-day readers—unwittingly using the
argument the Belgian government used to excuse its agents' atrocities—
to consider such terrorism as the rule in native life, and to excuse the
Europeans as merely entering into recognized modes of warfare to maintain
governmental authority. The obvious rejoinder to this was expressed by
Mark Twain in an outraged satire of the Congo's owner, the Belgian King
Leopold: "if a Christian king can perceive a saving moral difference between
inventing bloody barbarities, and *imitating them from savages*, for charity's
sake let him get what comfort he can out of his confession!"[8] It would
have been Conrad's rejoinder, as borne out by his scornful satire of Leopold
in *The Inheritors*.

Conrad's African tales, even more than his Asian ones, demonstrate that
the contact of Europeans and natives encourages the submerged barbarism
of the superficially civilized whites to express itself by genocide. Not only
are the natives stirred by up the rapacious policies of the imperialists, but
the whites become more savage than the "savages." The process known
colloquially as "going native"—already observable in such previous Conrad
heroes as Almayer, Willems, and Lingard—is fully realized in Kurtz.[9] The

---

[6] Pierre Mille, "L'Enfer du Congo Léopoldien," *Cahiers de la Quinzaine*, 7th
ser., No. 6, p. 62.

[7] Diary of colonist E. J. Glave, quoted in E. D. Morel, *Red Rubber* (London,
1907), p. 46.

[8] *King Leopold's Soliloquy: A Defense of His Congo Rule* (Boston, 1905), p. 19.

[9] A historical instance of such conduct that may have occurred to Conrad was
Rajah Brooke: "He thought of himself as a man whose aim was to uplift the natives of the Indies to the level of Europe, but in fact he was himself being lifted
up to their own level. He made war like the Malays, conducted diplomatic negotiations like them, and came in time almost to resemble a Malay" (Robert
Payne, *The White Rajahs of Sarawak* [New York, 1960], p. 162).

irony in Conrad's portrayal of the return to nature is that it is precisely the most destructive forces in native life which the primitivist acquires, rather than the social values that are also to be found in some native societies.

On the side of the natives, their retrogression to atrocities and warfare is only one effect of imperialism. Perhaps even a more profound disruption is the process of uprooting them from their tribal patterns of life and fitting them—awkwardly and ultimately unsuccessfully—into the patterns of white society. This process has been studied by sociologists and anthropologists under the name of "detribalization," but long before them Conrad had seized upon it as a major charge against imperialism.

The subject has been opened up for literary criticism with the publication of an important article by Harold R. Collins, "Kurtz, the Cannibals, and the Second-Rate Helmsman."[10] Against a background of anthropological information on the distinctions among the native tribes indicated in Conrad's stories, Collins points out the presence of a class of "such 're-claimed' Africans as the prisoners' guard with the unmilitary bearing and the rascally grin, the manager's boy, who announces Kurtz's death 'with scathing contempt,' and the unstable helmsman, who conducts himself so imprudently during the attack from Kurtz's 'adorers.' The guard, the manager's boy, and the helmsman are what the anthropologists now call 'detribalized natives'; that is, natives alienated from the old tribal life." Collins might have added the fireman on Marlow's riverboat: "He was an improved specimen; he could fire up a vertical boiler. . . . He ought to have been clapping his hands and stamping his feet on the bank, instead of which he was hard at work, a thrall to strange witchcraft, full of improving knowledge" (*Youth*, p. 97). Here the detribalized native is admirably—though inexplicably—following the work ethic, yet Marlow finds his mixture of primitive belief and modern technical ability a grotesque distortion. The implication might be drawn from Marlow's (not necessarily Conrad's) tone that it is better to leave the natives in the jungle than to try to civilize them. Yet it is fair to assume that Conrad could imagine the process of detribalization being accomplished without these human losses.

By breaking up the natives' traditional communities—which provided a provisional security, an ordered life pattern, and limited but realizable expectations—the Belgians opened a Pandora's box from which the troubles

---

[10] *The Western Humanities Review*, VIII (1954), 299–310; the quotation is from the reprint in Leonard F. Dean (ed.), *Joseph Conrad's Heart of Darkness: Backgrounds and Criticisms* (Englewood Cliffs, N.J., 1960), pp. 152–53.

of recent date have sprung. It should be noted that detribalization is endemic
to imperialism, not merely the result of Belgian policy, although that policy
did systematically undermine the tribal authority. The Belgians were doing
what seemed prudent to control an enormous territory with a small force,
just as the Dutch thought they were acting prudently in the Indies where,
faced with similar responsibilities and similarly limited resources, they
retained the tribal structure and used the rajahs as their regents. In the Congo,
the Belgians needed native laborers in regions far from where they were to
be found; they impressed them and transported them to growing cities like
Leopoldville and Elizabethville, and thus created an urban proletariat which
later became the breeding ground of the nationalist independence movement.
They found the tribal chiefs opposed to their appropriations of labor (which
undermined chiefly authority) and therefore extirpated them, thus breaking
down the tribal structure and the restraining mores that went with it. "Unfortunately the destruction of the chiefly system had been too complete, so
that by 1917 the Belgian officials stood face to face with a native rabble."[11]
When the Belgians thought of reversing the process in 1958, building up the
chiefs to delay independence, they were pathetically late.

The norm against which Conrad's account of detribalization was written
is ultimately the concept of the organic state. For Conrad shows that natives,
as well as Europeans, are destroyed by the breakdown of their relationship
with a stable order of society—by their loss of that sense of identity with a
larger reality that gives the otherwise anarchic individual a rule of life. If we
were to give a name to Kurtz's vision of "the horror," it might appropriately
be *anarchy*: that state of social decomposition at the opposite pole from
organic community. This anarchy is already latent in the individual—
individuality and anarchy are implicated in each other—and in the absence
of an ordering community it springs into action as terrorism.

As was suggested in the preceding chapter and as is to be set out in the
accounts of Conrad's three major political novels, his political imagination
and the dramatic form in which it is expressed rest on a vision of the ideal
society as a genuine community. Measured against this standard, the societies
of European nations show themselves to be shabby approximations, but
they *do* hold together and give the individual some relief from his anarchic
propensities. But in the Congo, in the absence of European civilization and
with native society falling all too easily into the corruptions imported by

[11] Stephen H. Roberts, "Native Policy," *Encyclopedia of the Social Sciences*, XI,
274.

the Europeans, that civilization is sorely missed. That is why, in Marlow's ruminations, the modern European state is held up to scorn but its loss is nevertheless considered dangerous.

Conrad's other African tale, "An Outpost of Progress," extends this view of society, generating an insight into the foundations of political organization that goes beyond the suggestion in "Heart of Darkness" that it is merely a restraining force or "policeman." Speaking of his nominal heroes, Conrad writes:

> Society, not from any tenderness, but because of its strange needs, had taken care of those two men, forbidding them all independent thought, all initiative, all departure from routine; and forbidding it under pain of death. They could only live on condition of being machines. And now, released from the fostering care of men with pens behind the ears, or of men with gold lace on the sleeves, they were like those lifelong prisoners who, liberated after many years, do not know what use to make of their freedom. (*TU*, p. 91)

These "strange needs" of the state bureaucracy and army—the institutions of which Kayerts and Carlier are, respectively, the products—require a suppression of personality especially marked in the modern state by its comprehensive, prison-like rigor. Conrad is prophetic in his awareness of the modern state's tendency to develop into demagogic totalitarianism, based on the anonymity of the "mass man":

> They were two perfectly insignificant and incapable individuals, whose existence is only rendered possible through the high organization of civilized crowds. Few men realize that their life, the very essence of their character, their capabilities and their audacities, are only the expression of their belief in the safety of their surroundings. The courage, the composure, the confidence; the emotions and principles; every great and every insignificant thought belongs not to the individual but to the crowd: to the crowd that believes blindly in the irresistible force of its institutions and of its morals, in the power of its police and of its opinion. (*TU*, p. 89)

Conrad's portrayal of imperialism is, then, tied up with a critique of the political communities which engage in it. Making excessive, though comforting, claims on the individuals who compose them, they render men incapable of autonomy outside them. They fail to stimulate internalized moral resources which could govern conduct when police restraint is removed. These societies finally send out to the colonies their least stable elements, their socially mobile adventurers, who run amok in the jungle, destroying themselves as well as the native communities upon which they intrude.

Conrad's sardonic description of the "crowd" stands in a tradition of criticism of mass society coming down from De Tocqueville (if not from Plato and Thucydides) to Ortega y Gasset and a host of lesser expositors. In this account, modern European society is the disease of the communal ideal, a tyranny of public opinion that is even more stultifying than its frequent accompaniment, a police state. Nevertheless, like others in the organicist tradition, Conrad maintains—with all due irony—the ideal of social solidarity despite its distortion in existing states. He accepts the merely negative state at its proper value, while looking toward some better association.[12] This wary acceptance is implied in Marlow's famous description of the English state; his listeners live "with solid pavement under your feet, surrounded by kind neighbours ready to cheer you or to fall on you, stepping delicately between the butcher and the policeman, in the holy terror of scandal and gallows and lunatic asylums" (*Youth*, p. 116), and are thereby protected from the experience and vision of Kurtz. But they lack the social values that would place them beyond Kurtz's individualism.

Lionel Trilling has noted the "strange and terrible message of ambivalence toward the life of civilization" in "Heart of Darkness" but has placed major emphasis on the appeal of the uncivilized life to overcivilized modern man, as evinced in his perennial retreat from a decadent civilization to a variety of primitive refuges.[13] But for all Conrad's respect for individual noble savages, and despite his suggestion that some village communities were better off without European influence, there is no romanticizing of primitive society to be found in his works. (Even the romantic native lover, Dain

[12] Bosanquet cites Hegel's theory of this aspect of modern societies: modern man is

> tied to others, in appearance, only by the system of wants and work, with the elementary function which is necessary to it, viz. its police functions and the administration of justice. It is this phase of social life, and the temper or disposition corresponding to it, which Hegel indicates by the expression Bourgeois Society. . . . It is, in mind, the presence of definite though limited aims, calculation and self-interest. It is the peculiarity of Hegel's view—probably the most definitely original, as it is the most famous, of all his political ideas—to contend that this aspect of society, with the form of consciousness belonging to it, is necessary to a modern state. (*The Philosophical Theory of the State*, pp. 272–73)

[13] "On the Modern Element in Modern Literature," *Partisan Review*, XXVIII (1961), 25. Reprinted in *Beyond Culture: Essays on Literature and Learning* (New York, 1965).

Maroola, is accepted by Nina Almayer only after she discovers that the whites are just as *barbaric* as the natives.) Kurtz is heroic because he reaches the depths of barbarism and gives them a name, but it is not recommended that we repeat his experience. Marlow almost does so when he is sorely tempted by the jungle drums to join in the dance. We are led to admire, however, not his quickness to regress but his forthright acknowledgment of a universal human weakness. *La nostalgie de la boue* is never allowed to become a moral alternative for Conrad, as it becomes for Lawrence and other moderns.

Professor Trilling is on much firmer ground in observing that the primitive life is attractive just *because* it is ugly. The landscapes described in "Heart of Darkness" are awesomely grotesque (though sometimes dispiritingly vapid). But the implication to be drawn is that European social order, material values, and technical competency are insufficient to the task of beautifying or ordering nature on the scale of the Congo. But the frank acceptance of the limits of human skill generates no love of the intractable medium.

It is, however, not as much the futility as the hypocrisy of the white-man's-burden claims that seems to irk Conrad. This sense of outrage at presumption, and not merely his mania for keeping things shipshape, charges his satiric account of the chaotic development projects at Matadi in "Heart of Darkness."[14] Not only are the works of imperialism, like the railroad, an insignificant pecking away at the fringes of the African jungle; they do not touch the problem of economic survival in an unbountiful nature, and merely accelerate the collection and export of cash crops like ivory or rubber. This economy fatuity is suggested in the story by the absurd payment of the boatmen in unredeemable copper wire: they have been elevated to a "money" economy, which calmly allows them to starve.

If the jungle is unmanageable as anything but a temporary clearing, do its inhabitants share its awesomely decadent qualities? In the Asian tales, apart from the sexually attractive natives like Dain Moroola and Dain Waris and the naïvely faithful Hassim and Immada, there are only ungovernable women (Mrs. Almayer and Aissa), rapacious chiefs (Lakamba), homicidal maniacs (the heroes of "Karain" and "The Lagoon"), and crafty sneaks (Babalatchi). There seems to be no *homme moyen sensuel* among Conrad's

[14] Nor does André Gide's discovery, on his Congo journey some thirty years after Conrad's, that the Matadi-Kinchassa railroad had, after all Marlow's skepticism, been built, alter the larger judgment of imperialism that Conrad implies (see "Voyage au Congo Belge: Carnets de Route," in *Journal: 1939-1949: Souvenirs* [Paris, 1954], p. 689).

Malays, but in an African setting he comes to speculate on the unmotivated restraint of the cannibal crew. Why, Marlow wonders, after being starved and bullied by the Belgians, do they not simply eat them?

> What possible restraint? Was it superstition, disgust, patience, fear—or some kind of primitive honor? No fear can stand up to hunger, no patience can wear it out, disgust simply does not exist where hunger is; and as to superstition, beliefs, and what you may call principles, they are less than chaff in a breeze. . . . And these chaps, too, had no earthly reason for any kind of scruple. Restraint! I would just as soon have expected restraint from a hyena prowling amongst the corpses of a battlefield. But there was the fact facing me—the fact dazzling, to be seen, like the foam on the depths of the sea, like a ripple on an unfathomable enigma. . . . (*Youth*, p. 105)

Human nature remains an enigma, but Conrad succeeds in avoiding the temptation to consider it merely evil or fallen. He elsewhere lists the virtues of certain native peoples (not omitting to qualify them in the process): "They have kept to this day their love of liberty, their fanatical devotion to their chiefs, their blind fidelity in friendship and hate—all their lawful and unlawful instincts" (*Rescue*, p. 3). The human endowment consists, here, of individualism *and* sociality, love *and* aggression, restraint *and* anarchy.

The final vision of Conrad's colonial tales is far from the tradition of the exotic tropics which was still alive in contemporary romantic fiction, particularly in French tales of native passion. For Conrad the jungle, with the people who dwell in it, is simply the wrong ground for Western civilization to choose in a struggle against the darkness: it had better cultivate its own garden rather than try to dispel a miasma. His controlling image of the tropics emerges as early as *Almayer's Folly*:

> all around them in a ring of luxuriant vegetation bathed in the warm air charged with strong and harsh perfumes, the intense work of tropical nature went on: plants shooting upward, entwined, interlaced in inextricable confusion, climbing madly and brutally over each other in the terrible silence of a desperate struggle towards the life-giving sunshine above— as if struck with sudden horror at the seething mass of corruption below, at the death and decay from which they sprang. (P. 71)

Given the teeming struggle for survival that everywhere breeds brutality, given the tenuous balance by which civilized society regulates in its own realm the course of nature, given the anarchic propensities of its human material both native and European, imperialism represents a bad bargain for all. Yet Conrad's strong fatalism allows for a possible and qualified amelioration if colonization is undertaken in some better spirit than Belgians or Dutch, Kurtz or Almayer, bring with them.

The Brooke Myth

Despite Conrad's broad skepticism of the constructive potentialities of imperialism, his frequent asseverations of respect for British colonial administration raise the possibility of defining an ideal of European influence in native societies. What would Conrad's colonial policy, had he ever given it extended formulation, have been? We may arrive at the basis of this policy by examining the values on which he based his qualified approval of British imperialism.

There is, of course, the well-known passage in "Heart of Darkness" in which Marlow comments on the red-colored areas of the map of Africa, while waiting to be interviewed at the Société Anonyme Belge pour le Commerce du Haut-Congo in Brussels. Referring to the British territories, Marlow concludes, "some real work is done in there" (*Youth*, p. 55). The work ethic alone is not the legitimating principle, however, else Conrad would have had to acknowledge the value of German ventures in Africa—for which he expresses contempt in the same passage.

Another discussion in "Heart of Darkness" comes closer to defining Conrad's position: it is his critique of Roman imperialism in Britain—a brilliant shift of perspective to see the greatest contemporary empire as a barbaric colony of the greatest empire of a past age. The narrator's account of Roman imperialism gives a hint of another and better form:

> But these chaps were not much account, really. They were no colonists; their administration was merely a squeeze, and nothing more, I suspect. They were conquerors, and for that you want only brute force—nothing to boast of, when you have it, since your strength is just an accident arising from the weakness of others. They grabbed what they could get for the sake of what was to be got. It was just robbery with violence, aggravated murder on a great scale, and men going at it blind—as is very proper for those who tackle a darkness. The conquest of the earth, which mostly means the taking it away from those who have a different complexion or slightly flatter noses than ourselves, is not a pretty thing when you look into it too much. What redeems it is the idea only. An idea at the back of it; not a sentimental pretence but an idea; and an unselfish belief in the idea —something you can set up, and bow down before, and offer a sacrifice to. (*Youth*, pp. 50–51)

Conrad's critics have not been much exercised to specify the content of the idea to which Marlow refers, preferring to take it as an instance of the saving-illusion theory on which Conrad's heroes are supposed to find a principle of action in a world without real values. Nevertheless, the passage itself describes the idea in fairly explicit terms, and it is a real one, based on an awareness of colonial history.

The distinction in this passage between "colonists" and "conquerors" can be applied throughout Conrad's tales and explains much about his varying judgments of imperialist ventures in his own time.[15] Of his early heroes, Almayer and Willems, Kayerts and Carlier, Kurtz and the Belgium "pilgrims" are exploitative conquerors; Lingard (at least by intention) and Jim are colonists. Clearly, long residence in the tropics does not by itself make for successful colonization, if the Lingard-Almayer company is considered, but it is a necessary precondition. Almayer, however, like Kurtz, tries to use the tropics as a way station in a triumphant return to Europe, whereas Jim and Lingard commit themselves to spend their lives among the natives and ally themselves with them.

Just as work alone and residence alone do not make the genuine colonist, neither does the mere refraining (on the Dutch model) from mixing in native life. In his review of Hugh Clifford's book on his experiences as an administrator in Malaya (Clifford was later to become Governor-General of Nigeria and a close friend of the novelist), Conrad gives another basis for his approbation of British imperialism:

> Mr. Hugh Clifford's anxiety about his country's record is needless. To the Malays whom he governs, instructs and guides he is the embodiment of the intentions, of the conscience and might of his race. And of all the nations conquering distant territories in the name of the most excellent intentions, England alone sends out men who, with such a transparent sincerity of feeling, can speak, as Mr. Clifford does, of the place of toil and exile as "the land which is very dear to me, where the best years of my life have been spent. . . . " (NLL, p. 58)

The "idea" that distinguishes the colonist from the conqueror is his commitment to the role, to the place, and to the men among whom he lives. This commitment constitutes an act of allegiance equivalent to the service of a state. It is an identification of oneself as a member of the native society,

---

[15] Here Conrad refines a distinction made by the economist J. A. Hobson, in his classic work *Imperialism: A Study* (orig. pub., 1902; London, 1905), between "colonialism," or emigration to relatively unpopulated areas and the establishment of a culture attempting to reproduce that of the home country (e.g., Australia, New Zealand, Canada), and "imperialism," in which the settlers form a ruling caste among an overwhelmingly native population.

which becomes the colonist's community in his escape from the home country. In a rough generalization, the individualist man projected by Liberal theory becomes in the tropics a conqueror, while the social man idealized by the organicist tradition becomes in action a colonist.

The discrimination of colonists and conquerors is conducted in Conrad's fiction within a fairly consistent type of tale involving a characteristic hero. When most of a novelist's heroes go through a definite pattern of change in their career, we may—as we speak of the Lawrentian myth or the Kafkian myth—speak of a Conradian myth: the myth of the White Rajah, based on the career of James Brooke. Its essential components are these: an individualist hero or anti-hero, outcast like Willems or Jim, self-isolated like Kurtz or Heyst, or illusion-ridden like Lingard or Almayer; and a primitive society, often originally benign, but presently in a condition of permanent warfare. Intervention by the hero sometimes brings order out of anarchy (Jim), but usually it changes the power structure for the worse (Willems), intensifies the destruction of the natives (Lingard), and in addition brings about the destruction of the self (Kurtz).[16]

What this myth represented to Conrad was the possibility of ordering a society almost completely along the lines of an individual's imagination. Hueffer claimed that "almost the only revolution that he contemplated with enthusiasm was one by which a successful adventurer seized the reins of power. Anywhere! Some King Tom!"[17] But Hueffer characteristically over-simplifies Conrad's enthusiasm: it was absorbing to watch the individual imagination at work with a free hand in politics, but the results to be expected were those rumored of Jim: "Some white man had gotten in there and turned things upside down." Yet some individualist imperialists had a more balanced record. The father of them all was Rajah Brooke, the type of the free-enterprise imperialist who ruled a kingdom independently of—even in opposition to—the mother country. For many years the symbol of the White Rajah for the British public, Brooke's fantastic success was a contemporary folk myth that Conrad could interpret and refine in his art.

[16] It will be seen that this myth bears a resemblance at critical points to the careers of Nostromo, of the Assistant Commissioner in the *The Secret Agent*, and of the rover, Peyrol, which are set in more civilized but similarly disordered societies. The background of myth serves to heighten the drama of the hero's complex relationship to society in these novels.

[17] Ford Madox Ford [Hueffer], *Joseph Conrad: A Personal Remembrance* (London, 1924), p. 60. The appelation is applied to Lingard in *The Rescue*, p. 95.

James Brooke was a seaman-trader who arrived in Sarawak in 1839 with
little more than the proverbial shirt on his back. After interludes in which
he aided a South Celebes chief in a local war and tried to stir up the Sultan
of Boni to revolt against the Dutch, he returned to help Sarawak's ruler,
Hassim, suppress his enemies. Brooke always claimed that he did so with
the promise of succeeding Hassim if he were successful. When Hassim
reneged on this strange alleged bargain (in which he stood to lose his realm
whether he won or lost), Brooke forced him to step down, and had his
conquest ratified by the Sultan of Brunei (to whom, as Rajah of Sarawak, he
was vassal). With these origins, inauspicious for the making of a colonist
rather than a conqueror, Brooke began a dynasty which his admirers and
hired biographers wrote voluminously to justify.[18]

"I go . . . to awake the spirit of slumbering philanthropy with regard to
these islands; to carry Sir Stamford Raffles' views in Java over the whole
Archipelago" (Keppel, I, 4): so Brooke declared his intentions early in his
career. Raffles, administrator of Java in its short period of British occupation
during the Napoleonic Wars, in turn based his colonial policy on that which
was beginning to be applied to Bengal and eventually to other parts of
India. With the precise economic policy which he advocated we need not
here be concerned (see the Appendix for the details). The chief political
rationale of the Raffles-Brooke policy was the displacement of The Netherlands in the East Indies by Britain. Their view of Dutch imperialism, as
formulated by a historian favorable to them, was that "the whole system
was evidently framed with but one object, not of doing something, but of
preventing anything from being done . . . ."[19]

Brooke was an enthusiastic colonizer who felt frustrated by the monopoly
the Dutch held but did not exploit: "Here a settler might hack and hew his
way to his heart's content if they would give him the land he cleared of
jungle. Here, likewise, with the industry and activity of the European and
the care of a fostering government, various articles of commercial produce

[18] Henry Keppel, *The Expedition to Borneo of H.M.S. Dido for the Suppression of
Piracy: With Extracts from the Journal of James Brooke, Esq.* (London, 1846); Mundy,
Borneo and Celebes; Baring-Gould and Bampfylde, *A History of Sarawak.* My own
account is based on the more recent evaluations of Stephen Runciman, *The White
Rajahs: A History of Sarawak from 1841 to 1946* (Cambridge, 1960); Payne, *The
White Rajahs*; and Jean Bruhat, *Histoire de l'Indonésie* (Paris, 1958). The sources of
the quotations from Brooke's writings will be identified parenthetically in the
text.
[19] Clive Day, *The Policy and Administration of the Dutch in Java* (New York and
London, 1904), p. 12.

might be grown. But the Company have the monopoly. *Basta cosi!"* (Payne, p. 17). Dutch policy was, indeed, based not only on excluding foreigners who might—and, in the case of Brooke, did—undermine their authority, but on limiting their own involvement to the fruitful Java and its immediate neighbors (not including Borneo) because of their limited funds for civil and military functions. It was only toward the close of the century, during the period in which Conrad was writing his tales of the Indies, that the so-called "non-active" policy was changed and the so-called "external" islands were opened to concerted development.[20]

The weakness of Dutch naval power was so glaring that the British early began to encroach upon the northern and western coasts of Borneo. Brooke's personal regime rested on the periodic visits of British men-of-war. Once he overcame the opposition of the Dutch authorities and native rulers, he energetically pursued the twin goals of colonial development and private gain. He cleaned up the pirate nests in order to make the seas safe for trade; he abolished slavery in order to create a labor force beyond the control of native slaveholders; he relieved the Dyaks from their traditional exploitation and periodic slaughter by the Malays in order to have them on his side in the perpetual jockeying for power with native rivals; he stipulated free trade but kept the monopoly of antimony ore for himself; he sanctioned international access to his realm but privately admitted that "I wish to prevent any foreign nation coming on this field" (Payne, pp. 75–76). Despite his conquering sword, Brooke was able to become a successful colonist. His example must, then, have suggested to Conrad the possibility of some other result of imperialism than the standard one.

Conrad's interest in Rajah Brooke is not simply a matter of the colorful details of his career, on which was modeled Jim's jump into a ditch during his escape from the natives, for example, and the signet ring carried by the

[20] An interesting sidelight on the question of how much more active and constructive a force the British imperialists were in the areas under their control than were the Dutch is the fact that Britain resisted German attempts at an international conference to define the minimal conditions for acknowledged sovereignty because its own territories were so widespread that it could not administer them all effectively. See S. E. Crowe, *The Berlin West Africa Conference: 1884–1885* (London, New York, and Toronto, 1942), p. 177. See also Ronald Robinson and John Gallagher, *Africa and the Victorians: The Climax of Imperialism in the Dark Continent* (New York and London, 1961): "That British governments before 1900 did very little to pacify, administer and develop their spheres of influence and protectorates, shows once again the weakness of any commercial and imperialist motives for claiming them" (p. 472).

trusty messenger from his doomed master to Lingard. The "idea" of benevolent colonization is vivid in Brooke's writings, and stands opposed to the
results of conquest: "The more virtuous, the more civilised, the more
educated a people, the more turbulent, indolent, and sullen, when reduced
to a state of subjection; the fewer qualities will they have to please their
masters, when foreign rule is oppressive, or looks solely to the advantage of
the country of the conquerors, and not the conquered" (Keppel, I, 127–28).
Furthermore, Brooke, like Conrad, was aware of the danger of regression
in turbulent native societies under the influence of white (even British) rule:
"The natives [of Madras] are despicable, and here, as at every other place
I have seen, have been corrupted by their intercourse with Europeans"
(Payne, p. 16). Sharing these opinions and (perhaps more important) re-
membering a boyhood ideal which he sought to apply in the political realm,
Conrad glowingly replied to a communication from the wife of Brooke's
nephew and successor:

> I am immensely gratified and touched by the letter you have been good
> enough to write to me. The first Rajah Brooke has been one of my boy-
> ish admirations, a feeling I have kept to this day strengthened by the
> better understanding of the greatness of his character and the unstained
> rectitude of his purpose. The book which has found favour in your eyes
> has been inspired in great measure by the history of the first Rajah's enter-
> prise and even by the lecture of his journals as partly reproduced by
> Captain Mundy and others. . . . [21]

So wrote Conrad in his later years, with his invariable special politeness to
influential persons. The letter is explicit enough about the relevance of
Brooke to *Lord Jim* (the book alluded to), but we must beware of taking at
face value its political approbation. Conrad could have known very little of
the workings of the Brooke regime, although it had been a *cause célèbre*
throughout the nineteenth century.

The controversy in England over the legitimacy of Brooke's undertaking
went through several commissions of inquiry, Parliamentary debates, and
journalistic campaigns. But the issue raised was not the justice of his government but rather the attitude the Empire ought to take toward the private
kingdom of a British subject, who depended on its naval protection yet contributed nothing directly to the Crown and was not bound by its laws. The
mystery of Sarawak remained, as anomalous as its founder, until after the

[21] Letter to Margaret Brooke, June 15, 1920, quoted in Payne, *The White Rajahs*,
pp. 247–48.

Japanese had occupied it and withdrawn, when the third Rajah, Sir Vyner Brooke, turned it over to the Crown. (It is today a proposed partner in the projected Malaysia Federation, with a native independence movement and until recently under periodic guerilla attacks by Indonesia.) In a letter to *The Times* in 1946, arguing against an article calling for his continued rule, Sir Vyner Brooke told the tale that was incompletely known to Conrad and his fellow Britons:

> What now is the stark truth about Sarawak in the past? My father's [and his grand-uncle James's] policy was to support the virile Sea Dyak tribes against all other tribes. Frequent expeditions, resulting in indiscriminate slaughter, were sent to subdue the recalcitrant natives. *Corvée* was the inveterate practice and the Malays loathed being ordered to take part in expeditions and to give gratuitous labour. There was no free Press, no means whereby the natives could ventilate their grievances without the haunting fear of incurring the displeasure of local British officers, who acted as "little tin gods," and no adequate educational or medical facilities for the mass of the people.
>
> The State revenues were mainly derived from opium, gambling, pawn and spirit farms, head and exemption taxes. The mineral wealth of the State was monopolised. And the small rubber holdings which Mr. Bryant extols were established at the cost of extinguishing thousands of acres of rice lands—rice being the staple food—with the result that poverty was rife whenever the price of rubber fell.
>
> In all the criticisms [of the abdication] which have appeared in Parliament and Press I have sought in vain for a single constructive suggestion which might contribute towards the establishment of a happier and brighter future for the natives. All that is urged is a return to "the good old days." But those days were good only for the British residents and not for the natives.[22]

Whatever the historians' final consensus on the first Rajah's administration, the results of his successors' carte blanche rule would detract from his idealistic pronouncements. Conrad may not have been aware of the shortcomings of Brooke's reign in Sarawak, but he was aware of the dangers of personal imperialism. Lingard, Kurtz, and Jim are instances of the various forms that individualist imperialism may assume. Two of them try to be colonists, and one partially succeeds in becoming one, but they all fail to realize completely their "idea." Egoism, which gave the impetus to their idealism, comes ultimately to determine their failure. It is this tragic interpretation

[22] Quoted in Payne, *ibid.*, pp. 259–60.

of the Brooke myth that is its author's most penetrating vision in his fiction on imperialism.

Lingard is of the Brooke mold not only in the romantic verve of his adventurousness but in the mock-heroic aspect of his career. In *The Rescue* he is a rather pathetic figure, for all his Marlovian refinement of consciousness. He is racked by the same guilt feelings that pursue Brooke after his failure to save Budrudeen, Hassim, and their sister (as Lingard similarly fails to do in the novel). We have seen above how his equivocal position precipitates the final disaster, due to a conflict of motives: the desire to reinstate his friends, Hassim and Immada, and the desire to save his beloved, Mrs. Travers. It is possible to account for the unexplained fading away of Lingard in *Almayer's Folly* (which was set later, though written earlier, than *The Rescue*) by the shattering experience he has had on the Shore of Refuge. The implication of his story is that the individualist imperialism of a would-be colonist like Lingard is as dangerous as that of a conqueror like Kurtz.

The use of the Brooke myth to define the limitations of his avatars is clearly set forth in the prologue to the novel:

> Almost in our own day we have seen . . . a true adventurer in his devotion to his impulse—a man of high mind and of pure heart, lay the foundation of a flourishing state on the ideas of pity and justice. He recognized chivalrously the claims of the conquered; he was a disinterested adventurer, and the reward of his noble instincts is in the veneration with which a strange and faithful race cherish his memory.
> . . . But there were others—obscure adventurers who had not his advantages of birth, position, and intelligence; who had only his sympathy with the people of forests and sea he understood and loved so well. . . . They were lost in the common crowd of seamen-traders of the Archipelago, and if they emerged from their obscurity it was only to be condemned as law-breakers. Their lives were thrown away for a cause that had no right to exist in the face of an irresistible and orderly progress—their thoughtless lives guided by a simple feeling. (*Rescue*, pp. 3–4)

Here Brooke is idealized for his recognition of the "claims of the conquered," for functioning (after his theft of the throne, at least) not as a conqueror but as a colonist. But Lingard is made to represent a class of less successful colonists, the "seamen-traders," who live by passion rather than by their limited intelligence. An undertone suggests that though they are pathetic and romantic, they must give way to the "orderly progress" of government colonizers.

The patronizing tone of Conrad's effort to absolve these "obscure adventurers" from general condemnation as "law-breakers" betrays the ambiguity in his view of them. The tone is found again in the course of the narrative, when the hero's political program is described:

> "We will stir them up. We will wake up the country!"[;] he was, without knowing it in the least, making a complete confession of the idealism hidden under the simplicity of his strength. He would wake up the country! That was the fundamental and unconscious emotion on which were engrafted his need of action, the primitive sense of what was due to justice, to gratitude, to friendship, the sentimental pity for the hard lot of Immada —poor child—the proud conviction that of all the men in the world, in his world, he alone had the means and the pluck "to lift up the big end" of such an adventure. (*Rescue*, p. 106)

"Idealism" and disinterestedness like Brooke's are the essence of the colonist, but when these selfless virtues are associated, as in Lingard, with egoistic sentimentality, pride, and impulsiveness, they become a danger to the colonist and to those whose betterment he seeks. And yet "devotion to his impulse" is the mark of Brooke himself, as Conrad's account admits. There seems to be something fatal in the very virtues that mark the best of colonists.

To see how strong is the degenerative force within all colonial activity, we turn again to "Heart of Darkness." Here even such rock-bottom values as the work ethic are re-examined in the light of the complexities of imperialism. Marlow, who, as a seaman, is the spokesman for the work ethic, evaluates imperialism as though it were merely a matter of work. Though he responds appropriately to the chain gang, the grove of death, and the high-handed treatment of the steamboat crew, his major criticism of Belgian rule is leveled against the inefficiency of the administration, the laziness of the "pilgrims," the sporadic blasting for the railway, the lack of straw for bricks and bolts for the steamboat, the waste of pipe in a gully, the general lack of devotion to the task.

Marlow does manage to make one corner of the Congo shipshape. Under his command, the fireman is attentive to his task, the cannibal crew refrains from eating the whites, and the helmsman keeps to the wheel—at least while Marlow is nearby. But the restraint of work, while it keeps Marlow himself from going off for "a howl and a dance" in response to the savage life ashore, is not sufficient to keep the helmsman from expressing his hostility toward the attacking savages, a reversion to the instinctual life which is punished by instant death. "Work is the law" for the colonist, but the law is puny before the lawless element of human nature.

After exposing this first limitation upon the idealism of the skeptical colonist, Marlow, the narrative switches to Kurtz, the conqueror. In considering his career, the appalling conviction grows upon us that in personally committing himself to native life, and in bringing a kind of organized purpose to native society, Kurtz is a devastating parody of the Brooke myth. Furthermore, Kurtz is designed to show the total bankruptcy of the work ethic: it is consistently his industriousness and indefatigability that are emphasized. At last Conrad discovers that it is not work but the means and ends of work that have ethical substance; mass destruction can evince the highest standards of efficient work. This further employment of the Brooke myth offers a severe test to the working distinction between colonists and conquerors that Conrad's tales suggest. What redeems the colonist, if anything can, is neither industriousness nor impulsive sentiment. In what, then, does the redeeming "idea" lie?

Lord Jim, the climax of Conrad's early development, not only in his art but in his political imagination, resolves the limitations of the work ethic and of colonial adventurism by leading its hero to find his identity in *political action*.[23] It portrays the political life of a community no longer as a conflict of tribal factions but as a conflict of social classes. Prefiguring Conrad's later novels, it establishes the possibility of political activity not merely as an expression of egoism but as the realization in social action of the otherwise hollow self.

Jim is another exemplar of the Brooke myth: not merely a copy of the historical Brooke (on whom his later career is modeled), but a higher development of Kurtz. In form, if not in content, their careers are remarkably similar: they come to remote native areas with driving personal aims; they attain absolute power over the natives by manipulating their personal

[23] The following remarks are not intended as a total reading of *Lord Jim*: it is too great to be exhausted by one line of interpretation. As if in confirmation of this principle, the best study of the novel (Tony Tanner, *Conrad: Lord Jim* ["Barron's Educational Series"; Woodbury, N.Y., 1963]) falls short of its brilliant analysis of Jim's early development in its cursory treatment of his Patusan experience: "Of Jim's successful battle with Sherif Ali, his control over the Rajah and his rapid, almost effortless, achievement of preeminence among Doramin's people, little need be said" (p. 47). Since Tanner's approach is a psychological one, it is to be hoped that the present "sociological" approach will provide a complement in perspective, as well as in the phases of the story emphasized.

charismatic power (that Jim disdains his idealization does not prevent him from employing it effectively); they take native (in Jim's case, half-caste) mistresses and otherwise assimilate themselves to native life; they organize war parties and successfully pursue armed campaigns; and they are both destroyed by their incomplete identification with native life.

The significant difference between them is one of politics: Jim learns to employ his power in reordering the structure of the community, rather than, like Kurtz, accepting and exploiting the community's worst potentialities. Like Kurtz, Jim is an energetic worker, but he turns to economic pursuits only after stabilizing the political situation and distributing social justice. (He plans to become a colonist by developing a coffee plantation in a land which had previously produced only subsistence crops and, far in the past, pepper.) Kurtz seeks to drain rather than develop the land; his primary concern is acquiring ivory. He is, therefore, a personification not only of Belgian but of Dutch (and, although Conrad might not have agreed, of British) imperialism, whose politics varied with its economic interest and without respect to the social welfare of the natives.

A brief review of Jim's activities in Patusan will help to make clear Conrad's discoveries in colonial politics, especially in relation to the problem of personal identity. Patusan, as described by the Malaprop, half-caste captain of the ship that takes Jim to the mouth of its river, is at the outset a society close to precivilized animality: the Rajah, as he puts it, is a "laughable hyaena" and the place is a "cage of beasts made ravenous by long impenitence" (*LJ*, p. 239). When Marlow visits Patusan two years later, this state of affairs is "ancient history"—indeed, history at Patusan may be said to begin with Jim's advent.

The war at Patusan is not merely another example of inveterate native factionalism but is specified as a trade war between the Malay population under Rajah Tunku Allang and the immigrant Bugis people from Celebes, under Doramin. The Rajah systematically terrorizes the surrounding countryside to force all produce from the interior to be marketed through his hands, but the more "intelligent, enterprising, revengeful" Bugis challenge his monopoly. A third party to the dispute is a tribe of Dyaks in revolt against their oppressor, Rajah Allang. They are led by an Arab half-caste, Sherif Ali, who is said to have religious motives (he is apparently attempting to convert them to Mohammedanism while leading them in war).

Jim's first political course is to organize the Bugis (who are commercially linked with Stein's trading company) for the task of subduing the Dyaks, thereby preventing the Rajah from bolstering his position by an alliance with Sherif Ali (who is perfectly willing to sell out the Dyaks). With the prestige of the successful expedition behind him, Jim begins his second phase: a thorough political reorganization of Patusan. He appoints new headmen for the outlying villages, liberates the slaves held by Ali—forming them into a work force under himself—and exerts pressure on the Rajah for relief of the local peasantry. Unfortunately, his political reform does not go far enough: he resists Doramin's desire for a war against the Rajah which would give exclusive power to the Bugis. The subsequent alliance of the Rajah and Gentleman Brown brings about Jim's undoing.

Meanwhile, he takes on the role of unofficial judge in the community. He arbitrates cases of civil law, such as the affair of the brass pots, which threatens to erupt in tribal feuding; he defends such groups as the coastal fishing villages from the Rajah's exactions (still using the terms of the work ethic, Jim condemns the robbery of their produce as an infringement of the right to work); and he abolishes the Rajah's system of feudalism, which is described as personal slavery (p. 333). Only then does Jim begin to look— and look well—after his own economic interests, building a fort with the labor of ex-slaves, planning his coffee plantation, and obtaining a monopoly on the gunpowder in Patusan.

In all this, altruism and egoism are closely identified: " 'And do you know what's the best in it?' he asked. 'I'll tell you. It's the knowledge that had I been wiped out it is this place that would have been the loser' " (p. 245). Jim's self-realization occurs through—is identical with—his identification with the native community: "Now and then, though, a word, a sentence would escape him that showed how deeply, how solemnly he felt about that work which had given him the certitude of rehabilitation. That is why he seemed to love the land and the people with a sort of fierce egoism, with a contemptuous tenderness" (p. 248). Indeed, Jim comes to stand as a virtual symbol of civilization itself, as Marlow suggests:

> He dominated the forest, the secular gloom, the old mankind. He was like a figure set up on a pedestal, to represent in his persistent youth the power, and perhaps the virtues, of races that never grow old, that have emerged from the gloom. I don't know why he should always have appeared to me symbolic. Perhaps this is the real cause of my interest in his fate. (P. 265)

At this point, Marlow recalls Jim's original sin of deserting the pilgrim ship: "I don't know whether it was exactly fair to him to remember the

incident which had given a new direction to his life, but at that very moment
I remembered very distinctly. It was like a shadow in the light" (p. 265). What
is the significance of this act, the key to the moral drama of *Lord Jim*, in
relation to the political revolution Jim later effects?

It would be possible to find in the abandonment of eight hundred brown-
skinned people to save one's own white skin a basis of racial prejudice,
but Jim's attitude toward the Malays is carefully distinguished from that of
the German captain, for whom they are "cattle," and from that of the chief
engineer, for whom they are "brutes." Jim has, indeed, some difficulty in
acknowledging the humanity of a horde of almost indistinguishable faces—
"eight hundred pilgrims (more or less)"—but he overcomes it, ironically,
when he pauses in his turmoil after the damaging of the ship to bring water
to a beseeching Malay. His identification with the native community is, in
fact, made the easier by his alienation from the white maritime world.

Jim's development is not from racial prejudice to missionary benevolence
toward the natives; it is from egoistic isolation to political solidarity. Marlow's
famous explanation of the jump—"He was not afraid of death perhaps, but
I'll tell you what, he was afraid of the emergency"—contains the clue to the
political meaning of this moral event:

> A certain readiness to perish is not so very rare, but it is seldom that you
> meet men whose souls, steeled in the impenetrable armour of resolution,
> are ready to fight a losing battle to the last, the desire of peace waxes
> stronger as hope declines, till at last it conquers the very desire of life.
> Which of us here has not observed this, or maybe experienced something
> of that feeling in his own person—this extreme weariness of emotions, the
> vanity of effort, the yearning for rest? Those striving with unreasonable
> forces know it well,—the shipwrecked castaways in boats, wanderers lost
> in a desert, men battling against the unthinking might of nature, or the
> stupid brutality of crowds. (P. 88)

"This extreme weariness of emotions"—what is this but a magnificent phrase
for the failure of nerve, the passivity that results from loss of engagement,
the retreat from the world of men's affairs into the bare self? While the
dominant imagery of the passage is drawn from the sea, the final illustration
has a wider relevance than that of a threatening natural realm. It describes the
isolation of the self, Jim's self, in the most extreme form of social chaos.
This awful vision of the "emergency"—the rush of eight hundred terrified
people for safety—is Jim's greatest fear, and the "stupid brutality of crowds"
is Marlow's general term for the anarchy that faces Jim as a brute fact. Jim

fails, of course, to find social roots in the maritime world; his wanderings, and the protean shapes he is led to take, represent the extreme of isolation, rootlessness, and loss of personal identity.

Then Jim creates his own community in Patusan: his jump takes him "into the heart of the community" (p. 258). It is this that gives him "the impenetrable armour of resolution" he had lacked. But he fails to make a total identification with the community, with the result that his resolution breaks down. When Brown appeals to him on grounds of their common moral failings and status as outcasts, Jim places Brown, who is to him the image of his own prior self, above his group ties. With this decision he is cast back into his hollow selfhood, and is sundered from his social group.

In his final act, Jim gives himself back to the group by accepting its justice and passively submitting to it his life. The denouement of *Lord Jim* has failed to satisfy many, who find in it too flamboyant a sacrifice of the self or too chilling an affirmation of retributive native justice. It is both of these, but above all it is an individual's act of identification with the higher claims of the community: "there is to my mind a sort of profound and terrifying logic in it," writes Marlow (p. 342). If we are to find the axiom of this logic it must lie in the philosophy of the organic state.

If there is anything like original sin in Conrad's morality, it is the temptation to stay outside the community, or to return from it to the sole self. As Freud would have it, this is the resistance of the self-conscious ego to the complete assimilation of men like Singleton, which is itself a kind of death— an end to personal existence. But the compelling appeal of this temptation leads men to become aware that, in this world, they must lose themselves to find themselves. In his initial impulse to lose or avoid his identity, and in his ultimate self-creation by social action, Jim takes his place among the modern heroes to whom Lionel Trilling has called attention in *The Opposing Self*: those who strive to find a place in which the self can survive in the modern world. For Jim the only refuge outside civilized atomism lies in creating an organic native community.

What distinguishes the colonist from the conqueror in the last analysis is not good works but faith—his personal act of faith in joining the community. The "idea" is, in the end, not the work ethic, not even political amelioration. It is a creed of religious proportions, "something you can set up, and bow down before, and offer a sacrifice to," and it is this creed that gives the sanction to political activity and efficient work.

This denouement is rendered in a bundle of letters from Marlow to an unnamed member of his original audience, some two years after his recitation of Jim's earlier career. The theoretical issue is introduced by some remarks from Marlow to his second persona:

> You said also—I call to mind—that "giving your life up to them" (*them* meaning all of mankind with skins brown, yellow, or black in colour) "was like selling your soul to a brute." You contended that "that kind of thing" was only endurable and enduring when based on a firm conviction in the truth of ideas racially our own, in whose name are established the order, the morality of an ethical progress. "We want its strength at our backs," you had said. "We want a belief in its necessity and its justice, to make a worthy and conscious sacrifice of our lives. Without it the sacrifice is only forgetfulness, the way of offering is no better than the way to perdition." In other words, you maintained that we must fight in the ranks or our lives don't count. . . . The point, however, is that of all mankind Jim had no dealings but with himself, and the question is whether at the last he had confessed to a faith mightier than the laws of order and progress. (P. 339)

Conrad's usual formulation of the "idea"—"We want a belief," etc.—is here given to a white supremacist ("selling your soul to a brute"). In his view, the idea is exclusively Western ("ideas racially our own") and reduces itself to the concept of the white man's burden ("the morality of an ethical progress"). Marlow, on the other hand, seems to state the opposite extreme, rugged individualism ("no dealings but with himself"). This is, however, only another way of stating the organicist doctrine: only by engagement with others, by "a faith mightier than the laws of order and progress," can the individual really have dealings with himself. The final implication is that the "faith" or "idea" is not limited to any particular historical content. It is not simply the meliorist ideal of Western civilization; it includes any form of genuine social community, even that which the natives might achieve. In the final analysis, colonization is a viable—the only viable—form of imperialism, not so much because it ameliorates the worst conditions of native life but because the commitment to social progress allows the individual to discover himself in the community formed or improved by his efforts. He can then egoistically surrender himself to the community, wearing, as Jim does, "a proud and unflinching glance" (p. 416).

Afterthoughts on Colonialism

Even before Conrad had finished elaborating, in *Lord Jim* and "Heart of Darkness," the distinction between conquerors and colonists, he was collaborating with Ford Madox Hueffer on a novel, *Romance*, which takes a dim view of colonists, as well as of British imperialism generally. It is not, of course, surprising that the joint production of two authors with a highly cosmopolitan culture and with family ties to the Continent should reveal ambivalent attitudes toward England and its empire. This was especially likely at the time the novel was written, for the Boer War was then arousing widespread indignation in England and creating a problem of loyalty for Conrad. What is striking, nevertheless, is the depth of hostility toward Britain revealed in the novel, for an Admiralty court and a British colony are among its worst villains.

According to Hueffer, Conrad conceived the tale as a conflict between an individualist hero and corrupt society:

> Conrad saw the possibilities that were for his own exotic note in the story. Above all, with the coming of politics: for John Kemp [the hero], in coming to blows with Mr. Topnambo, member of the Governor's council, then and there identified himself with the party in the island of Jamaica that at that date desired annexation by the United States.
>
> This at once made our leading character handleable by Conrad. John Kemp merely kidnapped by pirates and misjudged by the judicial bench of our country was not so vastly attractive, but a John Kemp who was in addition a political refugee, suspect of High Treason and victim of West India merchants. . . . That was squeezing the last drop of blood out of the subject. . . .[24]

Hueffer's remarks require us to make a distinction between colonists, whom Conrad previously idealized, and colonial aristocracies, which, as they have done in recent conflicts, act more in the manner of conquerors. The *colons* of Jamaica are regarded in *Romance* in the hard light of irony, and although it is not a very successful novel it is considerably more serious, complicated, and relevant than Conrad's critics have acknowledged. (The same is true of the other major collaborative effort of Conrad and Hueffer, *The Inheritors*, which will be examined in the following chapter.)

When John Kemp arrives in Jamaica he finds three political forces at work: the British challenge to Spanish dominance in the Caribbean, which takes the form of a naval campaign to make British trade safe from pirates (whom Spain has not succeeded in driving from their lairs in Cuba); the pressure in the British Parliament to require implementation of the Abolition Act in the colonies; and the efforts of the Jamaica *colons* to extend the former

[24] *Joseph Conrad*, p. 46.

campaign and to obstruct the latter. The first issue puts the colony's merchants at odds with the Admiralty for not pursuing their interests with sufficient vigor; the second brings out the slaveowning planters against Parliament, for Abolition is to deprive them of their property and means of production. These two economic interests are united in a party of "Separationists" against the loyalists, or "Ministerialists." Somewhat as Conrad himself had joined a reactionary royalist intrigue when he arrived in Marseilles as a young man from the provinces, John Kemp joins the Separationist cause. It is personal attachment to a family of participants that determines him, for his political imagination is as yet undeveloped. He is thoroughly victimized and almost destroyed by his connections with the reactionary party, but gains political maturity in the process.

Conrad's political judgment of the *colons* is established in the novel not only by dialogues which express their mercenary motives but by the plot, which traces their shabby treatment of the hero. The authors had, moreover, to invent plot elements which would help prevent the reader's sympathies from swinging to the opposite side, toward the loyalist party and British sovereignty. Such, indeed, was Hueffer's understanding of Conrad's political stance:

> it was an easy task to identify Kemp hangably with those traitors to the British Crown [the Separationists]. Conrad, however, was a Loyalist: a Loyalist to every régime that ever existed but passionately a Loyalist to Great Britain. It was therefore necessary to give the screw one turn more: Kemp had to be made a misjudged man, betrayed by the stupid cruelty of merchants and the administration. He thus became exactly a figure for Conrad to handle. For, if Conrad were the eternal Loyalist, nevertheless the unimaginative and cruel stupidity of Crown and Government officials was an essential part of his creed. . . . The British Empire was for him the perfection of human perfections, but *all* its politicians, all its public officials, police, military officers of the Crown, gaolers, pilots, port admirals and policies were of an imbecility that put them in intelligence below the first lieutenant of the French navy that you could come across. . . .[25]

Hueffer effectively contradicts his assertion of Conrad's blind loyalty to the Empire by the swell of his own rhetoric in describing Conrad's contempt of its policies and personnel. Be that as it may, it is clear that *Romance*, especially in the portrayal of British justice in its final pages, is an attack on British imperialism severely at variance with his previous fictional suggestions.

[25] *Ibid.*, pp. 47–48.

Conrad and Hueffer reserve for the character portraits an examination of a subject dear to their hearts: the cultural concept of Englishness. The Anglophile Latin of the novel, Don Carlos—who wishes to marry his cousin Seraphina to Kemp largely for the reason that Kemp is an Englishman—defines the values which the authors had under consideration: "English things last forever—English peace, English power, English fidelity. It is a country of much serenity, of order, of stable affection" (p. 150). Such was the myth of English culture to expatriates from much-troubled lands like Poland and the Latin American nations, but on any examination of Britain's political history the myth could not endure. It is harshly shattered by the villain of the novel, an Irishman named O'Brien, who speaks sincerely enough to be believed:

> These English—I've seen them, spit the child on the mother's breast. I've seen them set fire to the thatch of the widow and childless. . . . Sorrow? Ruin? Death? I am acquainted with them. It is in the blood; 'tis in the tone; in the entrails of us, in our mother's milk. Your accursed land has brought always that on our own dear and sorrowful country." (Pp. 470, 473)

An alternative view, somewhere between these extremes, is that of the faithful retainer, Tomas Castro. When Kemp fails to shoot the escaping pirate, Manuel, and blandly answers Castro's remonstrances with a shrug—"What can Manuel do to me?"—Castro replies, " 'Did the Señor Don Juan ask himself what Manuel could do to me—Tomas Castro? . . . Are all you English like princes that you should never think of anybody but yourselves?" (p. 306). Castro's concern is well founded, for he ultimately meets death at Manuel's hands: he gives himself up to Manuel when he, Seraphina, and Kemp are besieged in a cave. Kemp interprets his surrender as weakness—as inability to maintain an English self-restraint and repress his thirst for water—but Castro intentionally puts Manuel off the track of Seraphina and Kemp, sacrificing himself to save them.

What is ultimately called into question by *Romance* is the concept of national identity. The political situation is, as we have seen, one of tension between *colons* of English ancestry and their mother country. Kemp's antagonist is an Irishman with an over-riding hatred of England, who has identified himself with Spanish Cuba to the extent of becoming a judge and power in the land and surreptitiously fostering anti-British piracy. O'Brien singles out Kemp as his special enemy not only because he stands in the way of his plans to marry Seraphina and inherit her estate, but because he is a typical Englishman. The irony of his final plot against Kemp is to have the Englishman indicted as the Latin pirate El Demonio (who is actually a Nova Scotian Scot!). He is tried by an English Admiralty court, a majority of whose members are merchants in the West Indian trade. Their economic interest in destroying the pirates leads them to make a mockery of traditional British justice in trying Kemp. To stretch the confusion of national roles further, it is a Spanish emissary who brings news of the mistaken identity and demands the Englishman's release. The true-born Englishman has a hard time maintaining his identity in the complex world of colonial politics, just as the *colons* tend to lose their national allegiance in a revolutionary separatism. In this almost satiric conclusion, Conrad and Hueffer expressed their ambivalent views toward their own national identity and their mixed feelings toward England.

Conrad's broadened condemnation of colonial society and of British imperialism did not develop in his full-length fiction, though there are touches of it in his handling of the economic imperialists Gould and Sir John in his next novel, *Nostromo*. His interest turned from the tropics of his early experience to the Europe of his later years. After he had completed the last of his major political novels, *Under Western Eyes*, Conrad returned to writing tales of the tropics, two of which, published in *'Twixt Land and Sea* (1912), are of considerable interest. These stories, "A Smile of Fortune" and "Freya of the Seven Isles," represent the last versions of Conrad's view of imperialism, and it is a rancorous tone that they take—not only with the old target, Dutch administration, in the latter story, but with a French colonial society in the former.

Conrad's ambivalence toward English imperialism and its colonies might be presumed to extend to other nations and their forms of life in the tropics. There was French colonialism, which, as Hueffer has claimed, Conrad admired: "He used to shock the writer . . . by declaring that the French were the only European nation who knew how to colonise: they had none of the spirit of Mr. Kipling's 'You-bloody-niggerisms' about them, but regarded black or tan or black and tan as all one humanity with themselves. . . ."[26] By the time he came to write "A Smile of Fortune," Conrad had changed his mind.

The first half of this poorly integrated story describes a young captain's efforts to distinguish between illusion and reality in the social reputations of

[26] *Ibid.*, p. 241.

colonial businessmen. Ernest Jacobus, upon whom his employers have counseled the Captain to rely, proves to be a scoundrel, while Alfred Jacobus, who vulgarly forces his wares upon him, comes to be the object of his trust and, eventually, of considerable help to him. The distinction between the brothers is first posed in terms of the work ethic: Alfred is an indefatigable (though slow-moving) salesman, while Ernest is discovered extending his siesta into the late afternoon. The work ethic does not, at first, seem to sanction non-productive activities like salesmanship, and the Captain rejects Alfred as irritatingly pushy. Only when Ernest reveals a more serious moral flaw does the Captain accept Alfred's services. But this flaw goes beyond the conduct of work, and even beyond relations with employees: it is a matter of race. When his half-caste clerk wakes him to announce the Captain, Ernest cuffs and kicks the boy and welcomes the Captain scurvily. The full significance of this action dawns upon the Captain when he perceives that the boy's resemblance to his master can be accounted for only by his being the latter's illegitimate son.

The further relevance of this scene for a judgment of colonial society is revealed when the Captain discusses the brothers with a member of the highest society on the island, which is named "Pearl of the Ocean" but is based on Conrad's experience of Mauritius. "This acquaintance of mine," the Captain recounts, "belonged to one of the old French families, descendants of the old colonists; all noble, all impoverished, and living a narrow, domestic life in dull, dignified decay" (*TLS*, p. 34). It is a society that enchanted Conrad, according to his French biographer, Jean-Aubry, but it is revealed in this story as anachronistic (its old ladies speak "quaint archaic French of pre-Revolution period"), banal ("the emptiness of [the girls'] existence passes belief"), and morally decadent:

> I gave him the whole story of my visit, not forgetting the tell-tale resemblance of the wretched mulatto boy to his tormentor. He was not surprised. No doubt, no doubt. What of that? In a jovial tone he assured me that there must be many of that sort. The elder Jacobus had been a bachelor all his life. A highly respectable bachelor. But there had never been open scandal in that connection. His life had been quite regular. It could cause no offence to anyone. (P. 34)

The irony in this revelation of colonial values is increased by the *colon*'s account of Alfred Jacobus, which follows. In Alfred's case, colonial society's judgment of a sexual peccadillo takes the form of the strictest ostracism. Certain changes in the circumstances make all the difference: Alfred was married, took up with another woman (white, but a circus performer), did so *publicly*, and acknowledged her (and his?) daughter as his own. For these affronts to public opinion he is not received in what passes for society on the island, and as for his legitimate daughter and her *arriviste* husband, "of course, they don't know him" (p. 36). The Captain's—and, by implication, the author's—view of these morals is manifest. Speaking of Alfred's adopted daughter, Alice, he says to the *colon*:

> "I suppose if he employed her, say, as a scullion in his household and occasionally pulled her hair or boxed her ears, the position would have been more regular—less shocking to the respectable class to which he belongs."
> He was not so stupid as to miss my intention, and shrugged his shoulders impatiently.
> "You don't understand. To begin with, she's not a mulatto. And a scandal is a scandal. People should be given a chance to forget. I dare say it would have been better for her if she had been turned into a scullion or something of that kind. Of course he's trying to make money in every sort of petty way, but in such a business there'll never be enough for anybody to come forward." (Pp. 38–39)

At this point begins the latter half of the story, in which the Captain himself comes forward—at least far enough to conduct a rather uncertain courtship of the neurotic young lady. In the course of the confused narrative which follows, interest in the romance gives way to a new display of Alfred Jacobus' character. This economically aggressive colonist who works mainly for his daughter becomes the object of a sympathy greater than that given to Almayer or to Kayerts of "An Outpost of Progress," who had similar paternal motives.

Indeed, Alfred Jacobus emerges as the pathetic hero of the story, despite the amusing roguery of his dealings with the Captain. He encourages the latter's courtship of his daughter by promises of business dealings to the Captain's profit. When he sees that these efforts are futile, he decides to get what profit he can by foisting a load of potatoes on the Captain when he makes ready to leave—in effect, blackmailing him for his advances toward his daughter. On the other hand, once he commits himself to helping the Captain, he blackmails his brother to obtain the sugar bags needed in order to put him on his way. He does this at a profit, of course, to himself, but his promise of profit to the Captain comes true ironically, when the latter takes advantage of a potato shortage at his next port of call to sell his load at three times the price he had paid. The playful tone of these concluding pages makes it difficult to draw a moral from them. Conrad seems to suggest that, in the absence of genuine community, the self-interest of a resourceful entrepreneur can become the only attractive element of colonial society.

In "Freya of the Seven Isles," Conrad returns to the Indies for a last look at Dutch imperialism. Freya's father, Old Nelson (or Nielson—his non-English nationality is important), is dominated by his fear of the Dutch authorities, and with some justification, considering the denouement. He has bought or leased part of a small island in the Seven Isles group from its sultan but maintains his plantation there only under the sufferance of the Dutch administration; the narrator comments that had he been English the Dutch "would have discovered a reason to fire him out without ceremony" (*TLS*, p. 148). Nelson is even more afraid of Spanish intervention from the Philippines, but fears English imperialism not at all: "fair play" is still a viable myth for the Scandinavian.

Nelson in his fear is entirely blind to the fact that the Dutch Governor at Banka, "a charming, peppery, hearty, retired rear admiral," "had a distinct liking for him" (p. 155). It is, however, true that the Dutch look askance at the doings of Jasper Allen, Freya's fiancé, for his trading activities in unsettled native areas. "They considered him much too enterprising in his trading. I don't know that he ever did anything illegal; but it seems to me that his immense activity was repulsive to their stolid character and slow-going methods" (p. 154)—so comments the presumably English narrator. The story's initial view of Dutch imperialism is, then, sensitive to differences of national character and ironic enough to make comedy out of Nelson's excessive fears.

Into this unstable equilibrium the villain intrudes, in the guise of a Dutch naval officer who competes with Allen for Freya. The narrator cautions the reader against generalizing his villainy: "I don't mean to say that Heemskirk was a typical Dutch naval officer. I have seen enough of them not to fall into that absurd mistake" (p. 160). The affair between Freya and her suitors quickly takes on a political-economic form: Nelson encourages her indulgence of Heemskirk in order to avoid his displeasure, and discourages her romance with Allen—"What would the Dutch authorities say to such a match!" (p. 166). Heemskirk takes to administrative interference with Allen's trade, knocking down his beacons on the Borneo rivers he plies, threatening Nelson with expulsion from his plantation to get him to restrict Allen's visits to his harbor, and finally—after being ridiculed and rejected by Freya—taking Allen's ship in tow for entering a politically disturbed area. When Allen's ship is discovered to be missing its complement of guns (they have been sold by his kleptomaniac mate), Heemskirk has a clear field to destroy him by running it aground. "And now you may go ashore to the courts, you damned Englishman," Heemskirk says (p. 221).

It is at this point that the admittedly atypical official's abuse of power is generalized to indict the Dutch administration as a whole: the inquiry court seems to accept his perjured testimony and refers the case to the central authority in Batavia, "where no doubt it would fade away in a fog of official papers" (p. 232). Justice is uncertain for an Englishman in Dutch hands, whereas "naturally in our [English] papers the whole story came out before long" (p. 235). Finally, the ousted Nelson's comic fears are rendered pathetic by his inability to dispose of his property to anyone but a Dutch half-caste, at a tenth of its value. "The Dutch authorities would never have allowed an Englishman to settle there," he explains (p. 237).

For the episode of Allen's undoing, Conrad's mind turned to an incident in *The Rescue*, Jörgenson's anecdote of a trader named Dawson, which is re-counted to caution Lingard against interference in native affairs:

> He broke some trade regulation or other and talked big about law-courts and legal trials to the lieutenant of the *Komet*. "Certainly," says the hound. "Jurisdiction of Macassar, I will take your schooner there." Then coming into the roads he tows her full tilt on a ledge of rocks on the north side— smash! When she was half full of water he takes his hat off to Dawson. "There's the shore," says he—"go and get your legal trial, you—English-man—." (*Rescue*, p. 101)

The repetition of the incident suggests the possibility of a historical precedent for such high-handed dealing by the Dutch authorities. But Conrad does not give the event or its aftermath sufficient credibility to establish it as a critique of Dutch imperialism. Faced with such an appalling miscarriage of justice, Allen suffers a complete failure of nerve, becomes a beachcomber interested only in watching the decay of his formerly proud ship, fails to return to claim Freya because of his beggarly condition, and finally commits suicide. The dim end of Freya and her father complete the picture—a hazy one, at best—of total social dissolution in the tropics.

Lest it be supposed that Conrad's later severity with colonial societies excepts the British, the opening pages of a long story of the same period

(1911), "The Planter of Malata," satirize the residents of an obviously British colony, "a great colonial city," probably Singapore (Malata-Malaya). Its society includes the son of an "eminent colonial statesman," who is described as a "commercial monster" (*Within the Tides*, pp. 3-4); the pudgy young editor of the local newspaper, who thinks himself "the only apostle of letters in the hemisphere" (p. 49); and visitors from England who represent "the two big F's . . . Fashion and Finance" (p. 17). In this setting, there is little wonder that the hero, a man with marked peculiarities that eventually lead him to suicide, would rather live in almost complete isolation on his leased island. The story should be read in relation to *Victory*, on which Conrad was working at the very time he wrote it; the individual is destroyed by his loneliness, but the society which he rejects is abominable.

Imperialism and Capitalism

In these last installments of Conrad's running commentary on imperialism, there is a general rejection not only of colonial society but also of the economic system on which it is based: the capitalist economy of the home countries. Conrad was not an economist but a moralist in fiction, however, and his attention is claimed by the personal motives of the men who are caught up in the system, whether as conquerors or colonists. National distinctions become less important than the common worship of money, a theme to be found throughout Conrad's writings.

Early in his career, in a lush tale of native passion, "Karain: A Memory," Conrad had introduced a derisive note on the materialism of the Europeans, in contrast to the purity of the native's exclusive interest in sexual possession and personal honor. Karain, to free himself of the ghost of his guilt, wishes to go with the white gun-runners "to your people, who live in unbelief; to whom day is day, and night is night—nothing more, because you understand all things seen, and despise all else! To your land of unbelief, where the dead do not speak, where every man is wise, and alone—and at peace!" (*Tales of Unrest*, p. 44). This ironic image of the materialism of Western man is elaborated when the Englishmen free Karain from his spell with a charm made from a sixpence bearing the likeness of Queen Victoria. The spokesman's explanation of its potency catches up both the material and illusionist powers of money, and of imperialism generally: "She commands a spirit, too—the spirit of her nation; a masterful, conscientious, unscrupulous, unconquerable devil . . . that does a lot of good—incidentally . . . a lot of good . . . at times" (p. 49). The final scene in the Strand, London, with its judgment of modern civilization as circumscribed by illusions as powerful as the myths and passions of Karain, becomes an incisive comment on the economic and the irrational motivations which fed the imperialist drive.

When Conrad came to write "Heart of Darkness" about the central experience of his career as a seaman-trader, he set it within a frame-story, a recitation by Marlow to a group of yachtsmen. This group is made up of businessmen with direct connections with the substance and import of Marlow's tale. Here Conrad directly approached the subject of the responsibility of capitalism for imperialism and its crimes.

The group of five—the Director of Companies, the Lawyer, the Accountant, Marlow, and the unidentified narrator of the frame-story—are sitting aboard the Director's yacht in the mouth of the Thames. This is a situation in which Conrad must frequently have found himself in 1895–96, during the period of his close friendship with G. F. W. Hope, to whom *Lord Jim* is dedicated. Conrad had few dealings with businessmen (other than his publishers and agents) because of a profound distrust of them, which emerges in *Nostromo*, *Chance* and "An Anarchist." The motive that in these years brought Conrad together with such a group was a commercial speculation which Hope had invited him to join. Conrad engaged in a number of such grandiose schemes, none of which came to anything for him, but what distinguishes the Hope enterprise from the others is its colonial aspect. It was a speculation in shares in a South African gold mine.

In the story, a similar group of businessmen (and one seaman-trader) are musing on African imperial ventures as they sit in the mouth of the river that has carried English traders like themselves out upon the world. The narrator speaks in defense of materialistic motives, identifying them with the national tradition of the early explorers: "Hunters for gold or pursuers of fame, they all had gone out on that stream, bearing the sword, and often the torch, messengers of the might within the land, bearers of a spark from the sacred fire" (*Youth*, p. 47). But Marlow turns the subject to the mercenariness and brutality of imperialism and ends by insulting his patient audience for their participation in it:

> "The inner truth is hidden—luckily, luckily. But I felt it all the same: I felt often its mysterious stillness watching me at my monkey tricks, just as it watches you fellows performing on your respective tight-ropes for— what is it? half-a-crown a tumble—"
> "Try to be civil, Marlow," growled a voice, and I knew there was at least one listener awake besides myself.

"I beg your pardon. I forgot the heartache which makes up the rest of the price. And indeed what does the price matter, if the trick be well done? You do your tricks very well. . . . " (Pp. 93–94)

This bitter satire of his businessmen friends and of the capitalist ethos by which they live is extended in Marlow's narrative, in his account of the despicable company manager, the group of adventurers who are Marlow's passengers on the trip up the Congo to Kurtz's station (the "pilgrims," as Conrad masterfully dubs them), and—as the starkest vision of imperialist rapacity—the Eldorado Exploring Expedition: "there was not an atom of foresight or of serious intention in the whole batch of them, and they did not seem aware these things are wanted for the work of the world. . . . the uncle of our manager was leader of that lot" (*Youth*, p. 87). Conrad's manager in the Congo was Camille Delcommune, and the latter's uncle, Alexandre Delcommune, did lead an expedition in the Congo during the period in which Conrad was there (1890).[27] That expedition was to the region that is now Katanga Province of the Republic of the Congo, and the expedition was one of the key steps in opening its mineral resources to exploitation by the company that was to become the giant Union Minière.

After Conrad had written his accounts of Belgian imperialism in the Congo, he would seem to have dissected utterly the theme of economic greed, but in the stories with which we have concluded, Conrad returns to it and gives it a new turn. Alfred Jacobus and the Captain, Old Nelson and Jasper Allen, are all presented sympathetically yet all function almost exclusively on the basis of economic drives. It is true that they each have a woman in mind as the end of their labors—the older men work to support their daughters and the younger men to win them—but their strongest emotional reactions are to business reverses. All of them are pathetic in their efforts to wring a living from the man-traps of imperialism.

Even the work ethic breaks down in face of such meaningless activity, and the stories end on a note of futility, whether announcing the Captain's success or Allen's failure. It is this revulsion from work with a profit motive that informs Conrad's treatment of "material interests" in *Nostromo* (despite the fact that their leading proponent, Charles Gould, begins by using them

[27] Alexandre Delcommune's book on the Congo, *L'Avenir du Congo Belge Menacé* (Brussels, 1919), dedicated to Camille, contains a description of capital in terms usually reserved for a higher power: "le plus grande levier du monde dans tous les domaines, le crédit financier indispensable, tout-puissant et créateur." It also contains a journal of his expedition to Katanga in 1890–93; see his Appendix I.

for a higher ideal). It is this attitude that leads Conrad to portray his final version of the capitalist entrepreneur, the Great de Barral of *Chance*, as a man possessed by illusions which are almost fatal to others and ultimately fatal to himself. Conrad has not spared the culture of capitalism—the moral and psychological distortions which it creates—in his penetration to the sources of imperialism.

Conrad's view of imperialism is, then, an old-fashioned one in that it places major emphasis on the mercenary motives of the conquerors and their opposite numbers at home, rather than on the non-economic forces that led European nations into competition for colonies. This emphasis may be accounted for by the author's greater personal familiarity with the individuals who went out to the tropics than with the mass emotions which backed up imperialism at home. Nevertheless, there are resemblances between Conrad's portrait of imperialist man and the more complicated descriptions of him by recent historians.

For one, his revelation of the aggressive impulses that lie in the heart of the conqueror accords well with a line of thought that descends from the economist Joseph Schumpeter, in which imperialism is considered a modern expression of an instinctual aggressive tendency. Schumpeter's theory of imperialism is derived from his observation of the chauvinistic propaganda that accompanied it in Conrad's time:

> As early as the nineties [imperialism] meant a great deal to the youth of Oxford and Cambridge. It played a leading part in the Conservative press and at Conservative rallies. Commercial advertising grew very fond of employing its emblems. . . . This success is readily explained. In the first place, the plan had much to offer to a whole series of special interests— primarily a protective tariff and the prospect of lucrative opportunities for exploitation, inaccessible to industry under a system of free trade. Here was the opportunity to smother consumer resistance in a flood of patriotic enthusiasm. . . . Equally important was the fact that such a plan was calculated to divert the attention of the people from social problems at home. But the main thing, before which all arguments stemming from calculating self-interest must recede into the background, was the unfailing power of the appeal to national sentiment. . . . Driven out everywhere else, the irrational seeks refuge in nationalism—the irrational which consists of belligerence, the need to hate, a goodly quota of inchoate idealism, the most naive (and hence also the most unrestrained) egotism.[28]

[28] *Imperialism and Social Classes*, trans. Heinz Norden (orig. pub., 1919; New York, 1950), pp. 13–14.

Rabid nationalism is rarely present in Conrad's characters, but the belligerence, hate, idealism, and egoism are there in abundance.

Another force that contributed to imperialist fervor was a historical tradition of aristocratic dominance within the military and religious institutions, which expressed itself in adventurous expansionism and missionary zeal, respectively. Even in Conrad's time, critics of imperialism like Hobson were confronted with the glaring fact that many colonial ventures were uneconomical, yet were intensely supported along lines which smacked of cant. Were imperialist pretensions to spreading civil and religious civilization as hypocritical as the "Little Englanders" made them out to be? One historian has said of Hobson what may equally well be applied to Conrad:

> Hobson made no charge of hypocrisy. Hypocrisy, after all, is a product of the reason, an assessment of means. There is never any enthusiasm in it, and even barefaced greed furnishes no adequate stimulus to a long policy. The real trouble as Hobson saw it was that the imperialists—well organized in small but interlocking groups, wielding influence not in political theory only but in social life, in sport, in the public schools, in the cadet forces, in the scouting movement, in the Press, in the pulpit—believed in what they said and in what they were doing, and he knew he could not convince them by any words or by any pages of closely-reasoned argument that "every enlargement of Great Britain in the tropics is a distinct enfeeblement."[29]

This theory of the rampant irrationality that typified imperialists at home and abroad indicates the strength of the public sentiments which Conrad's stories set out to challenge. He did so by insisting that the men who went out to the tropics were not the knights or saints they were supposed, but petit bourgeois businessmen willing to dabble in crime.

If we compare Conrad's colonial fiction with its French, German, and other English analogues, as Susanne Howe has described them in her study of the genre,[30] we see another point of reference to the milieu in which he wrote. Conrad shares with the French a romantic feeling for the power and mystery of the jungle and for unbridled native passion; with the Germans, he shares an interest in the situation of the small businessman of the tropics (as in the so-called *Kaufmannsroman*) and in the European's tendency to degeneration there (known as *Kaffern-wirtschaft*); but he is closest to the

---

[29] A. P. Thornton, *The Imperial Idea and Its Enemies: A Study in British Power* (New York and London, 1959), p. 73.

[30] *Novels of Empire* (New York, 1949).

English novelists in his tendency to erect a relativist defense of its empire on the grounds that it was better run than those of other nations. Conrad began with this assumption, rooted in the gospel of work, but as he discovered the moral limitations of work in itself, and as he turned to British themes in *Romance* and *The Inheritors*, he tended to drop the distinction. As he had put it in "Heart of Darkness," "all Europe had contributed to the making of Kurtz." His later stories make the nationality of the conquerors far less important than their common trait of money-grubbing.

Finally, the very selection of colonial sites for his tales marks a selective judgment of the critical issues in late nineteenth-century imperialism. By focusing on the Congo, he could expose the Belgian conquest of central Africa as "the vilest scramble for loot that ever disfigured the history of human conscience" (*LE*, p. 17). By writing an allegory, in *The Inheritors*, of the transition from the Liberal tradition of free trade and non-intervention to the Unionist policy of economic and military expansion (as in the Boer War), he was able to catch his adopted nation at a crisis and turning point in its colonial policy. By setting his early tales in the regions of Borneo which were in dispute between Britain and The Netherlands, Conrad prefigured the clashes of empires which occurred with increasing frequency after the turn of the century and which were to lead to World War I.

Chapter V
THE OLD EUROPE
AND THE NEW

Joseph Chamberlain

Lord Randolph Churchill

. . . "il n'y a plus d'Europe!" There is, indeed, no Europe. The idea of a Europe united in the solidarity of her dynasties, which for a moment seemed to dawn on the horizon of the Vienna Congress through the subsiding dust of Napoleonic alarums and excursions, has been extinguished by the larger glamour of less restraining ideals. Instead of the doctrines of solidarity it was the doctrine of nationalities much more favourable to spoliations that came to the front, and since its greatest triumphs at Sadowa and Sedan there is no Europe. Meanwhile till the time comes when there will be no frontiers . .

—Autocracy and War

After his initial choice of imperialist themes for his fiction, Conrad turned to the world closer to home, contemporary Europe. With the exception of a muddled short story, "The Return," he avoided the domestic problems of modern life for broader social ones. (By the time he came to write *The Secret Agent* he was able to put the two realms together in an intertwined plot.) Although his earliest work which refers to European society, *The Nigger of the "Narcissus,"* appeared almost at the start of his writing career, it was only after the turn of the century that he devoted himself to the questions that were beginning to emerge as the main ones for our time: questions about social classes, their moral values and their political vitality; questions about capitalism, revolution, and counter-revolution; questions about nationalism, war, and cooperation. This is the period in which Conrad began to write his political essays, to take a public stand on topical issues, and to write his three great political novels. It is also the time in which his thoughts on society in general, and on the societies around him, began to evolve beyond his original assumptions, the time in which he began to look back to the past in order to re-evaluate his own political heritage and to formulate new attitudes toward aristocracy, bourgeoisie, and proletariat. It is these developing conceptions that inform his work in this period and give it its peculiar interest.

To measure the extent of Conrad's imaginative development, his earliest work serves as a fixed point. In *The Nigger of the "Narcissus,"* the seaman who narrates the tale expresses Conrad's ironic tone and political bias. He describes the crew with one eye on the reading public and its humanitarian sentiments, which he and the author hope to modify through a complex parable:

> Well-meaning people had tried to represent those men as whining over every mouthful of their food; as going about their work in fear of their lives. But in truth they had been . . . men enough to scorn in their hearts the sentimental voices that bewailed the hardness of their fate. . . . Their successors are the grown-up children of a discontented earth. They are less naughty, but less innocent; less profane, but perhaps also less believing; and if they had learned how to speak they have also learned how to whine.
> (P. 25)

This scorn of well-meaning "liberals" and of whining workers generates the plot and makes this Conrad's most didactic political tale.

In our time it is difficult to resist the temptation to read *The Nigger of the "Narcissus"* as a parable not only of class conflict but of racial attitudes. In such a reading one can see the Negro, James Wait, and the rabble-rouser, Donkin, as co-conspirators for the support of public opinion: using the same rhetorical means, they attempt to win the humanitarian sympathies of the crew. The burden of the fable would then be to check sentimentality toward the underprivileged and to affirm a conservative stoicism which accepts social evils and counsels the repression of resentments by immersion in work. Such is the implication of the description of Donkin:

> They all knew him! . . . The man who can't do most things and won't do the rest. The pet of philanthropists and self-seeking landlubbers. The sympathetic and deserving creature that knows all about his rights, but knows nothing of courage, of endurance, and of the unexpressed faith, of the unspoken loyalty that knits together a ship's company. The independent offspring of the ignoble freedom of the slums full of disdain and hate for the austere servitude of the sea. (Pp. 10–11)

The basis of moral criticism both of mutiny and, as we shall see, of revolution is the same: they are a breach of the work ethic—not mere laziness but a rejection of the restraining values of dedication to the task, abstract duty, and subordination to authority.

Yet elements of the plot will not fit this formula, though Conrad may have intended that they should. The main parable, the Negro's evocation of sympathy from the crew, is designed to create suspicion that he is faking illness in order to receive favors and attention. But the tale takes a new turn when Wait exonerates himself by the simple expedient of dying. Since his was a legitimate complaint, after all, it is necessary to introduce new elements to sustain the tension. This is done with detriment to the credibility of the plot. As soon as Wait dies, the doldrums that have impeded the ship's passage home are ended. The implication is that the crew is right in its superstitious belief that the weather is preternaturally linked with the dying man's presence on the ship.

The characterization of Donkin, on the contrary, has no room for obfuscation, only for sarcasm. It expresses, moreover, the imposition of the author's prejudice on the novel, rather than a discovery of moral significance in the dramatic working of the plot. In the almost contemporary "Heart of Darkness," the attribution to Kurtz of demagogic powers serves to give broad political relevance to the character study of the arch-imperialist: "He would have been a splendid leader of an extreme party." "What party?" asked Marlow. "Any party," the journalist answered (*Youth*, p. 154). The attribution of demagoguery to Donkin, on the other hand, expresses a political animus that seems excessive to the "objective correlative" of the story. Donkin, "who never did a decent day's work in his life, no doubt earns his

living by discoursing with filthy eloquence upon the right of labour to live"
(*NN*, p. 172). This net fails to catch all unionists, for Donkin is a poor
example of a labor organizer; he does not think in terms of the working man's
economic motivations. The proletarian crew immediately shuns him as
beneath their class: he is the type of what has been called the *Lumpenproletariat*, with his hobo's rags and criminal habits. Rather than reflecting on
the working class, Donkin anticipates Conrad's anarchists. He is moved by a
psychological, almost metaphysical, nihilism. When his crony, the dying
Wait, asks him, "Why are you so hot on making trouble?" Donkin fumbles
for an answer: " 'Cos it's a bloomin' shayme. We are put upon . . . bad food,
bad pay . . . I want us to kick up a bloomin' row; a blamed 'owling row
that would make 'em remember!" (p. 112).

Just as Donkin's role as an agitator is exposed as stemming from personal
resentments, the crew—which is nominally the collective hero of *The Nigger
of the "Narcissus"*—is shown to mutiny primarily because of its personal
attachment to Wait and because of childish grievances aggravated by
Donkin. The crew's clumsy protest against the supercilious commands of its
captain during a storm may be considered a commentary on strikes or
revolutions as well as on mutinies. The most poignant feature of the revolt
is its lack of formulation. When Captain Allistoun confronts the men and
asks with a challenge, "What do you want?" the narrator continues: "What
did they want? . . . They wanted great things. And suddenly all the simple
words they knew seemed to be lost forever in the immensity of their vague
and burning desire. They knew what they wanted, but they could not find
anything worth saying" (pp. 133–34). Conrad withholds sympathy, not
because their protest smacks of trade unionism but because their plight is
typical of the universal condition of mankind.

Even the moral sentiments of the lower classes are portrayed in an ambiguous light; we are not quite to approve the crew's pity for Donkin's indi-
gence (which is strong enough to overcome their contempt for his Lumpen-
proletarian origins and behavior), their similar sympathy for the dying Wait,
and their defense of him against Allistoun. Their ineffectiveness and cowardice
in the mutiny, together with their superstitiousness and gullibility, make the
novel's final judgment of their class a confused and unsatisfactory one.
Throughout the tale they are presented as spineless children, and their
officers compare them, to their disadvantage, with previous generations of
seamen, yet at the close of the narrative they are addressed as "brothers!

You were a good crowd. As good a crowd as ever . . . gave back yell for yell to a westerly gale" (p. 173).

This ambivalence toward the working class remains with Conrad throughout his career, though it detaches itself from the ultramontane politics which he had expressed in the 1885 letter to Kliszczewski. By the close of his career, as we have seen, Conrad expresses esteem for and identification with the *working* men of all classes (though he does accept the existence of a separate economic class of proletarians). But in *The Nigger of the "Narcissus"* and occasionally thereafter—as in *The Secret Agent*, where the lower-class characters, the cabmen and the charwoman, are caricatured as self-pitying and alcoholic—Conrad's sympathy with the labors and sufferings of the poor is mixed with a reserve that borders on contempt. It is an ambivalence that cannot, however, be used to characterize Conrad's politics, for it is to be found in the hearts of organicists, liberals, and conservatives alike.

The transition in Conrad's attitudes toward social classes came about through a series of tales hinging on the drama of class conflict, in which the motives and character of the upper classes were subjected to ironic scrutiny. The first of Conrad's collaborative efforts with Ford Madox Hueffer, *The Inheritors*, was, like the second, *Romance*, written to express primarily political concerns, although without sufficient seriousness to make them major works. For Conrad, the subject was laden with character types that could be treated only superficially in the novel's allegorical frame. There are the European capitalists conniving at imperialist coups, as in the colonial tales written in the same years; the aristocratic *émigrés* he went on to expose in detail in his later fiction ("Gaspar Ruiz," *The Arrow of Gold, Suspense*); the world of finance and fashion that he would derisively describe in such works as *Chance* and "The Planter of Malata." The most attractive challenge to Conrad's political imagination in *The Inheritors* was, however, the opportunity to portray in broad, allegorical terms the course which the modern world was taking at the turn of the century.

The subject of *The Inheritors* is the fall of a British government. The Foreign Minister of this government is named Churchill, unambiguously recalling Randolph Churchill (although he has also been compared to Arthur Balfour, Churchill's sometime political ally). He represents the traditional virtues of the English politician: self-restraint, disinterestedness, broad historical perspective—in short, the embodiment of the work ethic in politics. He has, however, favored British participation in the exploitation of a colonial area, "Greenland," which is described in precisely the terms used for the Congo in Conrad's African tales. He has thus allied himself with the Duc de Mersch, an international financier who heads a mythical grand duchy that bears every resemblance to Belgium, and who himself represents Leopold II, the initiator of the Congo exploitation and originally the private owner of its territory.

Churchill's rival in the cabinet, who assumes power after his fall, is a thinly veiled Joseph Chamberlain. His politics are not made clear, but his tactics and style suggest a new political world of bourgeois ambition and amorality, imperialist expansionism, and jingoist mass appeal—in sum, the politics of Kurtz. The problem of the novel is to account for this transition from the old school to the new, from the nineteenth century to the twentieth (the book was written largely in the winter of 1899–1900). The name Conrad and Hueffer gave to the new order of inheritors is the "Fourth Dimension," and despite its futuristic banality, the term comes to suggest the political forces that have succeeded to the modern world. "I heard the Dimensionists described," the narrator says, "a race clear-sighted, eminently practical, incredible; with no ideals, prejudices, or remorse; with no feeling for art and no reverence for life; free from any ethical tradition. . . ."[1]

Their plan is to discredit the traditional order by associating its exemplar, Churchill, with a shabby imperialist venture, and to make capital of the inevitable upheaval in political morality through the Dimensionist government of Gurnard (the name of a predatory bird). A precedent for these events did occur when Churchill, as Secretary of State for India in 1885, directed the military annexation of upper Burma, in the course of the Salisbury government's competition with France for colonies.[2] The alliance of conservatives with the new brand of imperialists was to occur again when many Tories joined Chamberlain's wing of the Liberal Party in the Unionist governments.

Conrad's vision of the politics of the deluge, and his choice of Chamberlain as its representative villain, was also conditioned by the historical circumstances surrounding *The Inheritors*. It was written toward the beginning of the Boer War, for which Chamberlain, who pursued an aggressive policy as Colonial Secretary, was in part directly responsible. To the extent that he was a "Little Englander" or "pro-Boer," Conrad was opposed to Chamberlain's

---

[1] *The Inheritors* (orig. pub., 1901; New York, 1914), p. 9.
[2] See Robert R. James, *Lord Randolph Churchill* (London, 1959), pp. 205–6.

prosecution of the war. Further, he would have sympathized with the judgment of Sir Henry Campbell-Bannerman, the leader of the pro-Boer faction
of the Liberal Party, who condemned the ungentlemanliness of the former
manufacturer, Chamberlain:

> I confess that the thing which concerns me most is to find that Chamber-
> lainism *pays* with our countrymen. They worship a forcible man, and a
> clever man, and if his methods are vulgar, dishonourable, unfair, they
> only smile and approve. The lowering of the standard of public life is a
> far worse evil, because more permanent, than Toryism, jingoism, or any
> other heresy. . . . The "commencement de siècle" morals, apparently.[3]

The Inheritors is, then, a minor tragedy of the undermining and fall of
traditional values to the level of modern demagogy. In the career of Churchill,
it raises the question of the future of Tory democracy, which had perhaps
been closest to Conrad's own creed. The survivors of Churchill's "Fourth
Party" group, which had begun with principles derived from the organicist
tradition, at the turn of the century were joining forces with the jingoists
in the colonial struggles over South Africa and Ireland. "The heart of an
immense darkness" that comes up the Thames at the end of "Heart of
Darkness" is seen in *The Inheritors* to be settling over all Europe, uniting
the evil and the good in a common gray.

The critique of the political tendencies of the lower and of the upper

---

[3] Letter of October 29, 1900, quoted in G. B. Pyrah, *Imperial Policy and South
Africa, 1902–10* (Oxford, 1955), pp. 25–26. Today there is reason to believe that
Conrad, along with most other Britons, misunderstood Chamberlain's long-term
intentions for imperial unity. His proposals for imperial tariff preference and other
organs of integration among Britain's colonies (on the model of Prussia's Imperial Council, *Kriegsverein*, and *Zollverein*) were an early form of the Common-
wealth idea (*ibid.*, p. 7). But for all his visionary power, Chamberlain seems to
have been infected with the racialism of England and of his admired Germany,
as is borne out by his rhetorical idiom: "I believe in the British race. I believe that
the British race is the greatest of governing races that the world has ever seen"
(speech at the Imperial Institute, November 11, 1895, quoted in George Bennett
[ed.], *The Concept of Empire: Burke to Attlee, 1774–1947* [London, 1953], p. 315).
Chamberlain was also not adverse to justifying imperialist crimes on grounds
which must have smacked of cant to Conrad: "You cannot have omelettes without breaking eggs; you cannot destroy the practices of barbarism, of slavery, of
superstition, which for centuries have desolated the interior of Africa, without
the use of force . . ." (speech at the Royal Colonial Institute, March 31, 1897,

classes in *The Nigger of the "Narcissus"* and *The Inheritors*, respectively, was to be pursued by Conrad in a series of short stories of European class conflict, collected in *A Set of Six*. His initial approach to the problem was to see it in what were to him fresh but familiar settings. He turned back to the tropics with a new determination to get to the economic and historical roots of class conflict. Turning to an area of the world, Latin America, which he knew only superficially, he wrote his *magnum opus, Nostromo* (which will subsequently be considered in the detail that it merits), and followed it with a long story set earlier in South American history, "Gaspar Ruiz."

The heroes of these two tales will bear comparison, as in them Conrad was striving to explore the nature of political motivation by showing the ironic reversals of allegiance possible in complex revolutionary situations. In *Nostromo*, the hero—who, according to Conrad, represents "the people"— faithfully serves his upper-class masters because of his desire for honor, later turns to making his own fortune while identifying himself with a radical movement, and finally is killed by the character who represents the pure revolutionary tradition. In "Gaspar Ruiz," the hero, a politically naïve Chilean peasant who is forcibly conscripted by the nationalists fighting for independence from Spain, is similarly shunted from cause to cause and ends outside society.

Ruiz is captured and turned against the Republicans by the Royalists, recaptured and almost executed as a traitor by the Republicans, sheltered by a Royalist family whose property has been expropriated and whose daughter plans to use him against the Republicans, pardoned and promoted by a Republican general (modeled on San Martin), turned against the Republicans by his wounded vanity, converted to diehard Royalism by the aristocratic girl (who is now his wife), and finally, as an independent guerrilla chief outside the pale of politics, destroyed. Such a plot amounts almost to a parody of political vacillation, but it serves to suggest a political nexus as binding as fate, impersonally destructive to all individuality (e.g., to Ruiz's flamboyant egoism), and incommensurate with its victim's powers of explanation. Conrad's dramatization of such political fatality reaches its crescendo in *Under Western Eyes*, where the hero is a more self-conscious but equally helpless, unwilling, and vacillating political actor.

---

ibid., p. 319). Chamberlain remained for Conrad the bête noire of modern politics and figured later as the probable model for the Parliamentary opponent of the Great Personage in *The Secret Agent*—"that brute Cheeseman."

Important, too, in "Gaspar Ruiz" are the modifications of Conrad's
political attitudes that are suggested by his characterization of situations and
individuals. The nationalist revolution is described in terms reminiscent of
Poland, terms which cast doubt on the validity of even nationalist causes:

> That long contest, waged for independence on one side and for dominion
> on the other, developed in the course of years and the vicissitudes of
> changing fortune the fierceness and inhumanity of a struggle for life. All
> feelings of pity and compassion disappeared in the growth of political
> hatred. And, as is usual in war, the mass of the people, who had the least
> to gain by the issue, suffered most in their obscure persons and their
> humble fortunes. (SS, p. 3)

It might well be asked in what sense the lower classes had least to gain from
a nationalist revolution. The answer lies in Conrad's condemnation of the
ruling class and the rebels equally. He shows both Royalists and Republicans
to be dominated by personal motives and prejudices that mar the principles
for which they stand.

The aristocrats are the more easily disposed of in the tale: the Royalist
family of Ruiz's wife is presented, for all its sufferings, as the comic forebear
of the self-deluding émigrés of *The Arrow of Gold* and *Suspense*. The Republican
leaders, on the other hand, are shown to be motivated mainly by class competition with the Royalists. The narrator, the Republican General Santierra,
says of the heroine's father:

> "I suppose I really despised him because he was an old Castilian, a Spaniard
> born, and a Royalist. Those were certainly no reasons to scorn a man;
> but for centuries Spaniards born had shown their contempt for us Ameri-
> cans, men as well descended as themselves, simply because we were what
> they called colonists. We had been kept in abasement and made to feel
> our inferiority in social intercourse. And now it was our turn." (Pp. 23–24)

The General, however—like the revolution itself—does represent the
social principles of the revolutionary tradition:

> "I am, as you know, a republican, son of a Liberator," he declared. "My
> incomparable mother, God rest her soul, was a Frenchwoman, the daughter
> of an ardent republican. As a boy I fought for liberty; I've always believed
> in the equality of men; and as to their brotherhood, that, to my mind, is
> even more certain." (Pp. 25–26)

Like Santierra, the figure of San Martin displays the egalitarianism of the
revolutionary army in his acceptance of the peasant Ruiz's services and in his
preferment of him after Ruiz's early successes. But it is another Republican,

a provincial governor, who distrusts Ruiz for his leniency to prisoners, for his marriage to a woman of the old regime, and for his low "antecedents"— and through this man's efforts Ruiz becomes alienated from the revolution.

Ruiz is, then, a victim of class antagonisms only partly sublimated in the nationalist movement, but sufficiently disguised for him ever fully to comprehend them. Only when they exclude him from the service of the people does he become an enemy of the newly independent nation, having been denied, like other Conrad heroes, the opportunity to identify his egoism with the social community. Ruiz's "burning sense of an irreparable wrong" is like that of Nostromo or of Feraud (in "The Duel")—all of them excluded by subtle class antagonisms from assimilation into a common cause.

The two anarchist stories in the same volume with "Gaspar Ruiz" (*A Set of Six*) turn to revolutionary politics on the European scene, but they do not, upon examination, make as simple a denunciation of radicalism as has been assumed. Both "The Informer" and "An Anarchist" study cases (they cannot be called heroes) who were originally radical and have become fanatic in their anti-anarchism. Sevrin and Horne of the former story, the police spy and the anarchist, are described as "two fanatics. They were made to understand each other" (pp. 96–97). Similarly, the lepidopterist who narrates the latter story says of the escaped convict, Paul, that "he was much more of an anarchist than he confessed to me or to himself; and that, the special features of his case apart, he was very much like many other anarchists. Warm heart and weak head—that is the word of the riddle . . ." (pp. 160–61).

In these stories (as in *The Secret Agent*, which they prefigure), apart from their analysis of revolutionary and counter-revolutionary mentality, the bitterest irony is reserved for the representatives of the bourgeoisie. They are exposed both as the dupes of their own liberal attitudes toward revolution and as the pillars of a decadent society. "The Informer" takes up the first aspect, the political illusions of the bourgeoisie. Its narrator is a comfortable antique collector who displays the limitations of the political imagination of his class. His response to the master anarchist, Mr. X, is typical:

> I don't understand anarchists. Does a man of that—of that—persuasion still remain an anarchist when alone, quite alone and going to bed, for instance? Does he lay his head on the pillow, pull his bedclothes over him, and go to sleep with the necessity of the *chambardement général*, as the French slang has it, of the general blow-up, always present to his mind? And if so how can he? . . . All I know is that Mr. X took his meals in a

very good restaurant which I frequented also. . . . He was alive and
European; he had the manner of good society, wore a coat and hat like
mine, and had pretty near the same taste in cooking. It was too frightful
to think of. (Pp. 75–76)

This failure of imagination leads the bourgeoisie into an indulgence of the
anarchists which amounts to a betrayal of its own security. The failing is explained by Mr. X in words that could be Conrad's:

"Don't you know yet," he said, "that an idle and selfish class lives to see
mischief being made, even if it is made at its own expense? Its own life
being all a matter of pose and gesture, it is unable to realize the power and
the danger of a real movement and of words that have no sham meaning."
(P. 78)

The proof of his point is demonstrated by one fable of the story, the
portrayal of the genteel girl who joins the anarchists in bluestocking fashion,
leads Sevrin to reveal himself as a police spy for love of her, and finally spurns
him as a traitor. The final irony is reserved for the climactic moment, when
the spy is being led away: "And then the appropriate gesture came. She
snatched her skirt away from his polluting contact and averted her head with
an upward tilt. It was magnificently done, this gesture of conventionally
unstained honour, of an unblemished high-minded amateur" (p. 98). The
irony here is supreme: class conventionality steeps the girl in boredom and
sentimentality, which in turn lead her to work against her own class. She
rejects the police spy who betrays himself in an attempt to save her—and
who is indeed working to protect the bourgeois order itself—and she does so
with one of the conventional postures of that class. This is the joke the
narrator, at the end of the story, confesses that he has missed.

Not the self-destructive obtuseness of bourgeois society but its moral
viciousness is the subject of "An Anarchist." Even before the tale proper
begins, the narrator makes an extended satiric comment on "a famous
meat-extract manufacturing company," B. O. S. Bos.,—particularly on its
advertising. There is no justification in the plot for this introduction, other
than the fact that the company owns the ranch on which the anarchist convict
finds refuge and enslavement. In moral terms, however, the company stands
behind the brutal manager who keeps Paul in virtual slavery and who justifies
his actions by his regard for his employer's profits.

Harry Gee's anti-anarchism is a simple affair:

"that subversive sanguinary rot of doing away with all law and order in
the world makes my blood boil. It's simply cutting the ground from under

the feet of every decent, respectable, hard-working person. I tell you that the consciences of people who have them, like you or I, must be protected in some way; or else the first low scoundrel that came along would in every respect be just as good as myself. Wouldn't he, now? And that's absurd!" (P. 144)

His behavior seems to be exclusively designed for self-advancement through financial responsibility to his employers; human values are not part of his petit bourgeois "conscience." He rides down the escaped convict like an animal, spreads rumors about him in order to hinder his escape, and gives him nothing but his keep in a toolshed in return for Paul's skilled services as an engineer on the company's launch. The ranch from which he cannot escape, with its herds of cattle which would trample him to death if he crossed the island, is an image of the society which has placed him in this position.

Paul is described as a loyal worker, whom self-seeking radicals have encouraged, with the help of liquor, into rebellion. But his crime—the shouting of anarchist slogans and the insulting of the police—is shown to proceed from deep-seated class antagonisms. Although a skilled and satisfied worker, Paul has deep within him the values of his class, the Parisian proletariat: "All the world outside the café appeared to him as a dismal evil place where a multitude of poor wretches had to work and slave to the sole end that a few individuals should ride in carriages and live riotously in palaces" (p. 146). This attitude the professional anarchists merely foster, not implant. When he emerges from prison, it is his class-conscious bourgeois boss who refuses him re-employment and thus puts him again into the hands of the anarchists. When he is caught holding a bomb and tries to explain himself to the court, "the president was amused." For all his political confusion, for all the circumstantiality of his career, his timid judgment is a comprehensive one: "All the same, there's something wrong in a world where a man can get lost for a glass more or less" (p. 149).

It has been noted that "An Anarchist" closely resembles, in its circumstantial plot and ironic tone, Anatole France's "Crainquebille," which Conrad had previously read and reviewed. What is significant in this literary parallel is the similarity of Conrad's judgment of society to France's, which Conrad might not be expected to share. More fundamental than its contempt of radicals is the presence in "An Anarchist" of a vision of the destructiveness of modern society as a whole—a vision which was elaborated as a panorama of London in *The Secret Agent*. Even before his attack on the liberalism of his friends Edward and Constance Garnett and John and Ada Galsworthy, Conrad had evolved an attitude toward the middle class which marked the growth in him of the typically French artist's disdain of both bourgeois exploitation and liberal sentimentality.

It may be remarked in passing that the burden of these stories, like that of *The Secret Agent*, is that the proper role of government and the dominant classes toward subversive activities is watchfulness, not repression. The most dangerous elements of society in these pieces are the extremist (Sevrin) and the opportunist (Harry Gee) of the right who further the growth of autocracy in the guise of a crusade against the left. Throughout his later career Conrad consistently denied making a crusade: from the apologetic letter to Cunninghame Graham on the publication of *The Secret Agent* (*LL*, II, 60, October 7, 1907) to another in his final year (*LL*, II, 322, September 1, 1923), he maintained that his attack was neither on the doctrine of anarchism nor on its theoreticians, but on certain types of revolutionists and their motives. Further, Conrad remarks in the former letter that he would like to criticize the "true anarchist, which is the millionaire." He did so later in *Chance*, in the portrait of the Great de Barral, who is a tragicomic grotesque of middle-class values—a Kurtz of high finance.

Another of the stories in *A Set of Six*, "The Duel," takes up the theme of class antagonism by setting it at a century's remove, in anticipation of the method of his late historical novels. The setting is a new one for Conrad (although it had long absorbed him)—the Napoleonic era—but the issues are social ones similar to those in *Nostromo* and "Gaspar Ruiz." The story is, to be sure, a comedy, but not the antiquarian *jeu d'esprit* it has been taken for. Rather, it is built upon two important forces of the period: the ideal of classlessness in the Napoleonic army and the class antagonisms which continued to manifest themselves within it. This dichotomy between ideal and reality partly accounts for Napoleon's failure to embody the French Revolution and is thus a central element of the "Spirit of the Epoch" which Conrad says in his Author's Note he was trying to evoke.

The plot traces the feud of D'Hubert, a Northerner, a Picardy aristocrat whose good breeding allows him to advance rapidly through staff positions, and Feraud, a Southerner, the gascon son of a Gascony blacksmith, who also rises to general's rank but, in his case, exclusively by gallant action in the field. Their quarrel arises when D'Hubert accosts Feraud, who is attempting to enter salon society, with orders to place him under arrest for dueling. Their own series of duels slowly reveals the motivations behind their apparently irrational hostility: competition for promotion, differences of manners, discrimination in their assignments, and, ultimately, the quality of their loyalty to the egalitarian ideals of the Revolution, as symbolized by Napoleon.

Feraud claims that D'Hubert "never loved the Emperor," and although the claim is used scurrilously against the Republican aristocrat, there is an element of truth in it. D'Hubert's letter to his sister on Napoleon's fall betrays an aristocratic reserve rather than the fanatic devotion of Feraud, which is born of class identification with the revolutionary cause. After the first Restoration, the Royalists retain D'Hubert as general because of Feraud's report of his defection from the Emperor, while Feraud retains his rank but is retired. During the Hundred Days, D'Hubert is too ill to join the Napoleonic forces, as he wishes to do, but Feraud does and is implicated. With the second Restoration, Feraud is scheduled to be executed, but D'Hubert, with his continued prestige and high connections, manages to have the sentence commuted to exile in a provincial town. Under the Bourbons, the cleavage between the two becomes complete: Feraud is declassed, while D'Hubert resumes his aristocratic privileges, retiring to the chateau of his well-married sister and preparing himself for an equally splendid marriage.

The Napoleonic code of honor ultimately reasserts itself when Feraud again challenges D'Hubert. When his fiancée's uncle, a returned *émigré*, suggests that he decline Feraud's challenge as coming from a person of a lower class, D'Hubert rejects the prerogatives of his position in favor of the manly equality of the officer corps. For all its absurdity—and for all Feraud's comic bluster—the dueling code emerges as the guarantor of equality, the fixed value among the vicissitudes of class antagonism. There is in "The Duel" a gradual transvaluation of values, in which not only do our sympathies toward the antagonists become more balanced but our enlightened attitude toward the dueling code becomes modified by its association with the democratic character of the Napoleonic army.

The final story in *A Set of Six*, "Il Conde," has been understood to be Conrad's dirge for the death of his own class, the nineteenth-century European aristocracy, under the attack of the destructive forces of the present age, as symbolized by the predatory young men of Naples and especially by the

Camorra leader who robs and threatens the aging Count. This reading of the story indicates Conrad's awareness of the changes in European society in the years just before World War I, but it does not suggest its specifically political import. "Il Conde" gains in relevance to modern politics by comparison with a story set in similar circumstances shortly after the war: Thomas Mann's "Mario and the Magician."

Like Mann, Conrad perceived the end of the traditional protections of free government in a society dominated by nationalism (in Mann, these forces are not merely nationalist but specifically fascist). The Count of Conrad's story had grown up in a world of traditional refinement and rectitude. Like Mann's narrator (who also comes from "beyond the Alps" and is a "good European"), his life was "ruled by the prescribed usages of good society and protected by the State" (p. 272). When attacked by irrational modern forces—the "young Cavaliere" who is, ironically, also "of a very good family"—the Count realizes he is powerless to protest to the police because the assailant could claim to have been molested by him. "What could I say?" the Count asks, "He was an Italian—I am a foreigner" (p. 281).

It is his realization of the end of equitable justice in a society dominated by nationalism that leads to the Count's retirement from the modern world (a kind of suicide, since he goes north to a climate that will kill him). "His belief in the respectable placidity of life having received this rude shock, he thought that now anything might happen" (p. 281). The more extreme instances of nationalistic prejudice which Mann describes did happen as the breakdown of legality burgeoned into the horrors of World War II. Conrad could not, of course, predict the precise form of subsequent events, but it is impossible to resist the suggestion of prescience in one of the concluding lines of the story: "he was going to his grave. He was going to it by the *train de luxe* of the International Sleeping Car Company, *via* Trieste and Vienna" (p. 289).

The five stories from *A Set of Six* which have been considered (the sixth, "The Brute," is of neither political nor literary interest) were written during the years 1905–7, between *Nostromo* and *Under Western Eyes* and concurrently with *The Secret Agent*. It is little wonder, then, that they unfold a series of incisive views of modern political life—its revolutions, its classes, and its historical transitions. It is not easy to summarize this series in a formula, for the prevailing impression the collection gives is not of a doctrine but of a sustained exercise of political imagination—the capacity of the artist to create dramatic embodiments of political tensions. It is this quality that makes *A Set of Six*, for all the modesty of its title and of its author's claims for it, a volume worthy to stand with the three great political novels.

In later years, during and after World War I, Conrad returned to one of his themes, the decline of European aristocracy, which was present in various forms in "Gaspar Ruiz," "Il Conde," and "The Duel." While the war was marking the end of that class's era, its death knell can be heard in the undertones of Conrad's prose. Even in a colonial tale of this period (1913), "The Planter of Malata," the debacle of the European aristocracy is anticipated. The hero judges the woman whom he loves, and who rejects him in favor of illusory ideals and guilts, as the symbol of a dying class. He calls her an aristocrat, and explains:

> Oh! I don't mean that you are like the men and women of the time of armours, castles, and great deeds. Oh, no! They stood on the naked soil, had traditions to be faithful to, had their feet on this earth of passions and death which is not a hothouse. They would have been too plebian for you since they had to lead, to suffer with, to understand the commonest humanity. No, you are merely of the topmost layer, disdainful and superior, the mere pure froth and bubble on the inscrutable depths which some day will toss you out of existence. (*WT*, pp. 76–77)

The tales of this period repeatedly turn back into the nineteenth century to discover how the aristocracy declined from its classical form. The intent of "Prince Roman" (1910), apart from its significant memoir of the author's childhood, is to draw the "character" of an ideal aristocrat. This definition is based on a distinction between two Polish attitudes toward Russian domination. It is a matter of extremists vs. compromisers, of revolutionists vs. evolutionists, of Reds vs. Whites—and Conrad in this tale declares for the former in each case! It has been pointed out earlier how the tension between the two parties was present in Conrad's own family heritage: his father and uncles were leaders of the "Reds" who created the revolt of 1863, while another uncle and his subsequent guardian, Tadeusz Bobrowski, was a moderate in politics, as he was in all his counsels to the restless youth. Thus the skeptical "Positivist" attitudes that were formed in his childhood were complemented by pride in his revolutionary heritage.

Conrad grew up in a milieu in which, after the failure of the 1831 insurrection, the higher aristocracy chose the course of collaboration in order to retain control of internal affairs in Russian Poland. Despite the conciliatory attitude of the new Czar, Alexander II, however, the lower gentry, including Apollo Korzeniowski, challenged the authority of the puppet Polish regime under Count Wielopolski. They disdained the conservative "Whites" as being more concerned for their lands than for their nation, and opposed Polish participation in municipal elections. Non-participation was the aim of Korzeniowski's agitation, for which he was exiled.

Conrad could not, then, have been under any illusions about the unheroic role of the Polish upper aristocracy, so that when he came, late in his career, to write a story of his native tradition, it is framed as a tribute to an exceptional aristocrat. By choosing this historical hero of the Revolution of 1831, he makes an effort to define the notion of genuine aristocracy, which he still cherished. He had defined it, in the Author's Note to *A Personal Record*, as an identification with the interests of all classes in the nation—as a kind of paternalistic nationalism—and it is that character that Prince Roman's *noblesse oblige* takes in the story. Here, in a European setting, is another version of the pattern in which the individualist hero finds it necessary to identify himself with a social community. This is the organicist burden of the aristocratic nationalism which "Prince Roman" promulgates.

As a member of the Polish aristocracy, Prince Roman has been assimilated into the ruling class of Russia and is an officer of the Imperial Guards. When confronted with the burgeoning revolution, he resigns his commission and unhesitatingly joins the Polish army. Roman's father, on the contrary, "speaking from a purely aristocratic point of view, mistrusted the popular origins of the movement, regretted its democratic tendencies, and did not believe in the possibility of success" (*Tales of Hearsay*, p. 40). The White tendency is thus attributed to aristocratic class interest; old Prince John fears the intimate connection of nationalism and republicanism in the nineteenth century. But Roman exploits other aristocratic values, winning his father over by his proud disdain of the Russian Czar: "Those people had never been heard of when our house was already illustrious" (*TH*, p. 41). It is his aristocratic pride of name that leads him to declare his true identity as soon as he is asked it by his Polish superiors, and it is his noble disinterestedness that leads him to make the damaging declaration to a Russian military court: "I joined the national rising from conviction" (p. 52).

Even in his defeat, Roman is an extremist in his devotion to principle, as opposed to his parents, who by bribery and influence secure the leniency of the judges and authorities but whose collusion with the Russians Roman disdains. In his old age, after twenty-five years of punishment, Roman remains the devoted nationalist, in contrast to his daughter and her Polish-Austrian husband, who live in cosmopolitan circles abroad. "They think that I let myself be guided too much by mere sentiment," he says, thereby distinguishing his aristocratic ideals—disinterestedness, identification with the nation, and egoistic pride—from the spirit of calculation which has penetrated the latter-day aristocracy.

Conrad may have known that the historical Prince Roman Sanguszko had changed profoundly in his old age:

> Prince Roman himself, after his experiences in Siberia and in the Caucasus, was simply appalled by the prospect of another Polish attempt against the Russian colossus and did not hesitate to throw the prestige of his great name in the balance in order to stop the young enthusiasts from joining the January Rising. In the beginning of 1863 Roman stayed in Cracow where he was one of the most outspoken and determined foes of the Insurrection.[4]

Conrad apparently chose to represent Roman as the aristocratic revolutionary, rather than as the more familiar temporizer that he was in reality, in order to celebrate the heroic ideal which transcends reality—to affirm revolution, not defeat.

The contrast between the ideal and the real, the exception and the rule, is, indeed, the point on which "Prince Roman" turns. The narrative systematically compares the decadence of the present aristocracy with the virtues of its ancestors:

> The aristocracy we were talking about was the very highest, the great families of Europe, not impoverished, not converted, not liberalized, the most distinctive and specialized class of all classes, for which even ambition itself does not exist among the usual incentives to activity and regulators of conduct.
>
> The undisputed right of leadership having passed away from them, we judged that their great fortunes, their cosmopolitanism brought about by wide alliances, their elevated station, in which there is so little to gain and so much to lose, must make their position difficult in times of political commotion or national upheaval. No longer born to command—which is the very essence of aristocracy—it becomes difficult for them to do aught else but hold aloof from the great movements of popular passion. (P. 30)

[4] Ludwik Krzyżanowski, "Joseph Conrad's 'Prince Roman': Fact and Fiction," in Krzyżanowski (ed.), *Joseph Conrad*, p. 58.

The anecdote recited as an exception to the norm only enforces the conclusion that aristocracy is dead. This sense is rendered dramatically by the
narrator's account of his introduction as a boy to the old Prince Roman:
"what concerned me most was the failure of the fairy-tale glamour. It was
shocking to discover a prince who was deaf, bald, meagre, and so prodigiously
old. It never occurred to me that this imposing and disappointing man had
been young, rich, beautiful . . ." (p. 35).[5]

Some six years passed before Conrad's next effort at historical fiction.
During the war period he returned, in "The Warrior's Soul," to the theme
of the aristocrat who holds to the code in a world that is witnessing the death
of honor. Tomassov departs from the military standard of the Russian army,
both by an excess of leniency—he sheathes his sword when the attack on the
fleeing Napoleonic troops turns into a slaughter—and by a supposed excess
of severity, in killing his prisoner. The principle of his conduct in each case
is the same: the clemency born of a notion of human worth that shuns its
degradation. The Russian narrator, compassionate after his fashion, is concerned to justify the slaughter of the French, but acknowledges the moral
transformation it brings about: "I don't know by what connection of emotions there came into my head the thought that the earth was a pagan planet
and not a fit abode for Christian virtues" (*TH*, p. 20).

Nevertheless, Tomassov hews to these virtues, which are in him mingled
with aristocratic honor. He shoots De Castel (the chivalric connotation of
his name is pungent) not only to redeem a debt for a past favor, not only
to put him out of his misery, but ultimately to relieve a fellow aristocrat
of a life without future, honor, and faith. The narrator suggests the con-

[5] "Prince Roman" was written in the year following Conrad's extended recall
of his Polish childhood in *A Personal Record*, and it is tempting to see him grap-
pling in the story with the same guilts which hover over his autobiographical
work. In Gustav Morf's reading, Roman would represent Conrad's father and
Prince John his uncle, while Roman's offspring would correspond to Conrad in
his position as a renegade from the homeland. Such biographical parallels do
not, however, suggest the political breadth of the story: it is not simply about
Conrad's guilt feelings, nor even about nineteenth-century Polish history, but,
most broadly, it traces the decline of the aristocratic ideals of obligation, freedom,
and selflessness, and their replacement in the latter-day aristocrats by vain attempts
to retrieve lost power. It is this observation that makes Conrad especially cutting
in his depictions of aristocratic *émigrés* in his later historical novels.

trast between their moral community and the uncomprehending world of modern morality:

> Destiny had led that De Castel to the man who could understand him perfectly. But it was poor Tomassov's lot to be the predestined victim. You know what the world's justice and mankind's judgment are like. They fell heavily on him with a sort of inverted hypocrisy. Why! That brute of an adjutant, himself, was the first to set going horrified allusions to the shooting of a prisoner in cold blood. (P. 26)

The relevance of Tomassov's morality, and its issue in social ostracism, to the war being waged while Conrad was writing is implicit in "The Warrior's Soul": traditional morality is dead in modern war, and the aristocratic tradition breathed its last in it. Conrad, at this moment of broad historical vision, chooses to suggest another vision beyond contemporary history. He does not state it directly, merely observing Tomassov in the act of contemplating De Castel's death meditation: "He was stooping over the dead in a tenderly contemplative attitude. And his young, ingenuous face, with lowered eyelids, expressed no grief, no sternness, no horror—but was set in the repose of a profound, as if endless and endlessly silent, meditation."

Toward the end of the war, Conrad made a concerted attempt to come to terms with his lingering ambivalence toward aristocracy and, at the same time, to resolve one of the political ambiguities in his early adventures. Writing of his gun-running days in the Second Carlist War, he had dismissed his own political motivation, and the historical value of that cause, with a phrase: "we were all ardent Royalists of the snow-white Legitimist complexion —Heaven only knows why!" (*The Mirror of the Sea*, p. 157). In *The Arrow of Gold*, Conrad told why. The answer is a devastating portrayal of the aristocratic milieu into which he had been introduced through family friends.

There is a lingering impression among Conrad's critics that the mature author retained the inherited pieties of his youth, that Conrad was a royalist to the end, and that *The Arrow of Gold* is his nostalgic swan song for an aristocracy with which he still identified himself. These illusions will be dispelled by attention to the statements of M. George, Conrad's hero and a fair copy of himself as a youth. When George is enlisted in the Carlist cause in defense of the "Principle of Legitimacy," he remarks:

> It sounded to my positive mind the most fantastic thing in the world, this elimination of personalities from what seemed but the merest political,

dynastic adventure. So it wasn't Doña Rita, it wasn't Blunt, it wasn't
the Pretender with his big infectious laugh, it wasn't all that lot of
politicians, archbishops, and generals, of monks, guerrilleros, and smug-
glers by sea and land, of dubious agents and shady speculators and un-
doubted swindlers, who were pushing their fortunes at the risk of their
precious skins. No. It was the Legitimist Principle asserting itself! Well,
I would accept the view but with one reservation. All the others might
have been merged into the idea, but I, the latest recruit, I would not be
merged in the Legitimist Principle. Mine was an act of independent
assertion. Never before had I felt so intensely aware of my personality.
(*AG*, pp. 88–89)

George's egoism is in the aristocratic tradition itself, to be sure, but he
sharply distinguishes his values from those of the royalists:

most of my acquaintance were legitimists and intensely interested in the
events of the frontier of Spain, for political, religious, or romantic reasons.
But I was not interested. Apparently I was not romantic enough. Or was it
that I was even more romantic than all those good people? The affair
seemed to me commonplace. The man was attending to his business of a
Pretender. (P. 8)

This suggests that a legitimist principle might have been one in which to
"merge" oneself, but is in its corrupt modern form no longer sufficiently
ideal for the genuine aristocrat; it is no longer "romance" but "business."
What brings George into the war, on the other hand, is personality—the
imposing appearance of Don Carlos, the haughty style of Blunt and Mills,
the sexual attraction of Rita. In contrast to George's gratuitous commitment
to persons, the modern aristocracy is seen fighting for mere power, dressed
up as legitimist principle.

Despite these political implications, Conrad disclaims the critical historian's
role and confesses himself a writer of nostalgic memoirs:

It is perhaps the last instance of a Pretender's adventure for a Crown that
History will have to record with the usual grave moral disapproval tinged
by a shamefaced regret for the departing romance. Historians are very
much like other people.

However, History has nothing to do with this tale. Neither is the moral
justification or condemnation of conduct aimed at here. If anything, it is
perhaps a little sympathy that the writer expects for his buried youth, as
he lives it over again at the end of his insignificant course on this earth.
(Pp. 4–5)

Forgetting this facetious view of the historian's role, Conrad goes on to
make discriminations of political and moral worth throughout the novel,

which becomes a typical tale of the young man from the provinces discovering the decadence of the beau monde.

The touchstone of political judgments in *The Arrow of Gold* is the genuineness of claims to noble standing, and it is consistently applied to the Carlist revolution. When George is prompted by his love for Rita to join the gunrunners, her aristocratic stature is the guarantor of the cause. It is significant that the definition of aristocracy implied in the novel, as in stories like "Prince Roman" and "The Warrior's Soul," is predicated on moral value, not on birth. Rita is of peasant stock, but she is genuinely noble—or so the hero wants his audience to believe. When, after the departure of Rita, George takes his orders from the Marquis de Villarel, the cause seems to George to have suffered a diminution in political value, as well as in romantic attractiveness: "I was convinced that this man of forms and ceremonies and fanatical royalism was perfectly heartless. Perhaps he reflected on his motives; but it seemed to me that his conscience could be nothing else but a monstrous thing which very few actions could disturb appreciably" (p. 252).

At a later stage of the war, a new type of administrator joins the Bourbon colors: "The Marquis of Villarel had of course gone long before. The man who was there was another type of Carlist altogether, and his temperament was that of a trader. He was the chief purveyor of the Legitimist armies, an honest broker of stores, and enjoyed a great reputation for cleverness" (p. 259). This bourgeois is made a baron by the tottering Principle of Legitimacy, and by thus confounding the standards of rank it loses its reason for existence. The judgment of the political forces at work in *The Arrow of Gold* is, in this way, to be inferred from their embodiment of standards of personal worth.

In addition to the political judgment of the Carlist movement, the moral weight of its members is also measured on the scale of their true nobility. George's competitor for Rita, the "American, Catholic and gentleman" Blunt, is defined as the villain by his excess of aristocratic manner and by the corresponding absence in him of gentlemanly morals. The boulevardier exterior, the threadbare impeccability, the exquisite taste, the service in American, French, and Spanish wars on the reactionary side, the romantic egoism—these are the marks of his breed. But his calumnies against his victor in the competition for Rita are the measure of his morals.

In contrast, George makes no issue of rank (he associates with bohemians and sailors as readily as with aristocrats) but is naïvely devoted to the aristocratic code of honor. When he enters the concluding duel, his idealism is contrasted with Blunt's coldness:

"Captain Blunt," he said, "the result of this meeting may go against me. In that case you will recognize publicly that you were wrong. For you are wrong and you know it. May I trust your honour?"

In answer to that appeal Captain Blunt, always correct, didn't open his lips but only made a little bow. For the rest he was perfectly ruthless. (Pp. 345–46)

The value of Blunt's breeding is attested to in the duel by his tenacity, skill at arms, and aplomb: after George disables his shooting arm, he calmly changes hands, takes careful aim, and shoots his rival through the breast. Yet it is George's moral idealism, rather than Blunt's manners or training, that is offered as the object of sympathy and the example of nobility.

George enjoys a less disastrous but equally enlightening encounter with aristocratic morals in the form of Mrs. Blunt. This southern (United States) aristocrat is, in fact, in the tradition of the comedy of manners, and George's longest conversation with her is a scene of high humor. Ultimately, moral vulgarity breaks through her mannered mask in a revelatory flash, as in a James novel about Europeanized Americans. After much hemming and hawing of the most refined and subtle sort, Mrs. Blunt reveals herself as the merest mercenary adventuress, who aims to recoup her family's fortunes— lost in the American Civil War—by marrying her son to Rita's money. Her distance from the traditional aristocracy is indicated when she resents George's citation of her son's boast, "I live by my sword":

"What nonsense! A Blunt doesn't hire himself."
"Some princely families," I said, "were founded by men who have done that very thing. The great Condottieri, you know."
It was in an almost tempestuous tone that she made me observe that we were not living in the fifteenth century. (P. 176)

And she warns George to take himself off or face her son, a crack shot. The final word on her sums up her class with delicious irony: "She was an aristocrat to the tips of her fingers; she really didn't care for anybody" (p. 186).

In his last years, Conrad turned further away from the present and reached back into history with an antiquarian's interest in the past-ness of the past. He was, nevertheless, able to portray episodes of Napoleonic history in ways that illuminate European politics in this century. It is easy to see in *The Rover* Conrad's self-dramatization as an old sailor come home to die in his long-abandoned native land, but the plot in which Conrad envelops Peyrol is more than mere autobiography. *The Rover* is a version of a fable which Conrad told and retold throughout his career but which in the war and postwar periods he conceived with increasing clarity, as in *Victory*. It is the story of a man alienated from community, nation, and humanity at large, who finds it necessary *and possible* to re-establish his ties with others in order to fulfill himself—or even in order to be able to die.

This increase in the simplicity of his fable is bound up not only with Conrad's advancing age but with his response to the crisis of civilization. What has been said of *Victory* applies with equal force to *The Rover*: "*Victory* interprets several of the events that foreshadowed the First World War. . . . Heyst's attitude is a clear indication of certain late nineteenth- and early twentieth-century ideas, which strongly imply that before 1914 man could make a pretense of detachment, but that, eventually, everyone must become involved in life."[6] The evocation of the past is due not entirely to nostalgia but is a response to the contemporary scene, and its aim is to discover the way from crisis to peace, the reintegration of self and society, and the resolution of conflicting forces in modern politics.

The Rover effects the resolution of many of the tensions in Conrad's work and thought: egoism and community, cosmopolitanism and nationalism, revolution and stability. It is the plan of the novel to offer us the example of a seaman who achieves the highest triumph of the work ethic in a political cause; to depict a rootless and proscribed adventurer who returns home to find his true identity in patriotism—indeed, in identification with the nation itself; and to lead the hero to die in the service of the Revolution, although bitterly condemning its anarchy. Finally, it is a personal portrait of an old man, past the love of life, who imparts fresh vitality to the world he is leaving by bringing the young together through the sacrifice of his life. It is the highest virtue of the novel that it accomplishes these resolutions (which if easily effected would be sentimental) by sustaining the full weight of the alternatives, weaving them together in a complex dialectic.

Peyrol's response to life at the start of the novel is that of a man anxious to retire. "J'en ai vu bien d'autres" (a phrase similar to the expressions of nostalgia and indifference which Jörgenson utters in *The Rescue*, which was completed in the same period)—this is the formula by which he assimilates all new experience to his romantic past, defeating the present by memory.

---

[6] Frederick Karl, *A Reader's Guide to Joseph Conrad* (New York, 1960), p. 247.

The attitude extends into his politics as well and defines his conception of history:

> By the time he had heard of a Revolution in France and of certain Immortal
> Principles causing the death of many people, from the mouths of seamen
> and travellers and year-old gazettes coming out of Europe, he was ready
> to appreciate contemporary history in his own particular way. Mutiny
> and throwing officers overboard. He had seen that twice and he was on a
> different side each time. As to this upset, he took no side. . . . What he
> had gone through . . . with all the gradations of varied experience of
> men and passions between, had put a drop of universal scorn, a wonderful
> sedative, into the strange mixture which might have been called the soul
> of the returned Peyrol. (*Rover*, p. 25)

The keenness of Conrad's irony is admirable, for it cuts himself as well:
Peyrol's translation of the Revolution into his own terms, mutiny, is a
glaring reduction of the immensity of the historical fact within a limited
perspective. His "universal scorn" is acutely described as a "wonderful
sedative," but his passive neutrality becomes impossible as the novel proceeds.

The central ambiguity of the Revolution is personified in *The Rover* by the
mad nihilist Scevola and the idealistic patriot Lieutenant Réal. They are
competitors not only for the hand of the heroine, Arlette, but for the reader's
estimation of the Revolution. After the novel was published, Edward Garnett
criticized Scevola on the same grounds as he had other Conrad anarchists:
if he were to be taken as a typical radical the novel would merely be partisan
caricature. Conrad replied to this as he had to Garnett's criticism of the
anarchists in *The Secret Agent*:

> now you have uttered the words he does look to me like a bit of a "scare-
> crow of the Revolution." Yet it was not my intention. . . . To me, S[cevola]
> is not revolutionary, he is, to be frank about it, a pathological case more
> than anything else. . . . As a matter of fact if there is a child of the Revolu-
> tion there at all, it is Real, with his austere and pedantic turn of mind and
> conscience.[7]

By making the true revolutionary the romantic hero of the novel, Conrad
not only succeeded in conveying the idealism and rationalism of the Revolution but made it more plausible that Peyrol should lay down his life for him.

We are now in a position to appreciate the prevalence of bloody descriptions of the Revolution in a novel which breathes its spirit. The harping on the

---

[7] Garnett Letters, pp. 331–32, letter of December 4, 1923.

reign of terror which followed the evacuation of the British from Toulon is in the tradition of Burke, but its tone is not that of Burke's shocked indignation at class war. Rather, the impression is more of Carlyle's brooding Nemesis, rising to do justice but leaving a stain of blood that remains impressed on the conversation, relationships, and dreams of the survivors—Republicans and Royalists alike.

Both Réal and Arlette are children of the New Regime, both have lost their *ci-devant* parents in the Terror, and both have become involved in the Revolution—Réal by rational choice, Arlette by momentary frenzy. They need a substitute for the dead older generation, a substitute father, who wil. confirm them in life, remove the stain of guilt, make possible their lovel Peyrol serves this function, both on the political and on the psychological level. The need is articulated in Arlette's dream:

> She had seen Réal set upon by a mob of men and women, all dripping with blood, in a livid cold light, in front of a stretch of mere shells of houses with cracked walls and broken windows, and going down in the midst of a forest of raised arms brandishing sabres, clubs, knives, axes. There was also a man flourishing a red rag on a stick, while another was beating a drum which boomed above the sickening sound of broken glass falling like rain on the pavement. And away round the corner of an empty street came Peyrol whom she recognized by his white head, walking without haste, swinging his cudgel regularly. The terrible thing was that Peyrol looked straight at her, not noticing anything, composed, without a frown or a smile, unseeing and deaf, while she waved her arms and shrieked desperately to him for help. She woke up with the piercing sound of his name in her ears. . . . the name that had sprung to her lips on waking was the name of Peyrol. (Pp. 245–46)

But Peyrol must first be brought out of his unseeing isolation into the life of the community.

Peyrol does not assume his indifferent attitude because he resists the Revolution but rather because he fulfills it: he stands for its principles in their ideal form, before they were incarnated in history. Early in the tale, Peyrol defends his piratical past to a French naval officer (to whom he delivers an English prize ship) by boasting, "we practised republican principles long before a republic was thought of; for the Brothers of the Coast were all equal and elected their own chiefs" (p. 5). Later these democratic principles are elaborated by Peyrol in terms of the revolutionary triad: "Liberty—to hold your own in the world if you could. Equality—yes! But no body of men ever accomplished anything without a chief. . . . He regarded fraternity somewhat differently. . . . In his view the claim of the Brotherhood was a claim for help against the outside world" (p. 132). In these passages Peyrol humanizes the abstractions of the Revolution by way of reducing them to his personal experience.

The most powerful element in Conrad's characterization of Peyrol is his stature as symbol—a symbol that fulfills the requirement that it participate in the reality it represents. Not only does Peyrol stand for France and for the spirit of patriotism, he becomes integrated with the history of the nation by the action of the plot and, because of the ironies of his career, he is shown, almost by definition, to be the son of the nation. Because he does not remember his mother or his exact birthplace, "here, on this Southern shore that had called to him irresistibly as he had approached the Straits of Gibraltar on what he had felt to be his last voyage, any woman, lean and old enough, might have been his mother; he might have been any Frenchman of them all, even one of those he pitied, even one of those he despised" (p. 98). Thus political animosities are transcended by the unity of Peyrol with the French people! His final action and his death are appropriately heroic and anonymous. For the British victors, too, he symbolizes the heroism of the French. They ritualize this identification when they raise the French flag on his captured ship as a salute, before they sink her with his body.

It is not quite true to say, as Morf does, that "in the novel the problem [of nationality] is easily and optimistically solved by the assumption that *true patriotism must needs be above political divisions*."[8] The final outcome of Conrad's lifelong nationalist sentiments—consistent with his view of the organic community—is to identify a political movement, the French Revolution, with the spirit of the people, the general will. The affirmation of revolutionary politics which *The Rover* develops in its drama, rather than in its explicit statements, suggests that Conrad had evolved a politics out of his nationalist sentiments and might have rephrased the Morf dictum thus: true nationalism must express itself in political choice—in Peyrol's case, the choice of dying for the Revolution.

In *Suspense*, Conrad's unfinished final novel, his last look at aristocracy, nationalism, and revolution is rendered subtly enough to make evaluation difficult in the absence of its conclusion. Some points are soon established.

[8] Morf, *Polish Heritage*, p. 182.

The father of the hero, Sir Charles Latham, is summarily characterized in terms of these political forces:

> In politics he was a partisan of Mr. Pitt rather than a downright Tory. He loved his country, believed in its greatness, in its superior virtue, in its irresistible power. Nothing could shake his fidelity to national prejudices of every sort. He had no great liking for grandees and mere aristocrats, despised the fashionable world, and would have nothing whatever to do with any kind of "upstart." (P. 20)

The portrait is not that of an arch-Royalist of the Old Regime but rather that of a perfect English squire, whose patriotism (like Prince Roman's) is not mitigated by class interest. He is an aristocrat of the humbler breed, the gentry, defending an ideal of honor against the new political forces, both aristocratic and bourgeois.

Cosmo Latham is his father's son, though not so much the mirror of his mind as the inheritor of its predicament. To maintain the gentleman's code is to be uncomfortably vulnerable in a changing world of "upstarts" and class war, at home and abroad. It is the pressure to redefine his aristocratic character that drives Cosmo on his grand tour. His quest for political experience is tempered in him both by his father's patriotism, which temporarily overrides his attraction to the Napoleonic revolutionaries whom he quickly encounters, and by his father's snobbery, which leads him to disdain the men without honor who have come to power in the Restoration. Such is Cosmo's view of the Council of Vienna: " 'I don't much care for the work which is going on there and perhaps still less for the men who are putting their hands to it.' This time Sir Charles's slow nod expressed complete agreement" (*Suspense*, p. 40).

In *Suspense*, Conrad extends his satire of the self-deluding *émigrés* to the French legitimists after their plots and dreams had actually come to pass. Their social position restored, they nevertheless express a new futility: "Most of us have exhausted almost all emotions. Life has grown suddenly very dull. We gossip a little about each other; we wait for the end of the Vienna Council and discuss the latest rumour that floats about. Yes. The play is over, the stage seems empty" (p. 90). Not only is this class ill at ease in the new world that the Revolution and Napoleon have made, but it is unable to adapt itself so as to wield its still considerable power effectively.

Power is the métier of the new aristocracy—those who have recently emerged from the military ranks, gained titles in exchange for money and support, and are now at the center of the Congress and its manufactured kingdoms. Of this type the villain of the novel, Count Helion de Montevesso, is the supreme example, but—what is more revealing of Conrad's sense of history—so is Napoleon himself. The affinity between the two is given in Adèle's account of her audience with the Emperor, in which he praises Count Helion, her husband, as an employer of labor—i.e., as a progressive capitalist in the process of taking up the reins of the nineteenth century.

It is Cosmo's gift to perceive clearly not only that the old order of things is a "rouged and powdered corpse putting on a swagger of life and revenge," but also that the new is on the ascendant: "We in England have a class of men who return from India enriched [as did Count Helion]. They are called nabobs. Some of them have most objectionable habits. Unluckily their mere wealth . . ." (p. 124). He breaks off, but the implication for the future of England is drawn by Helion himself: "There is nothing to compare with wealth. . . . When I was in England I had the privilege to know many people of position. They were very kind to me. They didn't seem to think lightly of wealth" (pp. 124–25).

The major action of *Suspense* is Cosmo's effort to locate himself in the post-Napoleonic world without attaching himself to either the old or the new debased versions of aristocracy. To do this he must discover a political force that carries on the ideal of honor. This moral requirement makes it necessary that his discovery be a personal one: he must discover genuine aristocrats, of whatever class, and follow them in political action, for whatever party. It is on these highly personal grounds that Cosmo becomes involved in the revolutionary underground, as it is represented for him by Attilio. Attilio's nobility is not presented merely as a function of his seamanship and fidelity; it extends to his politics as well. He

> had become familiar with the idea of revolt looked upon as an assertion
> of manly dignity and the spiritual aim of life. . . . he believed in the ab-
> solute equality of all men. He respected all religions but despised the
> priests who preached submission and perceived nothing extravagant in the
> formation of an Italian empire . . . since there was a great man—a great
> Emperor—to put at its head, very close at hand. (Pp. 256–57)

It is seemingly inevitable that Cosmo's course should be governed by the attractive power of Napoleon on Elba. In leading Cosmo to Napoleon, Conrad is not acceding to the latter's mystique as a liberator, since he seems skeptical of Attilio's naïve notion that the Emperor would honestly support any nationalism other than French. But Conrad does not stint the sugges-tion that Attilio's nationalism is closely identified with humanitarian radicalism, a tradition that descends from the principles of the French Revolution to the Italian independence movement. Cosmo's clandestine voyage toward Elba, with which the fragment of *Suspense* concludes, seems to prefigure a meeting with Napoleon that would result either in his being caught up in the Emperor's campaign of the Hundred Days or in disillusionment with him and in an allegiance to the Italian cause. In either case, any political career for this moral aristocrat seems to lie in the direction of revolutionary politics. As in "Prince Roman" and *The Rover*, Conrad leads his last hero to realize his moral ideals and his own identity by joining a revolution.

With this probable resolution of *Suspense*, Conrad's succession of forays into European history, past and present, concludes on the same note of ambiguity with which it began. He seems ready throughout his career to make caustic denunciations, if no longer of the lower class, at least of all revolutions but nationalist ones. Yet his fiction develops a broad sympathy with men caught in the toils of radical movements and shows an inveterate hostility toward the old ruling class, the aristocracy, and toward the new, the bourgeoisie. It is a fruitful ambiguity, however, as it allows his tales to trace their heroes' quests and vacillations among opposed political forces, none of which is given full credence and all of which are bound into a rich political milieu. Conrad acquired this capacity to conceive a complex political nexus fairly early in his career, and it is this that gives scope and power to his major political novels.

Chapter VI

NOSTROMO: CLASS STRUGGLE AS TRAGEDY

Theodore Roosevelt. Courtesy of Wide World Photos

Troops appear to be gaining the initiative in their long struggle against Colombian outlaw bands. . . . *The government has announced a social-economic rehabilitation plan for the area hardest hit by violence—in southwestern Colombia where the departments (States) of Tolima, Caldas, and Valle join [in the hinterland of Buenaventura].* . . . *The violence has its roots in a civil war between liberals and conservatives that killed 200,000 persons before a truce was declared between the two political parties in 1958.* . . . *Broadly speaking, the violence can be divided into two parts: political and social. Colombia's Attorney General has said the political groups are infiltrated by Communists. The violence resulting from social causes is the most deep-rooted.*

—The Christian Science Monitor
February 12, 1963

The narrative achievements of *Nostromo* have been amply praised—its complex characterizations, its rich texture of social life, its tragic view of man in the modern world—but not yet for the political maturity from which they proceed. The novel marks the fulfillment of Conrad's political imagination: it represents the history of a society as a living organism. Indeed, the complex narrative structure of the novel reflects this sense of history's unfolding processes. Men of varied classes and nationalities are shown caught up in a situation that their acts transform into history, that gives shape to their lives, and—what is rarer still in fiction—that is seen to continue beyond them. This personally created history gives meaning to individual destinies: it acts as a tragic nexus which, in the absence of organic community, is the only order that transcends the limits of personal life. "Where freedom is absent," Irving Howe has observed, "politics is fate." So, in a Latin American nation in which the forces of imperialism and capitalism, nationalism and socialism are brought into play, politics impinges on every point of individual and social life. But if politics is fate, history is freedom, and through Conrad's organic unfolding of Costaguana's past and future, the drama that is played out in *Nostromo* is given its meaning, as the past and future give meaning to the present.

Conrad himself conceived of the writing of *Nostromo* as an act of historical imagination. He describes it in *A Personal Record*, in a tragicomic anecdote about the intrusion of a neighbor while he was struggling with the novel:

> I had, like the prophet of old, "wrestled with the Lord" for my creation, for the headlands of the coast, for the darkness of the Placid Gulf, the light on the snows, the clouds on the sky, and for the breath of life that had to be blown into the shapes of men and women, of Latin and Saxon, of Jew and Gentile. . . .
> "How do you do?"
> . . . The whole world of Costaguana (the country, you may remember, of my seaboard tale), men, women, headlands, houses, mountains, town, *campo* (there was not a single brick, stone, or grain of sand of its soil I had not placed in position with my own hands); all the history, geography, politics, finance; the wealth of Charles Gould's silver-mine, and the splendour of the magnificent Capataz de Cargadores . . . all that had come crashing down about my ears. I felt I could never pick up the pieces—and in that very moment I was saying, "Won't you sit down?" (Pp. 98–100)

The language here subtly modifies the traditional metaphor of the artist as a creator in the image of God, and makes him specifically the creator of a *historical* world. The artist's vocation becomes not merely to be faithful to the forms of things but to give an account of them in their total unity. It is this quality of organic fullness that makes *Nostromo* a major novel, in the

161

tradition of those nineteenth-century fictions that endow themselves with the status of histories—from the local scale of *Middlemarch* to the international one of *War and Peace*.

What makes such novels histories (as distinguished from historical novels, which usually select authentic details as background to a plot) is their density, their approach in complexity to the actual condition of historical life. They dramatize the "history, geography, politics, finance" which are off-stage presences in lesser works. As Conrad himself put it in his Author's Note: "the few historical allusions are never dragged in for the sake of parading my unique erudition, but . . . each of them is closely related to actuality; either throwing a light on the nature of current events or affecting directly the fortunes of the people of whom I speak" (pp. xx–xxi).

Despite its advances over his earlier work, it is important to see *Nostromo* as an integral part of Conrad's achievement and to estimate its political meaning in the context of his developing social attitudes. The limits of such an undertaking must be borne in mind: the characters in the novel are unique beings and the situation depicted is a fictional creation, not a historical fact. We may nevertheless proceed with some confidence because of the consistency not only of Conrad's opinions of certain forces like imperialism, but also of his imaginative techniques for representing certain types of political actors: conquerors and colonists, aristocrats both real and ideal, alienated and integrated men. In addition, a new character form emerges in the novel and goes on to become the predominant heroic type in his political fiction.

Nostromo and Martin Decoud are the first in a series of young men in Conrad who bear a family resemblance to their ancestors in the Waverley novels. Such figures as the naïve Waverley and Morton, of *Old Mortality*, have been defined in a recent study of Scott:

> The hero can best be described by the words of Nigel Olifaunt—"a thing never acting but perpetually acted upon." But he is nevertheless the protagonist. He stands at the center of the struggle. He may not move, but his chances, his fortunes, are at stake. He is a victim, at the mercy of good and bad forces alike. He never aspires to property, nor actively courts the heroine. But he does not remain a victim, and he receives the heroine and property at the end.[1]

[1] Alexander Welsh, *The Hero of the Waverley Novels* (New Haven and London, 1963), p. 41.

This is not the place to examine the full relationship of Conrad to Scott and the Scott tradition of historical fiction, but we can isolate a few of the factors which account for the striking similarities between their characteristic heroes. We have seen the advantages Conrad gained, as Hueffer described them, from the peculiar position of John Kemp as a naïve outsider in a colonial society: from his perspective, and measured against his normality, *colons*, rebels, and English are shown to deviate from moral and political ideals. Kemp is squarely in the Scott tradition, and *Romance* is inspired by the same adventurousness, shifting background, and swashbuckling action as the most popular Waverleys.

Yet between *Romance* and *Nostromo* there is a difference that centers in Conrad's new conception of the hero. The point may best be made by looking at the Waverley hero again:

> The hero is not precisely Everyman, but every gentleman—not in some supercilious social sense, but in the profound conviction that society is a compact of independent owners of property. He is a passive hero because, in the words of Edmund Burke, a member of civil society surrenders the right "to judge for himself, and to assert his own cause. He abdicates all right to be his own governor. He inclusively, in a great measure, abandons the right of self-defense, the first law of Nature."[2]

In Scott, then, the hero emerges as the embodiment and protagonist of society itself. But in Conrad, the Waverley hero is made to represent the unpropertied classes which are exploited by and revolt against the social order, and he often is an intellectual, claiming the right to judge for himself. He remains, however, a waverer; his vigorous activity is still a shifting response to forces impinging upon him from without. Yet his career affirms not the stable order of civil society but its need to become an organic community that will no longer require the destruction of its most heroic members.

Nostromo has often been assumed to be a pathetic failure, rather than a tragic hero, because the critics have not identified him with the social movements in which he becomes engaged. By the same token, the final chapters of the novel, which depict Nostromo's melodramatic love and death, have been taken to be irrelevant because of a failure to see them within the symbolic pattern of the entire novel. In this pattern, Nostromo's career represents the history of an entire class, the proletariat—its enlistment and

---

[2] *Ibid.*, p. 57.

exploitation in the industrialization of the country, its entry into the separatist revolution (fighting for class interests not directly its own), its growth of self-consciousness and discovery of an independent political role, its temptation by the materialistic drives of capitalism, and its purgation by traditional idealists in its own camp.

The pattern is a tragic one, as we shall see, because it is founded on contradictions within the hero and his class, rather than on circumstance. As in classical tragedy, the hero is bounded by forces larger than himself, yet what happens to him is the expression of his own nature. Like classical drama, too, the novel connects the individual hero with a social group—which he represents not only symbolically but dramatically—in historical action. Conrad's special version of tragedy is that this very social rootedness of the individualist hero contains the contradictions which destroy him. The career and development of Nostromo follow a dialectic as incisive and ironic as one of the character studies of Hegel's *Phenomenology of Mind*.

Nostromo is to be understood as the symbol of a class. At the same time, and without avoiding the contradiction, he is an individual, a vigorous egoist, whose drives to maintain his gilded reputation and at the same time to become integrated in the making of a community cause him to oscillate between vigorous social action and almost total estrangement. Totally lacking in political sensibility, Nostromo joins the Waverley heroes in running the full gamut of political commitment. The climax of his career, in which he benefits society and establishes his highest honor, only leads to his deepest isolation.

Another form of this tragic pattern is presented by Decoud, whose intellectual aloofness from his comic-opera nation and simultaneous awareness of its precise historical needs lead to an oscillation similar to Nostromo's—and to eventual self-destruction. In political terms, however, Decoud's plan, the separation of the province of Sulaco from the state-of-nature anarchy of Costaguana, is a design for social integration, an attempt to render the province, as he puts it, "habitable"—that is, to make it a city of men, a civilization. But separatism brings with it the prospect of further revolutionary ferment and eventful fragmentation through class struggle, as well as the possibility of reintegration in new political forms.

Nostromo, prodigal of favors, has seen another of its characters considered as its hero. But Charles Gould is a hero in the Lingard (or Kurtz) tradition, a composite of the colonist and the conqueror—the former by virtue of his native birth and dedication to his property as a sacred trust, the latter by his placing of foreign material interests before those of the country. The mine, revived in an effort to vindicate his abused father, becomes an end in itself, leading to the estrangement of his excellent wife. The mining operation is repeatedly compared to the original slave mines of the Spanish conquerors (much as the Belgian conquest of the Congo is compared to the Roman conquest of Britain in "Heart of Darkness"). Gould's American backer, Holroyd, is portrayed in familiar terms as the imperialist man dominated by money hunger, with an admixture of the white-man's-burden missionary zeal characteristic of the period. These associations sharply limit Gould's role as hero, and make him instead Conrad's deepest probing of the captain of industry's soul.

The problem of interpreting *Nostromo* is often complicated by the interpreter's own sense of history, not to speak of his political sympathies. The most rewarding commentator on the novel, Albert Guerard, confesses as much when he writes, "the novel's own view of history is sceptical and disillusioned, which for us today must mean true."[3] Guerard goes on to describe the shortcomings of the society which emerges from the victory of "material interests" and identifies them with the present crisis in Latin America and other underdeveloped areas: "In my interpretation [the grim predictions by Monygham and Mrs. Gould] look forward to a period when—as in Guatemala yesterday, as in the Middle East today—the conflicts induced by capitalist exploitation outweigh the benefits accrued."[4]

Guerard is arguing against the view of Robert Penn Warren that, for all its human losses, the new state of affairs in the Occidental Republic (i.e., Sulaco, after separation from Costaguana) is preferable to the chaotic and unjust old order, with its succession of bandit governments and bloody coups. Warren finds his text in the novel's epigraph, "So foul a sky clears not without a storm"—presumably connecting the storm with the separatist revolution depicted in the novel.[5] It is one of the minor ironies of literary history that Warren, like other New Critics, has been critical of the values of modern industrial society, yet when a judgment of society is to be made he bases it on typically capitalist norms: political stability, the security of life and property, expanding production and trade. There is nothing to quarrel

---

[3] *Conrad the Novelist* (Cambridge, Mass., 1958), p. 177.
[4] *Ibid.*, p. 198.
[5] Robert Penn Warren, Introduction to *Nostromo* (New York, 1951), pp. xxix ff.

with in such values, but they are not the only results of the victory of "material interests."

A third party to the dispute on Conrad's judgment of Costaguana's future is Irving Howe, who attempts to reconcile both of the opposed views with the Marxist theory of the successive stages of social change. The bourgeois separatist revolution is a necessary one, but it breeds new, capitalist evils in its turn, which generate a proletarian revolution, the final stage of progress. Not bound by the Marxist theory, Howe interprets this prospect as an undesirable one: "Both critics seem to me right: the civil war brings capitalism and capitalism will bring civil war, progress *has* come out of chaos but it is the kind of progress that is likely to end in chaos.[6]

If there were no indication of Conrad's views on the future of Latin America, it would be impossible to evaluate the condition of society at the end of *Nostromo*. But in "Autocracy and War," written in the year after the novel was published, Conrad indicates fairly clearly how he envisioned the outcome of the dominance of "material interests" (as capitalis.n is referred to in *Nostromo*):

> A swift disenchantment overtook the incredible infatuation which could put its trust in the peaceful nature of industrial and commercial competition. . . . democracy, which has elected to pin its faith to the supremacy of material interests, will have to fight their battles to the bitter end, on a mere pittance. . . . The true peace of the world . . . will be built on less perishable foundations than those of material interests. (*NLL*, pp. 106–7)

Conrad does not stop with this prediction of capitalism's issue in imperialist war. There are narrative situations in *Nostromo* which support the view that he looked forward to the proletarian stage of the Latin American revolution not only with resignation but with a certain warmth toward the rising populace. A generally neglected but, to my mind, climactic and spectacular chapter of *Nostromo* (the third of Part Three) brings Gould together with an emissary of Hernandez, the leader of the insurgent peasantry. The peasants have yet to throw their weight into the battle between the capitalist mine owner, who is supported by the aristocratic Blanco party, and the Caesarist dictator Montero, who is supported by the *Lazarones*, or *Lumpenproletariat* of the city slums. As they were to do in the then-imminent Mexican Revolu-

---

[6] *Politics and the Novel*, p. 106. Howe cites Trotsky's theory of the permanent revolution, in which the proletariat takes over the function of the inept bourgeoisie in bringing an undeveloped country out of feudal stagnation, but this does not quite fit Costaguana, which will have a two-stage revolution.

tion, the peasantry (under leaders like Zapata, whom Hernandez resembles) hold the balance of power but because of their traditional estrangement from the urban proletariat are inclined to join the aristocratic-capitalist forces.

The peasants recognize their own power, manifesting it even in the humility of their emissary's proposal for a *rapprochement* with Gould:

> "Has not the master of the mine any message to send to Hernandez, the master of the Campo?"
>
> . . . .
>
> "You are a just man," urged the emissary of Hernandez. "Look at those people [the aristocrats] who made my compadre a general and have turned us all into soldiers. Look at those oligarchs fleeing for life, with only the clothes on their backs. . . . We need ask no man for anything; but soldiers must have their pay to live honestly when the wars are over. It is believed that your soul is so just that a prayer from you would cure the sickness of every beast, like the orison of the upright judge. Let me have some words from your lips that would act like a charm upon the doubts of our *partida*, where all are men."
>
> . . . Charles Gould, with only a short hesitation, pronounced the required pledge. He was like a man who had ventured on a precipitous path with no room to turn, where the only chance of safety is to press forward. (Pp. 360–61)

The passage prefigures the future power of Hernandez as Minister of War of the new republic and the proletarization of his peasant band as workers in the mine. It is also revealing because it expresses Gould's diminishing control of the course of the revolution, in which he must continue to participate even though it is inimical to his interests. The metaphor of the "precipitous path" is a perfect figure for the absoluteness of the historical process. Though Gould's moral imagination is outraged by an alliance with what he considers another of the anarchic and criminal forces in the country (it is clear that Conrad does not depict the peasant band in the same light), he must sacrifice principle to maintain his position. Indeed, he must become a party to the future proletarian revolution in the very process of securing the capitalist-backed separatist revolution.

If the internal and external evidence in Conrad's own words were not sufficient to indicate his view of Latin American history, the historical sources on which he drew would do so. It has recently been shown that he used South American travelogues by Masterman and Eastwick, and it be-

comes possible to deduce his own position by seeing his distance from them.
Masterman exhibits a typical attitude: "The history of South America, like
that of Mexico, has hitherto been written in blood and tears, and I fear
will continue to be so written until Anglo-Saxons or Teutons shall there
outnumber the Indo-Spanish race."[7] Conrad is equally far removed from the
opinions of Eastwick, who subtitled his account of life in a republic "How
To Make the Scum Rise to the Top," found the Creoles lazy and lacking the
Yankee's entrepreneurial spirit, and proposed imperialist annexation if a
country failed to pay its foreign debts.[8]

Conrad did, however, use many names and incidents from the history of
Venezuela and Paraguay cited in these accounts. (It was in Venezuela that
he had his own brief experience of South America.) But his creation of
Costaguana's past tallies not as closely with the history of these nations as
with that of Colombia.[9] The precise background of *Nostromo* needs to be

[7] George Frederick Masterman, *Seven Eventful Years in Paraguay: A Narrative
of Personal Experience amongst the Paraguayans* (orig. pub., 1869; London, 1870),
p. iv. Another recently discovered source is Ramon Paez, *Wild Scenes in South
America: Or, Life in the Llanos of Venezuela*, discussed in C. T. Watts, "A Minor
Source for *Nostromo*," *Review of English Studies*, XVI (1965), 182–84.

[8] E. B. Eastwick, *Venezuela: Or, Sketches of Life in a South American Republic* (2d
ed.; London, 1868); cf. Baines's belief in Conrad's affinity to Eastwick, in *Joseph
Conrad*, p. 296.

[9] Jerry Allen has provided excellent materials for studying Conrad's treatment
of historical data, although she does not pursue this study herself (*The Sea Years*,
p. 22 ff.). Colombia was the only South American nation in revolt when Conrad visited its sister republic of Venezuela, and there are good grounds for believing that he was engaged in smuggling arms to the Conservative revolutionaries,
which arms were being provided by the same ultras for whom he had engaged in
gun-running in the Second Carlist War. The evidence for identifying Costaguana
and Columbia geographically has been assembled in E. M. W. Tillyard, *The Epic
Strain in the English Novel* (London, 1958), pp. 199–203, although Tillyard is
moved by one inconsistency to reject the identification.

Despite the structural similarity of Colombia and Costaguana in what follows,
it is well to remember the differences. The immediate cause of the Colombian
Conservatives' revolt was the secular education program of the Liberals, but in
Nostromo the issues are primarily economic—control of the mine. While the
aristocratic Blanco party of the novel includes dedicated Church supremacists
(e.g., Father Corbelàn, who wishes the return of confiscated Church property),
its main impulse is the progressive one traditionally animating liberal parties: it
is the Blancos who invite foreign capital under the Ribiera regime, and who try
to create the rule of law under which it can flourish. Despite their forward-looking
tendencies, the Blancos are treated as moribund anachronisms, incapable of
controlling the industrial and popular forces at work in the land.

Although Conrad took this subtly critical position on the aristocratic party, determined not merely for historical accuracy but for literary interpretation, for in the history of Colombia are to be found some of the central concerns of the novel, concerns which might otherwise remain baffling.

Like Costaguana, Colombia emerged from its war of independence under Bolivar as an unmanageable confederation which included the provinces that were soon to become Venezuela and Ecuador. After the latter had broken away, the centrifugal tendencies continued (in both the historical and fictional countries) because of the virtual isolation of the provinces by the Cordillera—the mountain range in both Costaguana and Colombia. Colombia's history throughout the nineteenth and much of the twentieth century is one of extended civil war between Liberals and Conservatives, divided largely on the issue of federal or centralized government. It is a history of unstable constitutionalism with interludes of dictatorial sclerosis—much like the history of Costaguana, with its regime of terror under Guzman Bento and its subsequent reversion to a succession of weak or criminal governments.

The main political issue in both the fictional and the historical realm is the same: the centralist party in Colombia, like the Unionists under Guzman Bento, was opposed to the federalist party—which in Costaguana is made up of the aristocratic Blancos. Federalism of this kind is a separatist tendency that expresses the desire of the aristocrats to be free of the exactions of the central government, which they can rarely control. Defeated by Guzman Bento, the Blancos are satisfied to remain subservient to the political rule of the capital while economic masters in their own province, until the intervention of an outside force raises again the issue of provincial separation.

Such an outside force existed in both Colombia and Costaguana, and even the form of its intervention is somewhat similar. In the former, it was the European and United States' interest in building a mid-hemisphere canal which, with the encouragement and the active support of the nationalists by the United States government, led to the separation of the Province of Panama from Colombia. The creation of an independent Panama was deemed necessary in order to have a more tractable lessor of the canal route than Colombia,

---

having outgrown his youthful ultramontanism, he retained his original contempt of the *Lumpenproletariat* and of any party which appeals to it; in *Nostromo* the latter is described as Liberal, but it is not clear whether this is an inaccurate imputation by the rival Blancos. Conrad's main animus is against the militarist *caudillo* which harnesses this anarchic force (the same relationships are observable in most fascist revolutions in South America, as well as in Europe). The old socialist and nationalist revolutionary Giorgio Viola, who represents the real proletariat of the port and the mine, has nothing but contempt for the demagogic orators and their mobs.

and to get a better bargain on the rental fees. In the fictional country, the outside force is the Gould concession, backed by European and American capital and the naval presence of the United States, which also seeks a better deal by manufacturing a new state. Here, too, the result is the independence of a province which is tractable and will, it is hoped, be stable in its dealings with foreign enterprises. The connection between the historical and the fictional events lies not only in their parallelism; the United States intervention in Panama culminated in 1904, during the writing of the novel, and must be considered an active influence upon its creation.

Despite the popularity of Anglo-Saxon racist political theories during this period, which backed the United States as the natural ally of England, Conrad was hostile to the growth of United States power and its deployment in Panama. Earlier, during the Spanish-American War, he had professed support of Spain because of his sympathy with the Latin race and fear for its future (LL, I, 236, May 1, 1898). Subsequent references to "Yankee Conquistadores in Panama" (LL, I, 325–26, December 26, 1903) equate American expansion with that of Belgium in the Congo. In the same letter, Conrad tells of an invitation to visit Colombia from that country's ambassador in Spain and England, S. Pérez Triana; he may have heard the Colombian case against the United States from him, as well as receiving praise from the son of the former Liberal (!) President for his account of the Colombian civil war.

As for Theodore Roosevelt, Conrad vented on him the full measure of his scorn (dragging him into a review of a travel book):

> That peripatetic guide, philosopher and friend of all nations, Mr. Roosevelt, would promptly excommunicate [the author] with a big stick. The truth is that the ex-autocrat of all the States does not like rebels against the sullen order of our universe. Make the best of it or perish—he cries. (NLL, p. 62)

Conrad's exposure, in Nostromo, of Roosevelt's moralistic and providential rationalizations of imperialism takes the form of a satire of the American financier Holroyd's missionary Christianity.[10] Given Conrad's political

[10] In the early history of attempts to build a Panama Canal, there is a remarkably similar figure, the "mystical and imaginative New York capitalist" Frederick M. Kelley, who declared, "Seven years ago my thoughts were directed to this field of honorable enterprise and investigation by HIM who directs the minds of men to what does good or confers distinction; and I have labored ever since in an earnest and reverent spirit, to accomplish what seemed to be quite in accordance with the arrangement of providence" (quoted in J. Fred Rippy, The Capitalists and Colombia [New York, 1931], p. 46).

judgment of the United States, Holroyd's prophecy of its dominance not only over Latin America but over all the world—and not only economically but culturally—has the sound of a trump of doom (p. 77).

The history of Costaguana is to be judged in the light of Conrad's consistent attitudes toward imperialism. In his terms, the ascendancy of foreign "material interests" is a form of conquest. The separatist revolution, which is supported by these interests, must be read as a mixed blessing. It marks the triumph of imperialism but, as it is formulated by its theoretician, Decoud, it is also the beginning of a nationalist revolution that will intervene and liberate the other portion of Costaguana. Further, as we have seen, it will inevitably turn against the foreign elements which fostered it. Decoud emerges as the prophet of the nationalist movements of our time, in his understanding of imperialism:

> "Now the whole land is like a treasure-house, and all these people are breaking into it, whilst we are cutting each other's throats. The only thing that keeps them out is mutual jealousy. But they'll come to an agreement some day—and by the time we've settled our quarrels and become decent and honourable, there'll be nothing left for us. It has always been the same. We are a wonderful people, but it has always been our fate to be"—he did not say "robbed," but added, after a pause—"exploited!" (P. 174)

Decoud's historical perspective on the new imperialism is borne out in the denouement of the novel. The war between the newly independent Occidental Republic and its parent nation, Costaguana, is brought to a close through a show of force by ships of the imperialist powers, led by the "U.S.S. Powhattan" (p. 487). The United States is the first great power to recognize the new republic (p. 485). The visiting entrepreneur has a choice of the Amarilla Club of the Blancos or the Anglo-American Club—"Mining engineers and businessmen, don't you know," Captain Mitchell explains (p. 474)—or one may stop at one of the two American bars—"New Yorkers mostly frequent that one" (p. 479).

Given the intimate connection of the novel's themes with the history of imperialism in Latin America, it is possible to read (though by no means to exhaust) *Nostromo* as a record of the transition from precapitalist to capitalist— and, prospectively, to postcapitalist—society. To do so, it is necessary to analyze these stages of society by their component classes, and at the same time to consider the main characters in the novel as representatives of those classes.

172   CONRAD'S POLITICS

The People

The title of *Nostromo* has been found wanting by many who take seriously
its grand historical theme, but Conrad's choice of the name has something
to tell us about his larger intentions. The hero who bears this name is not
only a romantic individual but acquires dramatically the status of a complex
symbol. On the meaning of this symbol, Conrad is more explicit than is
elsewhere his practice:

> Nostromo does not aspire to be a leader in a personal game. He does not
> want to raise himself above the mass. He is content to feel himself a
> power—within the People. . . . He is a man with the weight of countless
> generations behind him and no parentage to boast of. . . . Like the People.
>   In his firm grip on the earth he inherits, in his improvidence and generos-
> ity, in his lavishness with his gifts, in his manly vanity, in ,the obscure
> sense of his greatness and in his faithful devotion with something de-
> spairing as well as desperate in its impulses, he is a Man of the People, their
> very own unenvious force, disdaining to lead but ruling from within.
> Years afterwards . . . listening in unmoved silence to anarchist speeches
> at the meeting, the enigmatical patron of the new revolutionary agitation,
> the trusted, the wealthy comrade Fidanza with the knowledge of his moral
> ruin locked up in his breast, he remains essentially a man of the People.
>   . . . Antonia the Aristocrat and Nostromo the Man of the People are
> the artisans of the New Era, the true creators of the New State. . . .[11]
> (Pp. xxi–xxiii)

It is thus the collective sense of his nickname—"our man" (like Lord Jim,
"one of us")—and not its Italian meaning, "boatswain," that is emphasized
in the title of the novel.

Nostromo's career, as outlined here, represents the exploitation of the
proletariat in behalf of the various political forces that contend for the
country without reference to the interests of its masses. He ultimately tries
to emancipate himself and materially supports the proletarian revolution, but
he does so through crime—the concealment of and slow theft from the
silver hoard. Nostromo's corruption by silver, which is, in part, a complex
symbol of "material interests," evokes the moral danger of taking on the
values of the propertied classes that yawns before revolutionary movements.

[11] Conrad wrote in the same vein to Cunninghame Graham that Nostromo is
"a romantic mouthpiece of the 'people' which (I mean 'the people') frequently
experience the very feelings to which he gives utterance" (*LL*, I, 338, letter of
October 31, 1904). Here and in the novel the term "people" connotes a specific
class—the peasant and working class— and not the community of all members
of the nation which it elsewhere suggests.

Nostromo is, however, not only the dramatic representative of the people but an individual—indeed, an individualist, a stern foreman, a would-be popular hero. His existence is a more complex affair than its primary symbolic function; it involves the relation of the individual ego to the collective identity of the people. It is the unwillingness to see the hero in this double aesthetic role that has obscured for most critics his tragic stature.

The focus of *Nostromo* is not "material interests" and their representative, Gould, but the people and their representative, Nostromo. Permeating the novel, densely filling the interstices between characters, providing motive and meaning to their actions, are the people. Costaguana is the most palpable presence in *Nostromo* by virtue of the gross human fact of popular suffering. It is "a great land of plain and mountain and people, suffering and mute, waiting for the future in a pathetic immobility of patience. . . . on all the lips she found a weary desire for peace, the dread of officialdom with its nightmarish parody of administration without law, without security, and without justice" (p. 88). The vision is Mrs. Gould's, and, despite her limited perspective (she finds, for example, that all Costaguanans look alike), she is able to perceive it because "having acquired in Southern Europe a knowledge of true peasantry, she was able to appreciate the great worth of the people" (p. 89).

The people stand in danger of that primary evil of industrialism: dehumanization. In the days before the revolution ("nobody had ever heard of labour troubles then") the naïve human spirit of the European-born Cargadores led them to strike every bullfight day. Nostromo's role as foreman, master of labor, is to roust out the men on the mornings after from their "black, lightless cluster of huts, like cow-byres, like dog-kennels" (p. 95). When he later rebels against his own exploitation, he becomes at the same time conscious of the proletariat over whom he has been boss: "What he had heard Giorgio Viola say once was very true. Kings, ministers, aristocrats, the rich in general, kept the people in poverty and subjection; they kept them as they kept dogs, to fight and hunt for their service" (p. 415).

Nostromo's career is, then, a record of growing class consciousness. His offended egoism first leads to withdrawal: "What did he care about their politics? Nothing at all" (p. 417). But egoism also turns him against his former employer; the mine "appeared to him hateful and immense, lording it by its vast wealth over the valour, the toil, the fidelity of the poor, over war and peace, over the labours of the town, the sea, and the Campo" (p. 503). Finally, he reasserts his origins and his ties to his mentor, recognizing himself "a republican like old Giorgio, and a revolutionist at heart (but in another manner)" (p. 525).

The "other manner" is his acquisition of silver. It is not mere rationalization by which Nostromo explains it to himself: "The rich lived on wealth stolen from the people, but he had taken from the rich nothing—nothing that was not lost to them already by their folly and their betrayal" (p. 541). The point is supported by the plot of the novel, for what provokes Nostromo to steal is the businesslike complacency of his employers towards their loss. To them it is only money, well lost for political gains. To him it is labor, courage (facing the dangers he encounters), and pride—in short, the values of the work ethic and their just reward.

Nostromo takes up the silver, which Conrad has carefully designated as a symbol of capitalism by making it the mine's actual product, and acquires a secret taint on his erstwhile "incorruptible" character. The taint of wealth goes further: when the revolutionary party leader visits Nostromo at his deathbed in search of the bequest of his fortune to the movement, he claims it because "the rich must be fought with their own weapons" (p. 562). It is, then, a mark of his dedication to the revolution that Nostromo does not answer, does not allow the curse to be passed on to the people.

And yet, for all his developing class consciousness, Nostromo remains bedeviled by the contradictions of his own character. An egoist whose pride has been hurt, he tries to identify himself with the people, but just when his egoistic desire for reputation is satisfied in the fullest measure, he is isolated by his guilty conscience and by his hidden crime. He then tries to take on another identity along with the old—that of Captain Fidanza, seaman-merchant and respectable patron of the radical party. How are we to regard this ironic mixture of alienation and integration, of individualism and social responsibility, of self-transcendence and self-destruction?

Nostromo's political career centers on four acts: the rescue of the escaping President Ribiera and the suppression of the rioting *Lumpenproletariat*; the "off-stage" secret mission to Hernandez; the removal of the silver from Sulaco to save it from the invading Monterist forces; and the summoning of General Barrios' army to defeat the Monterists and establish an independent Occidental Republic. In the first case, Nostromo's act is along strict class lines, favoring the aristocratic Blancos against the demagogic popular party. In the second, he is the emissary of Father Corbelàn, serving the efforts of the aristocracy (Corbelàn is of the Avellanos family) to put itself in league with its own peasantry, despite their "bandit" status. In the third, the interests of the mine—of the new capitalist order—are uppermost, but here Nostromo breaks with his role of upper-class factotum when he discovers his exploitation. In the last action, his guiding principle is the separatism of Decoud and is in the popular interest: to protect the community of Sulaco from the depredations of a ruthless military regime.

It is at this point that Nostromo identifies himself with the community most fully and most altruistically—at precisely the time of his greatest egoism, when he is already absorbed in his own plans to become rich. Individualism here fosters social action, but later, his social integration is eroded by personal preoccupations. This ironic relationship of communal identity and inveterate isolation is what gives Nostromo's career, like the larger historical action of the novel, its tragic character. Community and individual are found to be both interdependent and mutually exclusive: they create and they destroy each other—at least at this imperfect level of social development.

We are now in a position to justify the otherwise intolerably melodramatic conclusion of the novel, in which Nostromo, drawing off silver in order to "become rich slowly," is shot by his revolutionary mentor, Giorgio Viola, who takes him for the young worker, Ramirez, the unwelcome suitor of his daughter. Given the class conflicts and symbolic suggestions of the novel, the denouement reads like a myth of radical politics: Viola, the old-guard Garibaldino, rejects Ramirez because he is a native of Sulaco and therefore lacking in traditional class consciousness. (It is the European element that forms the working-class elite and the native half-breeds who constitute the tools of the demagogues Gamacho and Fuentes [p. 529].) The idealist Viola fails to recognize Nostromo because of his both literal and symbolic poor vision. The faded radical is out of touch with the new proletariat and is himself ridden by class prejudices (e.g., those of the European workers against the natives).

Nostromo is, even without Viola's myopia, directly destroyed by the contradictions between self-seeking and class consciousness. He uses the silver, at least in part, for the support of the radical movement, but he keeps his secret so well that he becomes totally isolated. He is killed by that isolation, through Viola's ignorance of his identity and designs. As in *Lord Jim* and other Conrad fables of the individual's relation to the social organism, there is in *Nostromo* a residual resistance to complete assimilation with the people, and this heroic individualism accounts both for the hero's demise and for his stature.

Like every tragic figure, Nostromo cannot be held by the world any longer—cannot be contained, at least within its usual morality. Like every tragic figure, he takes on himself the burden of guilt (or at least the illusion of it): the guilt of failing to bring a priest for the dying wife of Viola, the guilt of leaving Decoud behind to die. Nostromo is the sacrifice that societies make in order to live, and thereby he is made awesome. His very self-sacrifice leads him to rid himself of the conventional social bonds—to be, with the aged Oedipus, beyond society. Like every tragic hero, he achieves freedom, a certain recklessness born of the infinity of possibilities which opens before him when he acquires the treasure and becomes alienated from all classes and all men. He becomes the benefactor of the people, but the new order he has brought about is repressive in its turn. He joins the revolutionary party, but he never becomes ideologically committed to social or political action.

He is now free of everything but the treasure, the very instrument of his flight to freedom. There remains only to rid himself of that bond and he will be free, so free that there remains for him only to die. "In the exulting consciousness of his strength, and the triumphant excitement of his mind, he struck a blow for his freedom." He tells his beloved, Giselle Viola, of the treasure and when she asks how he got it, "He wrestled with the spell of captivity. It was as if striking a heroic blow that he burst out: 'Like a thief!' " (p. 540). In judging his own crime, Nostromo frees himself from "captivity," strikes a "heroic blow," fulfills himself as tragic hero. He points the way toward an ideal social hero who achieves full integration with his nation or his class. But he himself does not fulfill that ideal. He is, rather, another kind of hero, the tragic figure torn apart by the contradictions involved in his effort to transcend his historical situation and his own ego. This dialectical negation is as far as Conrad will go in leading our imagination toward the ideal of community.

The Intellectual

The parallel between Nostromo and Decoud is suggested by the latter himself: "I am no patriot. I am no more of a patriot than the Capataz of the Sulaco Cargadores, this Genoese who has done such great things for this harbour—this active usher-in [sic] of the material implements for our progress" (p. 191). The two characters are twin studies of the relationship between personal and social motives, between egoism and the urge for community. "A victim of the disillusioned weariness which is the retribution meted out to intellectual audacity"—so Conrad describes Decoud; a "victim of the disenchanted vanity which is the reward of audacious action"—so he describes Nostromo (p. 501). The man of action and the man of intellect are in the vanguard of the nation's progress, but they are no patriots, never ridding themselves of their skepticism or their selfishness.

Although Decoud claims that his motives are not patriotic, his patriotism is not merely an invention to win his beloved, Antonia Avellanos, whose enthusiasm requires similar sentiments of him. He often speaks as though this were the case, and has succeeded in convincing some readers, but Conrad betrays Decoud's psychic need to do so: "He soothed himself by saying he was not a patriot, but a lover" (p. 176). Perversely, to the woman herself, Decoud insists on his lack of idealism: "he seized every opportunity to tell her that though she had managed to make a Blanco journalist of him, he was no patriot" (p. 186). He goes on to explain: "First of all, the word had no sense for cultured minds, to whom the narrowness of every belief is odious; and secondly, in connection with the everlasting troubles of this unhappy country it was hopelessly besmirched; it had been the cry of dark barbarism, the cloak of lawlessness, of crimes, of rapacity, of simple thieving." Yet despite his wish to dissociate himself from his country's history, Decoud becomes the author of his province's declaration of independence and the father of its development into a community.

What are we to make of this lover of contradictions, this skeptic who becomes a national hero almost against his will? It is easy to identify him with Conrad in his ambivalence toward his Polish tradition, as Morf has done: the words "Pro Patria!" which he utters ironically are those with which Conrad bitterly describes his grand-uncle's wasted dedication to Polish independence (*A Personal Record*, p. 35). Conrad carried his Polishness ironically, yet in the time of crisis he finally returned to the fold. Decoud is subjected to Father Corbelàn's Dostoevskian anathemas, but he defends himself as Conrad might have done: "I believe I am a true *hijo del pays*, a true son of the country, whatever Father Corbelàn may say. . . . A Sulaco revolution. . . . The Great Cause may be served here" (pp. 213–14). Decoud's nationalism, then, partakes of the larger visions of Conrad's political imagination, the "Great Cause" or "idea" of community which may be served by national liberation.

If Decoud, for all his irony, does affirm his identity with the nation and with some larger community through his theory and practice of revolution, it is his separation from the revolution and from other men that brings about his suicide. Conrad is unusually explicit in his authorial comment: "the truth was that he died from solitude, the enemy known but to few on this earth, and whom only the simplest of us are fit to withstand. The brilliant Costaguanero of the boulevards had died from solitude and want of faith in himself and others" (p. 496). The meaning of this solitude may readily be found in the metaphysics of individuality and community. In a crucial passage, Conrad sets out in metaphysical terms Decoud's inability "to grapple with himself single-handed." Separated from "others," the self does not find its pure essence but on the contrary loses its identity:

> After three days of waiting for the sight of some human face, Decoud caught himself entertaining a doubt of his own individuality. It had merged into the world of cloud and water, of natural forces and forms of nature. In our activity alone do we find the sustaining illusion of an independent existence as against the whole scheme of things of which we form a helpless part. Decoud lost all belief in the reality of his action past and to come. (P. 497)

Individuality is an illusion, then, but it is a "sustaining illusion" necessary to life. Reality consists of natural forces and historical action, joined in an oppressive web of circumstance. Belief in the reality of one's actions, faith in oneself and others (with its complementary skepticism) are predicated on political engagement in history, for all its brute awesomeness. Without that involvment, the individual returns to primal nothingness: "He beheld the universe as a succession of incomprehensible images . . . the solitude appeared like a great void" (p. 498).

In the absence of social connection, the self's only link is to nature, but it is an empty nature and a hollow link. Wishing to sever this umbilical cord as well, Decoud has nowhere to go but into the abyss: "The cord of silence . . . must let him fall and sink into the sea, he thought" (p. 499). He can do nothing but die.

There is this difference between nature and society as bases of human existence: Decoud sinks into the bay and disappears "without a trace, swallowed up in the immense indifference of things" (p. 501), while society's loss of him is remembered and he becomes part of history, a national hero. For society, unlike nature, cares—or can care when it moves toward community. His suicide and its aftermath are an enactment of the philosophy which holds that man's life is social—or it is nothing.

Decoud's career dramatizes Conrad's view of the relation of the intellectual and his class, the intelligentsia, to the political world. One indication of

Conrad's intention, which must be qualified by the low reliability of the source, is Retinger's account of his collaboration with Conrad in 1914 on plans for a play based on *Nostromo*:

> There was to be a South-American intellectual, artist, and patriot leading the revolt in the name of the people against a ruthless dictator, who dies exclaiming: "Je meurs honteusement, mais glorieusement, pour des principes que je méprise," because in his heart he was an aristocrat, and here it came to him to lead the masses. . . . When years later I went to Mexico and there witnessed fighting and revolutions, and made friends with fat generals and visionary dreamers—all the time, while history was enacted in front of me, I was thinking: "Here they are staging Conrad's play for me alone." The dreamer, artistic patriot, was Diego Rivera, with his flamboyance, his readiness for action, and his complete scepticism as far as social or political problems were concerned.[12]

This transmogrification of Decoud into a kind of intellectual Gaspar Ruiz is consistent with the Conrad myth; the "intellectual, artist, and patriot" becomes a popular leader but remains a tragic figure separated from the community. Decoud, like Nostromo, gives direction to a whole society but resists the assimilation of his precarious identity in the community, to his ultimate downfall. Decoud and Nostromo are the sacrifices that revolutions exact in order to succeed; they are the leaders, like those described by the narrator of *Under Western Eyes*, who begin revolutions but do not survive to guide them.

The Capitalist

The characterization of Gould can be read as a parable of the sociology of capitalism, in its classical formulation by Weber, Sombart, and Veblen. Gould is a technician, trained in mining engineering in the course of his preparation to redeem the wrongs done his father; a speculator, investing little capital of his own but engaging the confidence of international financiers; and a puritan: although his wife indulges a taste for carriages drawn by white mules, Gould's abstemiousness keeps him in frequent residence at the mining camp—the dominant image one is left with has him in the saddle. His ideology is chiefly distinguished by its absence, so that it is not possible to describe him in the terms applied to his backer, Holroyd ("Holy Rood"), the very type of *The Protestant Ethic and the Spirit of Capitalism*, who wants to

[12] Retinger, *Conrad and His Contemporaries*, pp. 122–23.

spread Protestantism in Catholic countries and with it the culture and politics favorable to economic expansion.

Yet even more than Holroyd, Gould epitomizes the capitalist spirit of economic activity. He is an egoist seeking victory over obstacles natural, economic, and political, a victory which is in itself more to him than the material benefit either to himself or to others—investors, workers, or the nation at large. Benefit there is, of course, but—to use a technological metaphor—it is a by-product of the mining operation rather than its real product, which is silver, i.e., money, or its international standard. The silver underscores his peculiarly capitalist behavior, as Marx described it: it is wealth without value, money as a mere abstraction, an end without an aim. Silver thus becomes an ironic symbol of Gould's distortion of the work ethic. Economic activity comes to dominate his entire behavior; his politics imply the support of any government at all which will allow that activity to continue. The ultimate failure of Gould's original policy of reliance on "material interests" is dramatized by his wife's discovery that what were means for her husband have become all-absorbing ends in themselves.

Gould is also an imperialist, a composite of Conrad's two fictional types, the conqueror and the colonist. He is anxious to affirm his third-generation roots in the land and his commitment to its fortunes; he justifies his re-opening of the mine with foreign capital "because the security which it demands must be shared with an oppressed people. A better justice will come afterwards" (p. 84; he does not realize the historical irony of his last remark). Nevertheless, Gould remains unassimilated, not only because of the English cut of his clothes, but because of the temperament and values that go with them.

His own self-consciousness tells him as much, but it also tells us more:

> After all, with his English parentage and English upbringing, he perceived that he was an adventurer in Costaguana, the descendant of adventurers enlisted in a foreign legion, of men who had sought fortune in a revolutionary war, who had planned revolutions, who had believed in revolutions. For all the uprightness of his character, he had something of an adventurer's easy morality which takes count of personal risk in the ethical appraising of his action. He was prepared, if need be, to blow up the whole San Tomé mountain sky high out of the territory of the Republic. This resolution expressed the tenacity of his character, the remorse of that subtle conjugal infidelity through which his wife was no longer the sole mistress of his thoughts, something of his father's imaginative weakness, and

something, too, of the spirit of a buccaneer throwing a lighted match into the magazine rather than surrender his ship. (Pp. 365–66)

This remarkable passage suggests not only the image of the conqueror, the alien who wishes to take spoil from the country rather than to identify himself with it, but also the image of the nihilist, like the Professor of *The Secret Agent* or Jörgenson of *The Rescue*, who would rather bring everything down with him than accept partial or temporary defeat. Conrad's expressed view, we recall, was that the capitalist is the greatest anarchist, and Gould's terrorism connects him with the subjects of the anarchist tales. The connection is made when he reveals his preparations to blow up the mine, in rejecting Hirsch's offer to sell him dynamite; the chief engineer of the railroad remarks that his policy is "radical. . . . I mean going to the roots, you know," and Gould replies: "Why, yes. . . . The Gould Concession has struck such deep roots in this country, in this province, in that gorge of the mountains, that nothing but dynamite shall be allowed to dislodge it from there" (pp. 205–6).

Above all other connections of Gould with the Conrad canon, he must be seen as an ironic version of the Brooke myth, the story of the man who goes alone into a disturbed area and establishes personal order over it, for good or ill. Like many of the exemplars of this pattern, the "King of Sulaco," as he is called, is destroyed by his undertaking—his "Imperium in Imperio." He discovers, in the course of the revolution, that he cannot remain an *éminence grise* in the arena of history but must openly support the Separatist forces; he must agree to reconciliation with Hernandez, although he feels the moral taint of dealing with a bandit; he must sacrifice the stuffy idealism of which Decoud accuses him: "He could not believe his own motives if he did not make them first a part of some fairy tale. The earth is not quite good enough for him, I fear" (p. 215).

When, through Gould's support, the popular cause is victorious, he begins the process of his own destruction, first, by his absorption in the mine, which alienates him from his wife, and then by his creation of an industrial proletariat which will eventually drive him out. Monygham predicts that "the time approaches when all that the Gould Concession stands for shall weigh as heavily upon the people as the barbarism, cruelty, and misrule of a few years back' " (p. 511), and Mrs. Gould has a similar vision of her husband's enterprise:

She saw the San Tomé mountain hanging over the Campo, over the whole land, feared, hated, wealthy; more soulless than any tyrant, more pitiless and autocratic than the worst Government; ready to crush innumerable lives in the expansion of its greatness. He did not see it. He could not see it. (P. 521)

It is this failure to know himself (except in brief moments like the one quoted earlier), his failure to judge his own moral and political condition, that distinguishes Gould from his blood-brother, Kurtz. Lacking even that negative heroism that rises to acknowledge the horror within the self, Gould falls somewhere between the poles of heroism and villainy.

The Aristocrat

The sympathy with which Conrad portrays the old aristocratic leader Avellanos has rubbed off on his politics, but it is the sentiment felt toward an amiable anachronism—a softened version of the irony with which Conrad regards the aristocracy throughout his political writings. Avellanos earns this sympathy on two accounts, his long and honorable career and his present effeteness. He is an active leader in the artificial creation of the progressive Ribiera regime and energetically aids in its defense against the Monterist coup. But the dominant image of him is set in the council chamber of the Blanco party, after his cronies have gone out to welcome the conquering enemy, where Decoud finds him slumped over the table at which he had presided. What Decoud later writes of him could be said of the best of his class:

> as I looked at him, it seemed to me that I could have blown him away with my breath, he looked so frail, so weak, so worn out. . . . hasn't he seen the sheets of "Fifty Years of Misrule," which we have begun printing on the presses of the *Porvenir*, littering the Plaza, floating in the gutters, fired out as wads for trabucos loaded with handfuls of type, blown in the wind, trampled in the mud? . . . It would be unreasonable to expect him to survive. It would be cruel. (P. 235)

For the rest of the novel he is an invalid, and he dies during the evacuation to the interior.

If there is melancholy at the passing of the noble vestiges of the aristocratic tradition, there is only contempt for the present aristocracy. Decimated by years of struggle with the central government—in which their original program of federalism was an attempt to achieve local autonomy and, through it, their own dominance in the provinces—they have contented themselves with resisting further attempts to bring their hereditary fiefs into contact with the rest of the nation or with the outside world. Sir John, the visiting head of the railroad company (whose intrusion the Blancos resist until the Ribiera government convinces them it is in their interest), remarks of their provincial realm: "But I had no notion that a place on a sea-coast could remain so isolated from the world. If it had been a thousand miles inland now—most remarkable! Has anything ever happened here for a hundred years before to-day?" (p. 36).

Sir John is narrow-minded, of course, in his belief that only his railroad and other modern advances constitute history, but the static insulation of the aristocratic estates from the modern world under the rule of the Blancos gives point to the demagogic slogans which call them "Feudalists! Goths!" After the visit of Ribiera and Sir John they accept the coming of the railroad, as they later accept the reopening of the mine, but at the impending invasion of the Monterist forces they are ready to cringe before the conqueror. It is the contemptible speeches they make to rationalize their cowardice that prod their last active spirit, Decoud, to develop his plan for separation.

Decoud's separatism is in origin an aristocratic plan, closely resembling the federalism of the Blancos' original program. But it does not imitate the insularity aimed at by the latter. The new separatism is based on popular sovereignty, on exposure to the modern world—for better or worse—and on continued efforts to liberate and annex the remaining portion of Costaguana. That Decoud's plan is a genuinely popular one is evidenced by the league of forces that defeats the Caesarist generals and establishes the Occidental Republic. These forces include the peasantry, led by Hernandez; the proletarians, represented by the mine workers; and the military force under General Barrios, a disreputable "Indio" with a rough, native's manner. Decoud's genius lies in discovering not only the geographical rationale for the existence of a separate nation but the political coalition that represents, at least temporarily, the genuine interests of the people.

With the success of his plans and the establishment of the republic, the idea of separation becomes an end in itself—a florid statue is even erected to it (p. 482)—and Decoud's newspaper, the *Porvenir*, becomes merely "Conservative, or, rather, I should say, Parliamentary," according to Captain Mitchell (p. 478). The new state is headed by Don Juste Lopez, one of the most timorous of the aristocrats. This figurehead is sufficient indication of its debased character. It can be seen only as a transitional stage to some fuller realization of the interests of the people, of which the first stage will be the extension of the revolution to Costaguana.

There is one other member of the aristocracy who sees the decline of his own class and the emergence of the new, and who puts himself in touch with the new. That this role should be assigned to Father Corbelàn, later Cardinal-Archbishop Corbelàn, is somewhat surprising in view of his conservative stand on other matters, particularly on preserving the Church's economic and political power. Upon reflection, Corbelàn's politics can be seen to contain a mixture of aristocratic contempt for the rising capitalist class and a patronizing but deep-rooted affection for the peasantry. Both these attitudes emerge when Corbelàn replies to Monygham's prediction that "material interests" will not support the planned revolution in Costaguana: "We have worked for them; we have made them, these material interests of the foreigners. . . . Let them beware, then, lest the people, prevented from their aspirations, should rise and claim their share of the wealth and their share of the power" (p. 510).

Corbelàn's political activity throughout the novel shows a consistent responsiveness to the needs of the lower classes. It is he, through Nostromo, who establishes contact with Hernandez's band and brings the peasantry to support the first revolution; it is he who plots the coming revolution with Antonia Avellanos and the political refugees from Costaguana. The final irony of aristocratic politics enters here: "And do you know where they [Antonia and Corbelàn] go for strength, for the necessary force?" Monygham asks Mrs. Gould. "To the secret societies amongst immigrants and natives, where Nostromo—I should say Captain Fidanza—is the great man" (p. 511). It is in alliance with the people that "the last of the Avellanos and the last of the Corbelàns" find their political future.

Chapter VII

THE SYMBOLIC WORLD OF
THE SECRET AGENT

Sir William Harcourt

'Tis all in pieces, all coherence gone.

—John Donne

Political estimates of *The Secret Agent* usually tend toward the view implied in the subtitle (which Conrad later disclaimed as unauthorized) of the first periodical publication of the novel: "A Novel Dealing with the Anarchists and Revolutionaries of London, in which the Diplomatic Intrigue of a Foreign Power, together with Human Selfishness and Anarchist Treachery, Furnish the Amazing Complications."[1] On the other hand, since Thomas Mann's introduction to the German translation of 1926, it has been noted that the revolutionary (and the reactionary) attack on bourgeois society is akin to Conrad's own view of the modern world. Later attempts to justify or denigrate Conrad's portraits of the anarchists have usually exaggerated their case by veering toward one or another of these poles. More recently, the tendency has been toward reading the novel's politics in relation to the social world in which it is set.[2] We can perhaps move further in this direction by asking why Conrad bothered to take up anarchism at precisely the time (1906) that he did.

The event on which the plot is based was the only anarchist bombing on record in England, and some of the background material he acquired had to come from Irish nationalist activities. The Greenwich bombing had taken place back in 1894, and, while attacks on the Continent continued to arouse the British public, these died down after 1900. Even Conrad's explanation of the bombing as a counter-revolutionary provocation could not have been topical, since the International Conference of Governments that met in Rome in 1898 (the equivalent of the International Conference in Milan which Vladimir's plan is designed to provoke into harsher repressive measures) needed no such encouragement to pass resolutions prohibiting even free thought and expression—much less anarchist activities.[3] Conrad would have chosen the subject of anarchism, then, not as a topical issue but as a theme with broader political implications.

In the unusually revealing Author's Note to *The Secret Agent*, Conrad identified the two stimuli for the novel: the remark of a friend that the sister of the mentally defective anarchist who had blown himself up in Greenwich Park committed suicide afterwards, and a line in a book of memoirs in which the Home Secretary complains that his subordinates are keeping him

[1] *Ridgeway's: A Militant Weekly for God and Country*, I (1906), 502.
[2] Karl, *Reader's Guide to Conrad*, p. 200; Gurko, *Giant in Exile*, p. 167; John H. Hagan, Jr., "The Design of Conrad's *The Secret Agent*," *ELH—A Journal of English Literary History*, XXII (1955), 158.
[3] Cole, *A History of Socialist Thought*, II, 396.

in the dark.[4] The former datum provided the precise point of contact between the political events and the domestic plot he developed for the novel; the latter suggested the atmosphere of secrecy and distrust that pervades both its political and domestic scenes. But they did not provide the symbolic medium in which the two currents of action are related, each to the other and both to the modern political and social world.

To discover the personal sources of the imagery which unifies the novel, we must go back a decade to a letter in which Conrad thanks Edward Garnett for advice on his problems with *The Rescue*:

> Where do you think the illumination—the short and vivid flash of what I have been boasting to you came from? Why! From your words, words, words. They exploded like stored powder barrels—while another man's words would have fizzled out in speaking and left darkness unrelieved by a forgotten spurt of futile sparks. An explosion is the most lasting thing in the universe. It leaves disorder, remembrance, room to move, a clear space. Ask your Nihilist friends. But I am afraid you haven't blown me to pieces. I am afraid I am like the Russian governmental system. It will take a good many bursting charges to make me change my ways.[5]

The clean-sweeping explosion is present in *The Rescue*'s climactic scene, and Conrad's thinking about a conclusion to that novel may have provided the germ of the idea for *The Secret Agent*. The letter's description of the liberating results of an explosion is quite close to the images of liberating negation put forth by the Professor; it indicates an imaginative identification by the author with his most bizarre character. Conrad's need for a "clear space" in the artistic realm is the counterpart of the nihilist's desire for "the destruction of what is," as the Professor puts it (*SA*, p. 306).

To claim this much is by no means to propose that Conrad was a concealed anarchist—in art or politics. It suggests only that the imaginative perspective of *The Secret Agent* is consistent with the subject matter, both personal and social. This perspective is a vision of the modern world in a state of fragmentation—as if by explosion. It is an ironic vision because Conrad's fundamental social value was the organic community, while the present status of men is that of isolation from each other, alienation from the social whole, and, in

---

[4] The informative friend was, as he later claimed, Ford Madox Hueffer. In *Memories and Impressions: A Study in Atmosphere* (New York and London, 1911), p. 136 ff., he described the vast crowd at the funeral procession of Bourdin, the Greenwich bomber. His explanation of the public interest was a projection of his own response: the "spirit of romance."

[5] Garnett Letters, p. 79, letter of March 8, 1897.

consequence, loneliness and self-destruction. The dramatic action presents this vision simultaneously in two plots, one in the public, political realm and the other in the private, domestic one. The two plots, and the social sectors they represent, are welded together not as much by their point of contact in Verloc as by the imagery, which is maintained throughout the novel in both plots. This imagery is the symbolic equivalent of the theme of fragmentation, and takes the varied forms of personal self-enclosure (secrecy, ignorance, foolishness, madness, etc.) and of physical dismembering (explosion, butchering, islands, etc.).

Much of the imagery of *The Secret Agent* has already been discussed by R. W. Stallman in a highly suggestive article,[6] but much remains to be done to see in it a consistent view of the novel. The study of imagery allows us to circumvent such questions as the degree of Conrad's unconscious involvement with the anarchist theories of his characters and to find instead the burden of his symbolic art. Similarly, focusing on the imagery allows us to neglect Conrad's explicit derogation of the anarchists and to reach his artistic —rather than his polemical—view of them. We shall find him to be operating imaginatively, showing and pointing rather than stating his political judgments. The novel's vision of the modern world as fragmented is an attempt to radically reorder its substance, to turn it in the opposite direction, toward an ideal, organic community.

The imagery of *The Secret Agent* is sufficiently consistent to allow us to speak of it as a *symbolic world*, to be distinguished from an allegorical landscape or system of correspondences by the homogeneous embodiment of the theme in all elements of its terrain. Symbolism of this kind operates as a function of its author's sensibility rather than of his schematic plan, and it is therefore a moot question whether Conrad contrived the novel in this way, contrary to his usual practice (except in "Heart of Darkness"). It appears, rather, that the limitations of the novelistic form he chose allowed him to focus his perceptions, with the effect described above. In the Author's Preface he tells us only that the novel was designed as an intense perception of its subject within a limited space. The result, inevitably, is repetition. The effect is akin to that described by Caroline Spurgeon in her study of the similar phenomenon in Shakespeare, "iterative imagery." So frequently are such words as "secret," "knowledge," "private," or "fool" used, and so widely are they made to apply in the London of the turn of the century,

---

[6] "Time and *The Secret Agent*," in Stallman (ed.), *The Art of Joseph Conrad: A Critical Symposium* (East Lansing, Mich., 1960), pp. 234–54.

that we are justified in speaking of a world pervaded by certain dominant symbols.

Conrad himself described the stage in his creative process when, after assembling his kernels of inspiration, his imagination expanded to conceive such a world:

> Then the vision of an enormous town presented itself, of a monstrous town more populous than some continents and in its man-made might as if indifferent to heaven's frowns and smiles; a cruel devourer of the world's light. There was room enough there to place any story, depth enough there for any passion, variety enough there for any setting, darkness enough to bury five millions of lives.
> Irresistibly the town became the background for the ensuing period of deep and tentative meditations. (*SA*, p. xii)

The process described here serves to expand the role of the city from a mere setting for the action to a medium that expresses the kinds of life lived there. The symbolic world of *The Secret Agent* is London itself, and the characteristic of urban life which is repeatedly manifested in the novel is social fragmentation.

The Moral World

Immediately, on the title page, the fragmented condition of the world is expressed in the language of secrecy. "Secret" is used more than fifty times in *The Secret Agent* (the record in previous analyses of iterative images is probably held by William Empson's count of forty-seven uses of "fool" in *King Lear*). On about half of these occasions the word merely refers to Verloc or to his profession. But most of the other uses of the word characterize human states of being, emotions, conditions, and moral qualities: "secret ardor," "secret scorn," "secretly much affected," "secret griefs," "secretly outspoken thought," "secrecy of his heart," "secret liberation," "secret weakness," "secret fear," "secret of good nature," "secret of guilty breasts," "secret habits of mind." We may gather that the individuals of this novel live their lives enclosed within themselves. That this self-containment is a universal human condition is suggested by the more general uses of the term: "secret of fate," "secret ills of existence," "secret ways of the future," and (most generally) "secrecy."

The relationship among these three groups of uses—the merely professional references, the emotional or qualitative descriptions, and the universal generalizations—is embodied in the following passage. It may be considered the crescendo of the novel's variations on the theme of secrecy (when Verloc replies to his wife's accusations, "if you will have it that I killed the boy, then you've killed him as much as I"):

> In sincerity of feeling and openness of statement, these words went far beyond anything that had ever been said in this home, kept up on the wages of a secret industry eked out by the sale of more or less secret wares: the poor expedients devised by a mediocre mankind for preserving an imperfect society from the dangers of moral and physical corruption, both secret, too, of their kind. (P. 258)

Here Verloc's secret political profession and his secret cover-up dealings in pornography are brought together with the secret basis of his marriage— his illusion that he is loved for himself, whereas Winnie had married him only to gain security for her brother (whom he has just destroyed). These furtive activities are generalized to suggest all human institutions, particularly political ones, whose hidden purpose is to preserve the social order from its hidden tendencies toward dissolution and anarchy.

The system by which the political world is organized to perform its function of maintaining the *status quo* is a hierarchy of secrecy. At the operative level, Chief Inspector Heat has secret contacts with such *agents provocateurs* as Verloc, and uses their (often false) secret information in secret, in order to avoid the legal limitations which his superiors might seek to impose on his activities. When his direct superior, the Assistant Commissioner, learns of Heat's "private" sources of information, he quickly adopts the policy of secrecy and goes out in disguise to contact Verloc and conclude the investigations himself. He does reveal his intentions to his own superior, the Home Secretary (whose very title is appropriate to the theme of secrecy), but this latter, by means of his imposing personality and avoidance of details, manages to keep himself in the dark about the moral secrets which the Assistant Commissioner has discovered. Even within the governmental apparatus, then, men are divided from one another in their common undertakings. The same secrecy obtains among politically allied powers, like Britain and the nation (presumably Russia) which seeks to enlist British support in its anti-subversive campaign by secretly provoking a bombing attack. If such mutual mystification is the law of life among the forces of legality, how unstable must be the basis of social order.

Yet there are many indications in the novel that Conrad thought the multiplication of secrets, while alien to the ideal of social community, performs a recognizable function in a fragmented society. Under the conditions of widespread disorder in the present world, secrecy is expedient and partly effective in promoting social stability. The Assistant Commissioner is rendered as a moral ideal, though he engages with the world's secrecy. (It is he who dons a disguise and plunges into the decadence of London: "His descent into the street was like the descent into a slimy aquarium from which the water had been run off. A murky, gloomy dampness enveloped him" [p. 147]). By the same token, Heat does manage to maintain a firm grip on anarchist activities—at least as long as Verloc keeps him informed, and before genuinely destructive force is unleashed. Similarly, the Home Secretary, while made to look an inflated looby by his stock phrases in the highly comic scenes with the Assistant Commissioner, is yet possessed of a lofty gravity which may be the best the public can expect in its public figures. Secrecy can also be used, as it is by the Assistant Commissioner, as a means of freeing the individual from the toils of bureaucratic stagnation and of allowing him to act vigorously. The danger of such unchecked initiative is that it can become a kind of anarchism in government; the Assistant Commissioner avoids its worst implications by carrying his code of legal and moral responsibility within him when he engages in extra-legal activities.

Though secrecy has virtues that in part compensate for its fragmentation of the social world, it is only an expedient in dealing with the secret forces that are tearing that world apart. Secrecy by itself cannot unify men or nations. Its opposite, "knowledge," is, however, the solvent that brings resolution and partial community. Knowledge, in the last analysis, does serve to weld the world together, though its entry into darkened minds tends to disturb them enough to provoke violence. On the political level, knowledge is a system of mutual expectations that stabilizes conduct, which might otherwise be precipitate and self-destructive. Such a functional arrangement is the macabre relationship of Heat and the Professor: Heat knows that the latter can blow them both up with the bomb he carries, and gingerly bypasses him, while the Professor walks secure in the knowledge that "they know."

Despite these advantages, men in this world shun knowledge: the Great Personage avoids details, Heat believes that "to know too much was not good for the department," and Mrs. Verloc complacently assumes that "life didn't stand much looking into." Yet the dangers of being kept out of a secret are palpable: Verloc and his wife are both destroyed by their mistaken conceptions of marriage (Mrs. Verloc, by her belief that her husband's sudden interest in Stevie is a fulfillment of her wish that he treat Stevie as a son; Verloc, by his illusion that his wife loves him for himself, rather than for the economic security he brings her family). In contrast to their perceptual laziness, the Assistant Commissioner stands as the ideal of active investigation and lucid apprehension (although he, too, fails to plumb the mysteries of personal life when he is unable to understand how Verloc's accomplice could have been persuaded to go on his fool's errand, because of "his ignorance of poor Stevie's devotion to Mr. Verloc" [p. 220]).

It is one of the traditional ironies of knowledge, discovered by Oedipus and continually rediscovered, that the lack of it brings destruction but the finding of it only seals that destruction. Despite the integrative function of knowledge in *The Secret Agent*, it destroys those who have become inured to a life of secrecy. After Winnie Verloc learns of her husband's perfidy, an elaborate set of variations on the theme of knowledge is presented in the closing pages of the novel. Verloc complains to his wife, in extenuation of his crime, "You don't know what a brute I had to deal with. . . . You didn't know. . . . You had no business to know" (pp. 237–38). Indeed, Winnie does not know, for knowledge, when it comes to her, takes away her capacity for knowing anything beyond the brute fact of her brother's death. When Verloc asks (reversing his question), "You understand why—don't you?" she answers, "What are you talking about?" (p. 240). Finally, Winnie comes to realize her helplessness without knowledge, when she envies the escape routes of professional criminals: "they had knowledge" (p. 270).

Human separation, isolation, and loneliness are here portrayed in terms of secrecy, knowledge, and ignorance. The final image is that of a blank wall confronting the individual with the meaninglessness of his knowledge: "Mrs. Verloc gazed at the whitewashed wall. A blank wall—perfectly blank. A blankness to run at and dash your head against" (p. 244). In this vein, the novel closes, with the repeated newspaper phrases which ring in Ossipon's mind as he reviews his dreadful knowledge of Winnie's death: "*An impenetrable mystery seems destined to hang for ever over this act of madness or despair*" (p. 307). Knowledge, which in other circumstances would bring people together, in this world leads them to destroy each other when they learn of evils formerly veiled. In the absence of full knowledge or firm belief, knowing becomes an equivocal good. The finest irony of *The Secret Agent* is that it not only posits the value of the enemy, secrecy, but shows the curse on the protagonist, knowledge.[7]

Several terms for distortion of perception operate in *The Secret Agent* as antitheses of knowledge. They include "ignorance," "fool," and "madness." That Conrad characterizes the anarchists as madmen is not as much a political judgment as it is an imaginative projection of their conduct. The anarchists wish to break things apart because they do not see things as they are. The Professor, who knows so clearly that "they know," is distinguished by "the extreme, almost ascetic purity of his thought, combined with an astounding ignorance of worldly conditions" (p. 80). He is the son of a revivalist preacher, who has reacted against his father's religious fanaticism by a neurotic distortion of reality—making a religion of destruction (pp. 80–81). Conrad generalizes the Professor's psychological fantasy to revolutionaries as a class: "The way of even the most justifiable revolutions is prepared by personal impulses disguised into creeds" (p. 81). He goes beyond this fairly trite observation, however, and associates the anarchists' condition of unrest with that of humanity at large: "in their own way the most ardent of revolutionaries are perhaps doing no more but seeking for peace in common with the rest of mankind—the peace of soothed vanity, of satisfied appetites, or perhaps of appeased conscience" (p. 81). This tragic view of his characters' participation in the human condition allows Conrad to make the anarchists an instance—though an extreme one—of the decay of the social order through the widespread ignorance, secrecy, and madness of its members.

These mental deficiencies are not, however, confined to the underground world. In the bureaucratic structure, the Great Personage assumes that Heat, whose obstructive tactics the Assistant Commissioner is describing, is "some ass," while Heat himself thinks of the Assistant Commissioner as a fool. The former Ambassador at the foreign Embassy, Baron Stott-Wartenheim (whose counter-revolutionary fanaticism made even his own Foreign

---

[7] Another term used in connection with secrecy and knowledge, "private," exhibits similar ironies. Verloc considers himself the defender of private property and turns out to be its most active assailant. Heat defends his use of a secret relationship with a double agent as "private information," and makes a visit to Verloc as a "private citizen." Instead of acting in the public welfare, Heat places his private interest ahead of his official duty. (He has risen rapidly in the department by means of the information supplied him by Verloc, and wishes to protect his source of self-advancement by pinning the charge on Michaelis.) Privacy, which would seem to be the primary value to be defended against anarchism, comes to mean that which is inimical to open knowledge and public welfare, and the term acquires an ironic ring as it is repeated in the novel.

Office smile), is said to have exclaimed on his deathbed, "Unhappy Europe! Thou shalt perish by the moral insanity of thy children!" (p. 28). The counter-revolutionary bomb plot is itself mad, intentionally and unintentionally so, "the shocking senselessness of gratuitous blasphemy" (p. 33). (It is worth recalling that Conrad disclaimed, in the Author's Note, any intention of committing "a gratuitous outrage on the feelings of mankind" [p. xv].)

The inventor of the bomb plot, the First Secretary, Vladimir, with all his suavity and veneer of civilization, is Conrad's representative of the essential irrationalism, or barbarism, of Russia, which is represented by the attaché's oriental manners and features. It is Vladimir's point of connection with the anarchists who are his enemies that they employ the same style of speech, continually casting scornful aspersions on the sanity not only of their political opponents but of the English as a whole and of its middle class in particular: "every imbecile with an income," "intellectual idiots," "idiotic vanity," "imbecile bourgeoisie," "the middle classes are stupid." It is Vladimir who knows better than anyone the essential terror of nihilism and the moral significance of his scheme:

> the absurd ferocity of such a demonstration will affect them more profoundly than the mangling of a whole street—or theatre—full of their own kind. To that last they can always say: "Oh! it's mere class hate." But what is one to say to an act of destructive ferocity so absurd as to be incomprehensible, inexplicable, almost unthinkable; in fact, mad? Madness alone is truly terrifying, inasmuch as you cannot placate it either by threats, persuasion, or bribes. (P. 33)

Vladimir's vision refers not only to the operations of the revolutionaries, but also to certain legal, governmental activities, such as those he is engaged in. (This political insight, posed though it is in existential terms of the absurd, strikes me as being a more convincing explanation than others of a number of irrational events in modern history, for instance, the annihilation of European Jewry.) *The Secret Agent* is not merely an anticipation of the irrationalism of subversive activity in modern times, but a prophecy of the erection of madness into a governmental system.

The theme of madness in the public world has its parallel in the domestic tale, which hinges on Stevie's madness and on the suggestion of its presence in his sister, Winnie. Conrad described his enterprise as "telling Winnie Verloc's story to its anarchistic end of utter desolation, madness and despair" (p. xv). The description of her passionate devotion to her brother makes the quality of her attachment clear: "She could not bear to see the boy hurt. It maddened her" (p. 38). Her protection of Stevie from their father, at least once by means of a poker, had led him to say that the one was "a slobbering idjut and the other a wicked she-devil" (p. 242). Ossipon's pseudo-scientific diagnosis of her congenital derangement is therefore ironically true: Winnie's entire life is imbalanced and precarious by virtue of the distorted notions of Stevie on which she bases her conduct. Her incapacity for intelligent life is summed up in her belief that "life doesn't stand much looking into"; it is the motto not only of her intellectual laziness but also of her mental weakness. The widespread condition of impenetrability and insensitivity in mankind at large, which the novel describes, is represented in Winnie as a latent hysteria which manifests itself in murder and suicide.

Stevie's imbecility, on the other hand, is represented as having moral possibilities of both the most destructive and the most exalted sort. In considering him, the term which figures saliently is not "madness" but "fool." He is in the tradition of the comic jester who is free to reveal the madness and corruption of society with impunity. Further, his idealism renders him a fool of a special sort—the Quixote who is out of touch with the practical realities of the world but who reaches the heart of its moral condition by his awareness of its divergence from a lost ideal state. (It is worth recalling that Conrad had himself been called "an incorrigible, hopeless Don Quixote" by his boyhood tutor when they argued his childhood plan to go to sea [PR, p. 44].) The Assistant Commissioner, too, in his leanness and intensity, is described repeatedly as looking like the Don. Just as Ossipon considers Stevie a fool, Heat considers his chief a fool, but Heat, it is ironically emphasized, "was not quixotic." Quixotism comes to be equivalent to a clearsighted view of reality; in Stevie, it is his awareness of the reality of suffering, as in the cab ride of Chapter 8. Such naïve realism stands in contrast to the conscious or unconscious obfuscation of the truth by the other characters; it makes Stevie, for all his foolishness, one of the moral heroes of the novel.

The physical qualities of thinness and activeness, in contrast to those of fatness and laziness, come to represent the moral idealism which is at the heart of all three quixotic figures—the author, the fool, and the hero. In the crowd of figures in the novel—the Great Personage, Heat, Vladimir, Michaelis, Ossipon, Verloc, Mrs. Verloc and her mother—who are described as fat, Stevie and the Assistant Commissioner stand out as the only lean ones. Conrad's physiognomic system is not as dogmatic as Ossipon's, but the correlation of laziness, self-esteem, and complacency in the former group is in marked contrast to the moral energy, social commitment, and intellectual curosity of the latter. "Unlike his sister, who put her trust in face values, he wished to go to the bottom of the matter," Conrad says of Stevie (p. 173). The point is further enforced in the passage describing Stevie's drawing of circles while the anarchists discuss the cannibalism of modern society; it is a drawing of "cosmic chaos, the symbolism of a mad art attempting the inconceivable" (p. 45). Stevie is described, only in part ironically, as "the artist" when "in all his soul's application to the task his back quivered, his thin neck, sunk into a deep hollow at the base of the skull, seemed ready to snap" (pp. 45–46).

This is the height of intensity of the symbol of thinness, which is here physically connected with Stevie's imaginative energy. It remains to be seen that his art is a moral one. The aim of this art is impossible to fix, for it is "inconceivable," but the concentric circles may be efforts at an arrangement of spheres—of society, or of the planets—in harmonic relationship. The eccentric circles, according to mathematical definition, are parabolas; in the term is implied the Renaissance concept of the eccentricity of those, like Stevie, who cannot rest within the social order (in this case, because of its disorder), and who tend to undermine it. The circle is also a symbol of infinity, composed as it is of an infinite number of sides; and of perfection— perhaps because of its equidistance from its center. This suggestion of the ideal is traditionally accompanied by a certain fear: for some Greek thinkers, the circle was an object of suspicion due to the logical connotations of the boundless and irrational (it required the irrational number pi to solve certain of its relations). Stevie's circles suggest disorganized perfection, an irrational harmony; they are his plan of a utopia.

The circle becomes in the novel the emblem of moral freedom—with all its dangers. It is contrasted with the triangle, the delta of Verloc's code designation, which becomes the sign of enclosure and secrecy. In the pattern of the circles which Stevie draws is seen the devastating temptation of freedom— which Winnie, for example, discovers after she has killed her husband (she is free, she realizes, but for what?—"she did not exactly know what use to make of her freedom" [p. 254]). The triangle, in contrast, is the device of safety sought in isolation and hiding. It is the mark of the spy's secret identity; it is the shape of Brett Place, the site of the Verloc home; it is the form which Verloc's coattails assume when he sits down to the table. (Ironically, it is also the design of Stevie's identifying tape, which accidentally brings about the solution of the crime.) Pre-eminently, it is associated with human solitude and with the indifference of the non-human world: Winnie faces Ossipon "under the falling mist in the darkness and solitude of Brett Place, in which all sounds of life seemed lost as if in a triangular well of asphalt and bricks, of blind houses and unfeeling stones" (p. 276).

The Physical World

The two symbols, circle and triangle, may be considered to mark the poles of an axis on which the world of the novel revolves. To review the layout of this symbolic world, the themes of secrecy, ignorance, and madness describe a condition of social fragmentation which is Conrad's vision of the modern world and which is designated by the triangle. As we shall see, the enclosure and separateness of this figure correspond to states of physical isolation, as well as to the mental isolation described above. Physical fragmentation is represented in the emphasis on the private life (including private property), in the environment of stone which surrounds the characters and to which they assimilate themselves, in the insularity which is prized in all realms of life, from dwelling place to nation. The safety of physical isolation is, however, only an expedient and temporary one: its diseases are physical disorder, decay, and explosion—just as "madness and despair" were the diseases of mental isolation.

Physical disintegration begins in the tendency to reduce the human being to its component parts. Men are seen first as animals, then simply as fat, flesh, or meat. In this connection, the notion of cannibalism is introduced with telling effect. With the ultimate reduction of the human being to fragments of matter ("He's all there. Every bit of him. It was a job" [p. 87]), man is imaginatively—and literally—annihilated. Conrad is the English writer who saw, as Brecht did, that in modern life "man feeds on others."

Closely related to the reduction of man to fragments is his reduction to inorganic matter:

And Mr. Verloc, steady like a rock—a soft kind of rock—marched now along a street which could with every propriety be described as private. In its breadth, emptiness and extent it had the majesty of inorganic nature, of matter that never dies. The only reminder of mortality was a doctor's brougham arrested in august solitude close to the curbstone. The polished knockers of the doors gleamed as far as the eye could reach, the clean windows shone with a dark opaque lustre. And all was still.

But a milk cart rattled noisily across the distant perspective; a butcher boy, driving with the noble recklessness of a charioteer at Olympic Games, dashed round the corner sitting high above a pair of red wheels. A guilty-looking cat issuing from under the stones ran for a while in front of Mr. Verloc, then dived into another basement; and a thick police constable, looking a stranger to every emotion, as if he too, were part of inorganic nature, surging apparently out of lamp-post, took not the slightest notice of Mr. Verloc. (Pp. 13–14)

This passage, describing the approach of Verloc to the Embassy where the bomb plot will be hatched, is based on the image of "inorganic nature." The street is broad, empty, extensive, even majestic—and it is alien to man. It is stone—"matter that never dies." Incapable of death, the world of inorganic nature is equally incapable of life, and the doctor's brougham enforces the associations of sickness and death. The brougham is "arrested in august solitude close to the curbstone": even an instrument of motion becomes assimilated to the motionless and lonely world of stone. This inorganic world is not only of stone but of metal; the polished knockers gleaming "as far as the eye could reach" evoke a wall of armor shutting out the human spectator and enclosing a realm of private property which does not emerge from behind its doors.

"And all was still." With this masterly sentence, Conrad changes the pace of his prose and concludes the depiction of inorganic nature in its silence and immobility. At the same time he prepares for the eruption of vitality which will disturb the trance-like stillness of the street, for the butcher boy who next appears has a symbolic significance far beyond his peripheral place in the novel; "driving with the noble recklessness of a charioteer at Olympic Games," he introduces the absent world of the vital and the human. The language of the sentence gives the mundane boy heroic stature by its allusion to classical scenes of athletic glory. His reckless freedom is a style of life different from that of the holders of private property. (We remember that Winnie's romantic beau, whom she was forced to renounce because of economic necessity, was also a butcher-boy.) The other living beings in the street, however, have assimilated themselves to inorganic nature. The cat issues "from under the stones" and quickly returns to a basement world of stone. The policeman appears to surge out of a lamppost, takes no notice of the only other human present (Verloc), and seems a stranger to human emotion, "as if he, too, were part of inorganic nature."

The text following the passage quoted appears to be a gratuitous and somewhat frivolous divagation by Conrad on the subject of the irrationality

of London streets and house numbers. It emerges, however, that the irrationality of the social order is crystallized in the confusion of the urban landscape.
Its relation to the larger absurdities of society is suggested by Verloc's very
acceptance of it: "Mr. Verloc did not trouble his head about it, his mission in
life being the protection of the social mechanism, not its perfectionment or
even its criticism" (p. 15). Verloc accepts this, as he does other appearances
of the absurd, with an impassivity which is itself absurd. Like the police
constable surging out of the lamppost, like the gleaming knockers on the
exclusive doors, Verloc is opaque and inactive, having found his means of
survival in the human world by succeeding, in some measure, in turning
himself into a rock—"a soft kind of rock." (Similarly, Mrs. Verloc becomes
petrified by the loss of her brother: the sound waves of Verloc's speech
"flowed around all the inanimate things in the room, lapped against Mrs.
Verloc's head as if it had been a head of stone" [p. 260].)

In addition to the inorganic, another realm of nature is employed by *The
Secret Agent* to represent the non-human world of whatever is inimical to
genuine social life. This other realm is the animal world and its presence in
man as physical animality—represented in the extreme case by gross fatness.
In the interview at the Embassy, after Chancelier d'Embassade Wurmt has
told Verloc that he is corpulent, Vladimir remarks to the former, "You are
quite right, mon cher. He's fat—the animal" (p. 19). Men describe others
as animals in this world quite as readily as they scorn them as fools, idiots,
or children. Even Conrad indulges in the tendency, when he describes Verloc
as "undemonstrative and burly in a fat-pig style" (p. 13). The imagery of the
animal world acquires further symbolic force in the great chapter on the
cab ride of Winnie's mother to the old age home. The cabman's classical
reflections on human misery are manifested in the scrubby horse which
draws them. After Stevie philosophizes on the equally scrubby cabman's
theme, "Bad world for poor people," he concludes with wide resonance,
"Beastly!" (p. 172). The imagery of animality reaches its crescendo in the
pages following Verloc's detection by Heat and the Assistant Commissioner;
he calls his nemesis, Vladimir, "a hyperborean swine" (p. 212).

From this point on, allusions to animals follow thick and fast. The Assistant Commissioner, before reporting to the Great Personage—who is
engaged in a Parliamentary debate on a fisheries bill—passes the time with
the latter's secretary, "Toodles," in an extended metaphorical allusion to the
bomb plot based on various sorts of fishes. When Toodles inquires about the
investigator's "sprat," the latter answers that he has caught him, then de-

clares his intention of using Verloc as bait to catch a "whale." When Toodles
inquires further, the Assistant Commissioner characterizes the target,
Vladimir, as a "dog-fish." "It's a noxious, rascally-looking, altogether
detestable beast, with a sort of smooth face and moustaches," says Toodles;
his interlocutor tells him that his own target is cleanshaven, "a witty fish."
When told that the dogfish is a member of their gentlemen's club, Toodles
sums up the conversation unwittingly by exclaiming, "That's the beastliest
thing I've ever heard in my life" (pp. 215–16).

Shortly thereafter, when the Assistant Commissioner confronts Vladimir
with his knowledge of the latter's complicity in the bomb plot, the metaphor
shifts to dogs. Vladimir calls Verloc, his accuser, "a lying dog of some sort,"
and the word enters the investigator's mouth: "What pleased me most in
this affair . . . is that it makes such an excellent starting-point for a piece of
work which I've felt must be taken in hand—that is, the clearing out of this
country of all the foreign political spies, police, and that sort of—of—dogs"
(p. 226). To the Professor, who is described in the last line of the novel as a
"pest in the street full of men" (p. 311), the human community, in turn,
seems to lead an animal existence: "They swarmed numerous like locusts,
industrious like ants, thoughtless like a natural force, pushing on blind and
orderly and absorbed, impervious to sentiment, to logic, to terror, too,
perhaps" (p. 82). The entire society comes to be seen as a jungle of animal
forms obeying the laws of predatory survival. Alien to this world, forced to
live in it yet inevitably devoured, men acquire the characters of beasts. The
image of human animality is, when reduced to its lowest point, that of Mrs.
Neale, the Verloc's charwoman: "On all fours amongst the puddles, wet and
begrimed, like a sort of amphibious and domestic animal living in ashbins
and dirty water" (p. 184).

Having reduced men to stones in one cluster of images and to pigs, dogs,
and fish in another, *The Secret Agent* goes on to break them down into smaller
components—into pieces of flesh, or (potentially) meat. Verloc, who regards
Stevie as a sort of domestic animal, is thereby made ready to employ him
in a way that will reduce him further, to bits of flesh. Vladimir, in instructing
Verloc in the "philosophy of bomb-throwing," had disclaimed the intention of organizing "a mere butchery" (p. 33), yet that is just what the event
becomes: "the Chief Inspector went on peering at the table with a calm
face and the slightly anxious attention of an indigent customer bending over
what may be called the by-products of a butcher's shop with a view to an
inexpensive Sunday dinner" (p. 88). Despite his initial shock and revulsion,

Heat's dispassion—the indifference of a trained investigator—is characteristic of a society that regards human beings as things and that can easily see them as mere meat once their bodies are reduced to fragments. These fragments are possible food for those who exploit the men they once were. Heat disdains these "by-products of a butcher shop," but the remains of Stevie are compared to the "raw material for a cannibal feast" (p. 86).

When Verloc returns home, his wife places a cold roast of beef before him, "examining the sharp edge of the carving knife" as she sets it down (p. 193). After the visits of the Assistant Commissioner and Heat indicate his game is up, Verloc falls to eating again: "The piece of roast beef, laid out in the likeness of funereal baked meats for Stevie's obsequies, offered itself largely to his notice. And Mr. Verloc again partook. He partook ravenously, without restraint and decency, cutting thick slices with the sharp carving knife, and swallowing them without bread" (p. 253). What Verloc is eating is the very flesh of Stevie: the metaphor of a funeral banquet suggests Stevie's remains laid out on the table in the morgue. But Verloc becomes mere meat in his turn: the carving knife with which he savagely cuts the beef will shortly become the instrument of his wife's revenge. Then Verloc himself will be fragmented: the shadow of his corpse, his blood dripping like the ticking of a clock, his hat "rocking slightly on its crown" in the middle of the floor— all the images of the dead are of dismemberment into organic flesh or inorganic objects. Finally, his blood forms a "beastly pool" around his solitary hat, both separated from his human body (p. 287).

The imagery of cannibalism is in accord with anarchist doctrine. It is Karl Yundt, the most repulsive of the sham revolutionaries, who suggests this vision of modern society: "Do you know how I would call the nature of the present economic conditions? I would call it cannibalistic. That's what it is! They are nourishing their greed on the quivering flesh and the warm blood of the people—nothing else" (p. 51). In this form, the image seems an exaggeration and a piece of anarchist lunacy. The novel proves it to be an accurate description of the relationships among men in a fragmented society. In this condition men are dismembered not only accidentally or metaphorically but systematically—as in the report of the German recruits whose ears were torn off by their officers. It is this condition that Stevie wishes to rectify; he had seized the avenging carving knive and "would have stuck that officer like a pig if he had seen him then" (p. 60). However, it is for him to be dismembered and for his sister to stick his porcine destroyer dead.

The ultimate reduction of man, even beyond fragmentation into flesh and transformation into matter, is his total annihilation. The death of Verloc brings on the same kind of crescendo of "nothing" as occurs in *King Lear*:

> Nothing brings them [the dead] back, neither love nor hate. They can do nothing to you. They are as nothing. . . . now he was of no account in every respect. He was of less practical account than the clothing on his body, than his overcoat, than his boots—than that hat lying on the floor. He was nothing. . . . that man, who was less than nothing now. . . . (Pp. 266–67)

This metaphor of the nothingness of man was made literal on a mass scale in the concentration camps of recent history. On this basis, we are prepared to see Winnie's incoherent muttering—"Blood and dirt. Blood and dirt" (p. 290)—not only as a reflection on the state to which her brother has been reduced, but as a vision of the course of human history. It is this vision which stands behind the Professor's statement that "blood alone puts a seal on greatness. . . . Blood. Death. Look at history" (p. 304).

Space and Time

The themes of isolation, secrecy, and ignorance achieve a spatial form in *The Secret Agent* in images of insularity. The world is composed of a scattering of islands, which separate men from each other as effectively as Verloc and his wife are separated in their own home. The prevalence of islands resembles a childhood game: the Verlocs are islands to each other, their home is an island of life—such as it is—in the gloom of Brett Place, the street is in turn an island of seclusion in the busy streets of London, and the city of gloom becomes an island of activity on the darkened island of Britain. There is some contact between these islands: Verloc is as Continental as he is English, he makes frequent trips to the Continent to buy pornographic materials for his shop, and he goes there during the action of the novel to try to find someone to do the bombing. But for him, for Mrs. Verloc after she has killed him, and for Ossipon when he seeks to escape with her, England is an enclosing space, a prison. Their visions of escape to Spain or South America (Verloc), Spain or California (Mrs. Verloc), Spain or Italy (Ossipon) seem fantastic in the context of the limited world of the novel. Ossipon sees it so when he seeks to escape with Mrs. Verloc: "The insular nature of Great Britain obtruded itself upon his notice in an odious form. 'Might just as well be put under lock and key every night,' he thought irritably, as non-plussed as though he had a wall to scale with the woman on his back" (pp. 282–83).

Here the images of island and wall come together to reinforce the sense of physical isolation which corresponds to the prevailing social and personal isolation. The ultimate version of this isolation is Winnie's sense of existence as an undifferentiated continuum completely surrounding her: "Mrs. Verloc gazed at the whitewashed wall. A blank wall—perfectly blank. A blankness to run at and dash your head against. Mrs. Verloc remained immovably seated" (p. 244). Similarly, Verloc's "intense meditation, like a sort of Chinese wall, isolated him completely from the phenomena of this world of vain effort and illusory appearances" (p. 154).

Dominated by such images, *The Secret Agent* becomes as much a novel of London, as much a reflection of its author's sense of place, as *Our Mutual Friend* or *The Princess Casamassima.* Conrad confessed: "I had to fight hard to keep at arms-length the memories of my solitary and nocturnal walks all over London in my early days, lest they should rush in and overwhelm each page of the story" (p. xiii). Places in this world are separated from one another like concentric circles that never touch. For this reason, any movement through London seems an uncanny experience. Verloc's trip to the Embassy is described in a tone of amazement: "Mr. Verloc was going westward through a town without shadows in an atmosphere of powdered old gold" (p. 11). In Ossipon's long walk home after sending Winnie to her death—"He walked through Squares, Places, Ovals, Commons, through monotonous streets with unknown names where the dust of humanity settles inert and hopeless out of the stream of life" (p. 300)—London appears as an engulfing fog in which men live in ignorance of other men and of their surroundings. Perhaps the most perfect image of this static relation of men to their environment is that of the macabre cab that brings Winnie, Stevie, and their mother to the old age home: "in the wider space of Whitehall, all visual evidences of motion become imperceptible. The rattle and jingle of glass went on indefinitely in front of the long Treasury building—and time itself seemed to stand still" (pp. 156–57).

Not only are men isolated from their world, but their world is hostile to them. It is an "enormity of cold, black, wet, muddy, inhospitable accumulation of bricks, slates, and stones, things in themselves unlovely and unfriendly to man" (p. 56). In such a world it is the habit of men to protect themselves through indifference. The irony of Vladimir's bomb plot, intended though it is to shake public opinion (which is indifferent to everything not practical and "scientific"), is that it does not succeed even though the bomb goes off:

the grimy sky, the mud of the streets, the rags of the dirty men harmonized excellently with the eruption of the deep, rubbishy sheets of paper soiled with printer's ink. The posters, maculated with filth, garnished like tapestry the sweep of the curbstone. The trade in afternoon papers was brisk, yet, in comparison with the swift, constant march of foot traffic, the effect was of indifference, of a disregarded distribution. (P. 79)

Ultimately, for the asocial murderess, the city becomes the abyss: "She was alone in London: and the whole town of marvels and mud, with its maze of streets and its mass of lights, was sunk in a hopeless night, rested at the bottom of a black abyss from which no unaided woman could hope to scramble out" (pp. 270–71). The felt spatiality is thus summed up: "The vast world created for the glory of man was only a vast blank to Mrs. Verloc" (p. 270).

The Secret Agent establishes the city of London as the spatial expression of its moral universe. Equally, the sense of time lies at the heart of the novel's theme. Much has already been observed and written of the importance of time in the plot to destroy the First Meridian, but it remains to be noted how precisely the events of the story are fixed in time, and how the effort to destroy time is symbolically an effort to end history—thereby theoretically achieving the revolutionary goal of a world beyond history and without time. In the present world, time is of the essence; almost everyone complains of lack of time, and all are perpetually conscious of the presence of time and their dependence on it. In the absence of community, a common time standard is a mechanical substitute to create social order.

The first step in estimating the action of time in *The Secret Agent* is, therefore, to establish a chronology of events, for which purpose Conrad has deftly provided precise information. The action of the novel takes place in the spring of 1886: Winnie's wedding ring is found (after her suicide), inscribed with her marriage date, June 24, 1879 (p. 309), and the Verlocs have been married seven years at this time (p. 276). Verloc is called to the Embassy and while there notices "his first fly of the year—heralding better than any number of swallows the approach of spring" (p. 27). (A confirmation of the date is given when Heat tells the Assistant Commissioner that he first met Verloc seven years before, and that Verloc was reported to have married at that time [pp. 129–30].) About a week later, on the day when Winnie's mother goes to the old age home, Verloc announces he is going to the Continent. He returns from the Continent ten days later (p. 182); after another interval of about a week, during which he takes Stevie out with

him on his walks, he announces he will take the boy to Michaelis' country
retreat, and does so on the following day (p. 189). Again an interval of perhaps a week follows, and Verloc takes the boy on his fatal mission. The rest
of the novel's action, apart from a short coda, takes place on that day, which
is specified as a month after the beginning of Verloc's worries (p. 240)—
thus the accumulation of three periods of about a week each, plus the definite
lapse of ten days.

The events of the decisive day of bombing, murder, and suicide are indicated with even greater specificity. Verloc goes out "very early that morning"
(p. 190), according to his wife's recollection. He picks Stevie up at Michaelis'
country retreat in Kent at 8 A.M., according to the Assistant Commissioner
(p. 218). The newspapers report, as Ossipon tells the Professor, that the
explosion occurred at "half-past eleven" (p. 70). The news is out at 2 P.M.,
when Ossipon buys a paper and runs into the Silenus hall, where he sits an
hour before meeting the Professor (p. 63). The Professor, coming from the
cafe after 3 P.M., meets Heat, who is on his way to report to the Assistant
Commissioner from the hospital morgue, where he has discovered Verloc's
address among Stevie's effects.

The subsequent detective work by the Assistant Commissioner takes place
in the late afternoon and evening. First he worms out of Heat the incriminat-
ing label and the secret of his special relationship to Verloc. He then receives
permission from the Great Personage to conduct the investigation in his
own way. He changes his clothes and acquires a foreign appearance, dines in
the Soho restaurant, converses with Mrs. Verloc, and takes Verloc away
with him to the Continental Hotel for an interview. He returns to Whitehall
to report to the Great Personage, then joins his wife at the home of Michaelis'
patroness. He imparts his knowledge of Vladimir's complicity to the latter
as they leave the party, and ends the day as he turns away from the Explorer's
Club at "half-past ten. He had had a very full evening" (p. 228).

Events in the underworld are not as fully elaborated, but at one point
they acquire an almost minute-by-minute notation. After Verloc returns
home, he has interviews first with the Assistant Commissioner and later with
Heat. During the latter talk, his wife discovers that he has caused her brother
to be killed. He attempts to dissuade her from leaving at "five and twenty
minutes past eight" (p. 255). She kills Verloc at 8:49 P.M., for one minute
later it is "ten minutes to nine" (p. 264). As she is about to rush out to kill
herself, she sees the clock: "she could not believe that only two minutes
had passed since she had looked at it last. . . . As a matter of fact, only

three minutes had elapsed from the moment she had drawn the first deep, easy breath after the blow, to this moment . . ." (pp. 268–69).

At this point, Winnie encounters Ossipon, and he, seeking a way out of the country, remembers that there is a channel boat at midnight and a boat train at 10:30 (p. 283). Ossipon drops Winnie as the train leaves—it is exactly the time at which the Assistant Commissioner drops Vladimir and concludes his day. Winnie sails at midnight, and is last seen alive at about 4:55 A.M., for when the stewardess and chief steward on the boat return to her "less than five minutes" after leaving her, she is gone: "It was then five o'clock in the morning" (p. 309). Ossipon's movements after leaving Winnie are also temporally fixed: he walks, presumably from Waterloo Station, passes Westminster and Victoria Station, returns to the river, and sees and hears a clock tower ringing "half-past twelve of a wild night in the Channel" (p. 300). He walks all night, sits up openeyed all day, and falls asleep "when the late sun sent its rays into the room" (p. 301). The coda occurs ten days later, when Ossipon and the Professor have their second conversation at the Silenus; the former produces the newspaper "ten days old" (p. 306) that tells of Winnie's suicide.

Time in *The Secret Agent* is not, however, merely a determinate measure of events precisely recorded and sequentially related. The chronology given above may be considered the objective history of the novel's world, but it is rendered in the narrative by indirection and out of sequence, according to the subjective impressions of the persons concerned with given events or moments of time. The "indirect" method of impressionist fiction is employed by Conrad to create a time structure of events in the form in which they are experienced. As has been pointed out by such modern philosophers as Bergson, Husserl, and Whitehead, there are other sorts of time then chronological or historical time. There is lived, subjective time, the shape that time assumes in consciousness as events impress themselves upon it with varying emotional force. In addition, there is abstract time, the logical construct which appears in astronomy and physics. An abstract view of time somewhat of the latter sort appears also in the millenarian visions of historical theories like Marxism. Both these aspects of time, the subjective and the abstract, figure largely in *The Secret Agent*.

Expressions of subjective time are made by or about almost every character in the novel. They include repeated complaints by the Great Personage about his limited time, Verloc's lack of time to escape his death blow, Vladimir's urgent requirement that the bombing shall take place before the Congress of

Milan has dispersed, Ossipon's sense of being trapped by the timetable of the channel boat, and the Professor's need of time to perfect the perfect bomb— the bomb that will end human time. It is only Mrs. Verloc, after the murder, who feels free of time (at least temporarily); she looks at the clock with incomprehension, for she "cared nothing for time, and the ticking went on" (p. 264). She has only a few hours to live, and only the living are bound by time.

Like the revolutionary, Heat is aware that his job is never finished—is inherently incomplete as long as time and history go on: "A given anarchist may be watched inch by inch and minute by minute, but a moment always comes when somehow all sight and touch of him are lost for a few hours, during which something (generally an explosion) more or less deplorable" happens (p. 85). Men are weighed down by time; the Assistant Commissioner expresses his boredom with his desk job and the weather: "Horrible, horrible. . . . We have been having this sort of thing now for ten days; no, a fortnight— a fortnight" (p. 100). Another type of subjective time is Verloc's illusory sense of assurance that "there would be always time enough" to tell Winnie of his orders to blow up the Observatory. On the other hand, the conclusion of his reveries suggests that he has some awareness of his impending doom:

> She let the lonely clock on the landing count off fifteen ticks into the abyss of eternity, and asked:
> "Shall I put the light out?"
> Mr. Verloc snapped at his wife huskily.
> "Put it out." (P. 181)

It is under this same clock that Stevie mopes as he awaits his destiny (p. 185). The clocks in the Verloc household are omnipresent in the characters' feelings, behavior, and consciousness. The distortion of time consciousness extends to the transformation of clocks themselves, which Winnie experiences after murdering her husband:

> Nothing moved in the parlour till Mrs. Verloc raised her head slowly and looked at the clock with inquiring mistrust. She had become aware of a ticking sound in the room. It grew upon her ear, while she remembered clearly that the clock on the wall was silent, had no audible tick. What did it mean by beginning to tick so loudly all of a sudden? Its face indicated ten minutes to nine. Mrs. Verloc cared nothing for time, and the ticking went on. . . . Dark drops fell on the floorcloth one after another, with a sound of ticking growing fast and furious like the pulse of an insane clock.

At its highest speed this ticking changed into a continuous sound of trickling. Mrs. Verloc watched that transformation with shadows of anxiety coming and going on her face. It was a trickle, dark, swift, thin. . . . Blood! (Pp. 264–65)

Winnie experiences what existential psychoanalysts have called the "flight of time," its apparent acceleration after the subjective congealment that had occurred just after the murder, when time seemed to stand still. Now time rushes away from Winnie, for her time has run out. Time has become eternity, for as the speed of the drops of blood increases, the interval between them decreases. When the interval is eliminated and the dripping becomes a steady stream, there is no longer a procession of moments but a fusion of them into one timeless moment. The final measure of time becomes personal in the crudest sense, for Winnie substitutes her husband's body for the ordinary clock of public chronology. The flow of his blood becomes the measure of the passage of time and of the diminishing substance of her life. She has destroyed time and made a timeless present—death.

If in *The Secret Agent* the substance of the plot is an attempt to destroy the historical order of time by blowing up the First Meridian, the novel also proposes a vision of time beyond history. Concerned as it is to provide an image of historical reality by giving the fragmentation of the city and its secret ways of life the force of a symbol, the novel seeks also to consider a world without time, a world free of the moral and physical decay of history. The ultimate suggestion of the novel is that there are no utopias and no timeless heavens, not because of original sin or revolutionary evil, but because man is inherently a historical being, time-bound and time-filled.

The first indication that man is bound by history is given in Conrad's version of anarchist doctrine (which is actually much closer to the economic determinism of Marxism):

History is made by men, but they do not make it in their heads. The ideas that are born in their consciousness play an insignificant part in the march of events. History is dominated and determined by the tool and the production—by the force of economic conditions. Capitalism has made socialism and the laws made by capitalism for the protection of property are responsible for anarchism. No one can tell what form the social organization may take in the future. Then why indulge in prophetic phantasies? At best they can only interpret the mind of the prophet, and can have no objective value. Leave that pastime to the moralists, my boy. (P. 41)

Ironically, this mechanical-determinist speech is uttered by Michaelis, the most utopian of the anarchists and the one who later immerses himself in visions of a future society run, as the Professor says, like a hospital, "in which the strong are to devote themselves to the nursing of the weak" (p. 303). Conrad seems to have ascribed an exaggerated form of Marxism to the anarchists, and then showed its issue in non-Marxist utopian dreams.

What is equally ironic is that at least the opening of the speech echoes Marx closely enough to raise the question of Conrad's knowledge of the philosopher. In the Marxist formulation of the limitations of utopian planning, historical change depends not only on the history of economic forces, but also on men's tradition-shaped *consciousness* of the past, and on the special conditions of each nation's development:

> Men make their own history, but they do not make it just as they please; they do not make it under circumstances chosen by themselves, but under circumstances directly encountered, given, and transmitted from the past. The tradition of all the dead generations weighs like a nightmare on the brain of the living. And just when they seem engaged in revolutionizing themselves and things, in creating something that has never yet existed, precisely in such periods of revolutionary crisis they anxiously conjure up the spirits of the past to their service and borrow from them names, battle cries, and costumes in order to present the new scene of world history in this time-honored disguise and this borrowed language.[8]

Michaelis' fatalistic sense of history is as crude a distortion of Marx's thought as is his utopianism. The anarchists' utopianism is not the less scorned for being presented through the eyes of the Professor; if the latter finds it contemptible because of its humanitarianism, Conrad finds it so because of its rejection of time. Conrad's distance from utopianism is as explicit as that of Marx; they are similarly committed to history as the source of the consciousness and the momentum by which men project their future from their present politics. As Conrad put it elsewhere, "There can be no evolution out of a grave" (*NLL*, p. 99); likewise, there can be no utopia born of destruction, without an organic historical development.

The anarchist, represented in his extreme form by the Professor, is dissatisfied not only with the difficulties presented by life in history but with

[8] Karl Marx, *The Eighteenth Brumaire of Louis Bonaparte*, quoted in *Marx and Engels: Basic Writings on Politics and Philosophy*, ed. Lewis S. Feuer (Garden City, N.Y., 1959), p. 320.

the "poor expedients" devised by man to keep himself alive within it—
"accepted morality, self-restraint, and toil" (p. 53). He is oppressed by
human limitation and by historical contingency; as the Professor puts it:
"They depend on life, which, in this connection, is a historical fact surrounded by all sorts of restraints and considerations, a complex, organized
fact open to attack at every point; whereas I depend on death, which knows
no restraint and cannot be attacked. My superiority is evident" (p. 68). By
putting himself on the side not of life but of death, the anarchist seeks to
overcome the constraint of time. The failure of the Professor's position,
however, is not only that there are too many men for him to kill, as he is
himself aware (p. 82), nor only that he lacks adequate time to accomplish universal destruction, as Ossipon taunts him (p. 305). Modern science and
politics have changed that, and it is now possible to destroy the world rather
quickly. But the would-be destroyer of time cannot transcend the limitations
of human life which is lived in time. His ideal bomb is an impersonal machine,
but it must have a fallible human mind as well—it must be "a really intelligent detonator" (p. 67). The Professor's bomb works by "a combination of
time and shock" (p. 76): it is dependent on the very medium it seeks to
destroy. Finally, it is mortal, like its maker: the Professor, who seeks to
annihilate the present, "had no future" (p. 311).

The severest critic of the Professor's philosophy of history is Ossipon, who
has listened patiently as he explained it at the Silenus hall early in the novel.
In the final chapter, Ossipon suddenly turns upon him:

> Just now you've been crying for time—time. Well, the doctors will serve
> you out your time—if you are good. You profess yourself to be one of the
> strong—because you carry in your pocket enough stuff to send yourself
> and, say, twenty other people, into eternity. But eternity is a damned
> hole. It's time that you need. You—if you met a man who could give you
> for certain ten years of time, you would call him you master. . . . Wait
> till you are lying flat on your back at the end of your time. . . . Your
> scurvy, shabby, mangy little bit of time. (Pp. 305–6)

Ossipon has been a spokesman for science—that is, for the narrowly materialist view of science popular at the turn of the century. He has examined and
categorized Stevie with an impersonal interest in his earlobes and drawings.
He has scoffed at the historical predictions of the anarchists as unscientific:
"There is no law and no certainty" (p. 50). In the later scene, Ossipon faces
the problem of history from an altered viewpoint. He is preoccupied with his

responsibility for Winnie's death, the newspaper phrases on her suicide are ringing in his mind, and he now makes paramount the fact of life in the present. From this viewpoint, the possession of time is the only good, for "mankind wants to live—to live" (p. 305). By another standard, time is a moral reward; the doctor-rulers of his own scientific utopia will confer it "if you are good." It is also a political weapon, for men would become slaves of the person who could confer time—life itself—upon them. Above all, the shortness of life and the frailty of man are seen against the magnitude of the universe's time, eternity, which is, for the human life that is drowned in it, "a damned hole." Ossipon is converted, in his agony of conscience and awe of death, into a believer in the ultimate value of human life and of the oppressive, yet necessary, rootedness of humans in time.

The Secret Agent is, then, not as much a novel about political anarchism as it is a novel about social anarchy. It is a dramatic portrayal of the sociological concept of "anomie"—radical disorder in the social structure and consequent personal dislocation. Despite its ironic skepticism, the novel carries with it certain implications for conduct. It does not amount to a political program, to be sure, any more than it amounts to a moral code, but it suggests an ideal of social order by its very representation of a world without order. Above all, it proposes the value of human community. As Heat discovers, shortly after his reflection on the absurdity of things human, "the murmur of town life, the subdued rumble of wheels in the two invisible streets to the right and left, came through the curve of the sordid lane to his ears with a precious familiarity and an appealing sweetness. He was human" (p. 94). After the images of fragmentation, the "street full of men" is the positive note on which the novel closes.

Within this view of the novel's concern with social community and social fragmentation, it is possible to make a balanced estimate of its political implications. Not the irrational caricature of revolutionists it has occasionally been taken to be, the novel makes an implicit appeal for restraint in public policy towards them. The Professor accurately says, "Nothing would please me more than to see Inspector Heat and his likes take to shooting us down in broad daylight with the approval of the public. Half our battle would be won then; the disintegration of the old morality would have set in in its very temple" (p. 73). A more questionable but equally prominent implication of the novel is also formulated by the Professor: "Like to like. The terrorist and the policeman both come from the same basket. Revolution, legality— counter moves in the same game" (p. 69). The novel effectively dramatizes this equation, at least as far as Verloc, Vladimir, and Heat are concerned. The Assistant Commissioner, on the other hand, by his willingness to act against all disturbers of the social order, counter-revolutionary as well as revolutionary, is the exception in the continuum of secrecy, fragmentation, and absurdity which constitutes modern political life.

We can sum up the political values suggested in the character of the Assistant Commissioner by referring to the career of the statesman whose reflection, in the shape of the Great Personage, looms up in *The Secret Agent* as a symbol. Sir William Harcourt was the Home Secretary, described in former Assistant Commissioner Robert Anderson's *Sidelights on the Home Rule Movement*, who made the well-known germinal remark about being kept in secrecy by his department. He does not, however, emerge in the novel with his full political significance. It is rather his delectable ponderousness and his muddled acerbity of which Conrad makes capital. Harcourt's quasi-socialism—he was the author of the "death duties" bill which began the modern English process of social equalization by high inheritance taxes— does not become an issue. Yet it is a fisheries bill, presumably regulating private use of public property, which is being debated at the time of the novel's action. "That brute Cheeseman," his virulent opponent, is, by association, Joseph Chamberlain, Harcourt's colleague in Gladstone's second ministry and also originally a Radical, who later turned away from social reform to promulgate militant jingoism.[9]

Sir William Harcourt represents a traditional English political type, and in *The Secret Agent* both the Great Personage and the Assistant Commissioner dramatically embody it. As his official biography sums it up:

> He himself delighted in proclaiming his Philistinism, by which he meant the plain interpretation and acceptance of the realities of life as he perceived them. "It was the Philistines who made England," he would say, and for those who, like Cromwell, sought to mould the politics of this world on the assumptions of the next he had small respect. "I am of the earth, earthy," he said, and his idealism in affairs was bounded by the horizon

[9] Harcourt, on the other hand, was close to Conrad's position as a leading "pro-Boer." Cf. Elie Halévy, *A History of the English People in the Nineteenth Century*, Vol. V: *Imperialism and the Rise of Labour, 1895–1905*, trans. E. I. Watkin and D. A. Barker (6 vols., orig. pub., 1926; New York, 1961), p. 51 ff.

of the visible and the known. But within that horizon his mind worked under the governance of powerful moral ideas which were the heritage of generations of public service. . . .[10]

It is this faintly comic figure, with his disarming acknowledgment of his own and the world's limitations, who stands before the madness of the political world of *The Secret Agent*—and before the mass insanity of recent history—as a pillar of dignified strength. He has behind him the weight of an organic community and its moral and political values, though these are threatened by modern anomie.

[10] A. G. Gardiner, *The Life of Sir William Harcourt* (New York, n.d.,), II, 595.

Chapter VIII

UNDER WESTERN EYES:
CONRAD'S VISION OF
COMMUNITY

Michael Bakunin

Evno Azoff

. . cet *Eldorado bourgeois où, sous les
apparences les plus républicaines et
démocratiques, la bourgeoisie suisse se
constitue et développe ses intérêts de classe
en toute tranquillité—la révolution sociale
étant impossible dans un pays où la légalité
et l'esprit de progrès sage ont si profondément
pénétré les moeurs politiques.*

—A Swiss Anarchist
Geneva, 1879

The strengths and weaknesses of Conrad's political fiction may best be estimated in the last of his full-scale tales of contemporary affairs, *Under Western Eyes*. After this novel, published in 1911, Conrad embarked on the commercially successful stage of his career, later returning to political themes only at the remove of historical perspective. Yet this book, neither as substantial a realization of living history as *Nostromo* nor as imaginative an expression of ideas as *The Secret Agent*, is psychologically the most mature of his political novels.

Under Western Eyes was the subject of an angry exchange of letters when Conrad's slowly cooling friend, Edward Garnett, remarked on the personal bias in Conrad's depiction of the Russian characters. The debate had previously taken another form when Conrad rejected Garnett's invitation to participate in a political rally at which he would have had to share the platform with Russian political figures. At that time, Conrad justified his refusal as based on racial antipathy rather than political judgment. On the present occasion, Conrad wrote:

> are you like the Italians (and most women) incapable of conceiving that anybody ever should speak with perfect detachment, without some subtle hidden purpose, for the sake of what is said, with no desire of gratifying some small personal spite—or vanity. . . . anyhow if hatred there were it would be too big a thing to be put into a 6/-novel.[1]

Conrad's detachment was clearly less than perfect, but it may not be a loss to the novel that it is more heavily invested with passion than any other of his political writings. The much-remarked dampening effect of the narrator of the novel, the Western eye of the English teacher of languages, has been regarded as Conrad's attempt to mute the intensity of his involvement with the subject, but the impression is only magnified by his efforts.

In the Author's Note to the novel, Conrad acknowledged the possibility of prejudice against his Russian characters because of his antipathy to Russians generally, and revealed the difficulty of his effort to overcome it:

> My greatest anxiety was in being able to strike and sustain the note of scrupulous impartiality. The obligation of absolute fairness was imposed on me historically and hereditarily, by the peculiar experience of race and family. . . . I had never been called before to a greater effort of detachment: detachment from all passions, prejudices and even from personal memories. (*UWE*, p. viii)

Yet if he had succeeded in writing with such detachment, the novel would not be the intense aesthetic experience it is. Fortunately, some of the passion

[1] Garnett Letters, pp. 249–50, letter of October 20, 1911.

penetrated his artistic sensibility—not enough to disturb the artistic economy of the novel by exceeding the objective correlative of his characters, but enough to inform the hero's situation with personal urgency.

The Author's Note to *Under Western Eyes* makes a further effort to obviate Conrad's personal relationship to his work. He points out his lack of specialized knowledge and disclaims credit for the accuracy of his predictions of the Russian Revolution; his object was to "express imaginatively the general truth which underlies its action, together with my honest convictions as to the moral complexion of certain facts more or less known to the whole world" (p. vii). Conrad goes on to insist on the general rather than specific character both of his knowledge and of his portrayal, not once but twice on a single page ("It is the result not of a special experience but of general knowledge"; "The various figures playing their part in the story also owe their existence to no special experience but to the general knowledge of the condition of Russia" [p. viii]). Yet Conrad's art belies his pretensions both as to generality of sources and as to generality of expression. If the novel were reducible to a general formula, as he implies, it would not be the passionate rendering of political experience it is.

What special knowledge could Conrad have had of the subject of *Under Western Eyes*, which treats of revolutionary *émigrés* in Russia and Switzerland? The subject lacks even the immediacy of the English setting of *The Secret Agent*—a novel whose subject was felt to be outside the scope of an entirely English writer in the first decade of this century. It has been said of the latter novel also that it presupposes a direct knowledge of radical psychology that was at best questionable in an apparently respectable and conservative author. The precise details taken from history for the Russian-Swiss novel even more markedly reveal a familiarity with revolutionary matters which cannot be explained merely by Conrad's periodic residence in Switzerland for health cures.

A list of these modelings from facts at that time not widely known constitutes substantial evidence, if not of special sources of information, at least of Conrad's dedicated interest in the subject. The main anarchist figure, Peter Ivanovitch, is elaborately patterned after Michael Bakunin, who had been a dissolute aristocratic youth and repentant convert to revolution; an escapee from imprisonment whose route went eastward across Siberia; a populist, nihilist, and elitist (cf. *UWE*, pp. 211–12); a man who idealized womankind and lived largely on the contributions of his infatuated followers (which included a villa on a Swiss lake); an inflated, almost comic figure in mind and body.[2] Bakunin also led an unsuccessful naval expedition to bring several hundred men to the Polish revolutionary army, taking ship from England for Lithuania; a similar affair is plotted by the revolutionaries at Peter Ivanovitch's apartment (p. 330). Such minutiae identify the model as Bakunin, even though another anarchist martyr and prophet, Prince Kropotkin, was lionized in England at the time. Conrad knew his anarchists well enough to distinguish their politics and personalities.

The assassination in which Razumov is falsely implicated takes its details from the assassination of Alexander II in 1882, not, as Conrad misleadingly suggested, from that of the Interior Minister, De Plehve, which occurred under different circumstances in 1904. A bomb damaged the Czar's sleigh, causing him to alight and inquire about the injured, upon which a second bomb went off at his feet, killing him and others in the crowd that had gathered.[3] Detailed knowledge was also necessary for the depiction of the police investigation under Councillor Mikulin, who, like Zubatov of the Ochrana (the czarist secret police), made a procedure of selecting for brainwashing one man among the revolutionaries arrested in a given case, even taking a fatherly interest in him and helping to restore his career if he implicated the others.[4] It would have required some sophistication to know that the betrayer of the assassins of Alexander II was one of their own number, Rysakov, whose name resembles that of the novel's hero..

At least one of Conrad's published sources can be traced, that of the incident in which Mikulin discloses to Peter Ivanovitch the duplicity of the *agent provocateur* Nikita while they are traveling in a railway carriage outside Russia. A. A. Lopuchin, a chief of the Ochrana, similarly revealed the police spy Evno Azoff to the revolutionary leader Vladimir Burtsev while they were thrown together by chance on a German train. Both the historical and the fictional spy chiefs were demoted and exiled for their indiscretions (see *UWE*, pp. 306, 381). Conrad must have known the story of Lopuchin's undoing from an article, "The Russian Spy System: The Azeff Scandals in Russia," signed D. S., in *The English Review* (I, 816–32)—the magazine on

[2] See E. H. Carr, *Michael Bakunin* (London, 1937); cf. also Michaelis of *The Secret Agent*, who is similar to Bakunin in name, in physiognomy, and in some points of ideology.

[3] Franco Venturi, *Roots of Revolution: A History of the Populist and Socialist Movements in Nineteenth Century Russia*, trans. Frances Haskell (orig. pub., 1952; New York, 1960), p. 713 ff.

[4] A. T. Vassilyev, *The Ochrana: The Russian Secret Police*, ed. René Fülöp-Miller (Philadelphia, 1930), p. 60.

which Conrad collaborated with its editor, Ford Madox Hueffer. Indeed, this article, published in 1909 as *Under Western Eyes* was begun, stands for the same principles in counter-revolutionary police activity as those proposed in *The Secret Agent* by the Assistant Commissioner—which are unquestionably those of Conrad himself.[5] This article may also be the source of Conrad's allusion to Father Gapon, in the reference to a Father Zosim who gives Razumov a letter of introduction to the revolutionaries, but who is actually a police spy (pp. 136–37).

Conrad had at least one other readily identifiable source of information about the private fortunes of revolutionaries—his own family. A close analogue of the plot of *Under Western Eyes*, at least of Razumov's predicament and the blasting of his hopes of advancement, lies among the Bobrowski letters which have recently been translated. His uncle recounts in several letters the stages of the arrest, trial, and sentencing of Conrad's cousin, Stanislaw Bobrowski, and as these tell the story with many of the details that appear in the novel, they may be quoted in sequence:

> Stanislaw has a worthy character and is already a man, but less pleasant— very presumptuous and rather a doctrinaire. Possibly he has, in fact, ultra-democratic notions which, however, he keeps to himself either out of consideration for his paternal Uncle or else not wishing to "cast pearls before swine." He is rather reserved and rather cold.[6]

> I can't recollect if I had already mentioned to you that the poor lad got arrested on the 3/15 January this year, and accused of some political or rather social propaganda. He is still under lock and key in the Warsaw citadel. It seems to me to be nothing more than simply a case of un- authorized teaching of artisans—but as there is about it a tint of nationalism, it becomes complicated. The exceptional ad hoc procedure is carried out in secrecy and an exceptional penalty may be imposed on the poor devil,

[5] The article describes Azoff's remarkable career, in which he began selling out his playmates as early as childhood, rose to a leading position in the Russian Social Revolutionary Party while maintaining contact with the chief of the Ochrana, organized the assassination of De Plehve by the Social Revolutionaries, then joined the head of the Ochrana in instigating an attempt on the life of Nicholas III, whom his chief wanted to replace with Prince Michael. The writer concludes with an eloquent warning of the dangers inherent in police employ- ment of *agents provocateurs*, paraphrasing the Assistant Commissioner's observa- tion that such men are professionally inclined to manufacture terrorism where none exists, thus disturbing public tranquility and even, as in the Azoff affair, threatening the stability of the state.

[6] Najder (ed.), *Conrad's Polish Background*, p. 149, letter of August 14/26, 1891.

ruining his present life—for he was just about to finish the University—and possibly even his whole future.[7]

. . . in any case this poor boy has spoiled his future, and knowing him, it is difficult to believe him to be as guilty as he seems. His reputation must have been tarnished by false appearances or friends.[8]

You wish and expect before your departure to have some definite news of Stanislaw. Alas, it is not as easy as it seems. . . . Whichever way it goes he is a lost man—especially as he has studied law—he could never become either a government official, a solicitor, or a notary—not even in Kamchatka!! His whole life had gone off the rails—together with all the hopes and confidence I had placed in him.[9]

On the 8/20th May, Stanislaw was taken to St. Petersburg to serve his sentence—a year and a half in prison. . . .[10]

Although the quietist uncle tended to discount the radicalism of his nephew and thought the Russians would feel threatened by his teaching of artisans only if it had a nationalist cast, it is fairly clear that Stanislaw Bobrowski was not another version of the family's nationalist heritage in the last decade of the century, but was—to put it in the term used in the first letter—"ultra-democratic."

Conrad could not, therefore, have been as naïve about revolutionary politics as he was sometimes disposed to maintain. Why he should have tried to do so will remain a matter of speculation, although it seems reasonable to believe that a show of intimate acquaintance with the politics and personalities of eastern Europe would have rendered him alien in the "Western eyes" of his public. That his critics have by and large been convinced by this pose is explainable only by their employment of political rather than literary standards of judgment—their critical pieties notwithstanding. On the strength of his knowledge of revolutionary history, Conrad's view of the revolutionaries in *Under Western Eyes* developed into an incisive and humane one, rather than the narrowly prejudiced attitude some of his critics have thought he shared with them.

Throughout the text of the novel there are outspoken and apparently definitive statements of Conrad's view on revolutionaries and revolution.

---

[7] *Ibid.*, p. 162, letter of May 2/14, 1892.
[8] *Ibid.*, p. 163, letter of July 2/14, 1892.
[9] *Ibid.*, p. 168, letter of October 5/17, 1892.
[10] *Ibid.*, p. 172, letter of July 1/13, 1893.

In the much-quoted Author's Note, the simple estimate of revolution as "merely a change of names" and the classicist skepticism of the utopian belief that "a fundamental change of hearts must follow the downfall of any given human institutions" are, when taken in context, relevant not to revolution generally but to Russian revolution in particular. The passage concludes: "The oppressors and the oppressed are all Russians together; and the world is brought once more face to face with the truth of the saying that the tiger cannot change his stripes nor the leopard his spots" (p. x). The cliché implies a strain of racism in Conrad's thoughts on Russia, and not fatalism about all revolutions.

To assess Conrad's position on Russia and its then-impending revolution, it is worth recalling the essay he wrote after the 1905 revolution, "Autocracy and War." There he put forward the following points: (a) czarism is barbaric, outside the stream of human progress, and entirely sterile; (b) "there can be no evolution out of a grave," therefore revolution is inevitable; (c) the Russian Revolution will create a new form of tyranny because of the political immaturity of the people; (d) revolutions *can* serve as short cuts to progress; and (e) progress would consist in the creation of states which genuinely express the will of the national community, and this development would lead ultimately to the breakdown of national rivalries (he even speaks of the elimination of frontiers and the unity of Europe). These are the political premises from which *Under Western Eyes* derives.

It proceeds to tell the tale of an exemplary young man, Razumov, who is both the victim and the hero of czarist Russia. As Conrad had already seen in the 1905 essay:

> The worst crime against humanity of that system . . . is the ruthless destruction of innumerable minds. The greatest horror of the world— madness—walked faithfully in its train. Some of the best intellects of Russia, after struggling in vain against the spell, ended by throwing themselves at the feet of that hopeless despotism as a giddy man leaps into an abyss. (*NLL*, p. 99)

It is in precisely these terms that the Ochrana chief Mikulin tells Razumov that Providence has called him to the service of his country: "You shall be coming back to us. Some of our greatest minds had to do that in the end" (p. 295). *Under Western Eyes* is distinguished from other Conradian tales of the isolated individual both by this oppressive political environment and by the intellectual status of its hero. The maturity of the novel lies in its focus upon the intellectual in the modern world; it may be read as a novel of ideas in a way in which no other Conrad work may.

The specific ideas it takes up are those of Russian populism, including the versions of Dostoevsky and Tolstoy, at whom Conrad obliquely glances in his references to the "best intellects" who end at the feet of autocracy.[11] It is one problem of the novel to distinguish their organicist ideas from Conrad's own notions of human community, just as it is his parallel aim to distinguish utopian faith in the revolution from his own hopes for progress. The judgment of Irving Howe that the novel lacks Dostoevskian dialectical force must therefore be brought into question. It will be found that Dostoevsky is one of the antagonists in the novel, that the struggle with him is conducted not in terms of literary taste but in terms of social values, and that the dramatic action of the novel is akin to that of Dostoevsky's fiction —a progressive discovery of modes of thought and behavior in the conflict of characters who not only speak but represent ideologies.

Conrad appears to have shared a widespread Russian view about Russia which was as much alive in the West in his own day as it is in our own. A typical formulation of the view is Berdyaev's:

> the Russian people may be characterized as imperial-despotic and anarchic freedom-loving, as a people inclined to nationalism and national conceit, and a people of a universal spirit, more than others capable of oecumenic views; cruel and unusually humane; inclined to inflict suffering and illimitably sympathetic. . . . Russians are always inclined to take things in a totalitarian sense; the sceptical criticism of Western peoples is alien to them. . . . The Russian spirit craves for wholeness. . . . It yearns for the Absolute and desires to subordinate everything to the Absolute. . . .[12]

In every stratum of Russian society probed in *Under Western Eyes*, this set of contradictory urges is found to be the basis of political ideology.

At the extreme right, in the highest class, the absolutist strain appears in the sensibility of General T—, with his ludicrous conception of himself ("I detest rebels of every kind. I can't help it. It's my nature!" [p. 50]) and his unequivocal political role: "They shall be destroyed." At the opposite remove, absolutism colors the mystical philosophy of the terrorist Victor Haldin, who has elaborate visions of the Russian soul but who cannot ac-

---

[11] See Conrad's scathing remarks on these authors in Garnett Letters, pp. 260 (May 27, 1912) and 265 (February 23, 1914).

[12] Nicolas Berdyaev, *The Origins of Russian Communism* (orig. pub., 1937; London, 1955), pp. 18, 21.

curately determine the political sentiments of a fellow-student (Razumov), whom he implicates in his crime. He tells Razumov, mystically, "My spirit shall go on warring in some Russian body till all falsehood is swept out of the world. The modern civilization is false, but a new revelation shall come out of Russia" (p. 22). In its most prophetic form, absolutism is at the basis of the dream of mass human sacrifice in Peter Ivanovitch's theory of history:

> "for us at this moment there yawns a chasm between the past and the future. It can never be bridged by foreign liberalism. . . . It has to be filled up." . . . And he added that surely whole cart-loads of words and theories could never fill that chasm. No meditation was necessary. A sacrifice of many lives could alone—He fell silent without finishing the phrase. (Pp. 211–12).

At the root of all forms of Russian thought, as exemplified in these speeches —the czarist general's autocracy, the mystical student's populism, the revolutionary's nihilism—lies a conception of society as an organism, a real unity of its members, which has not only a historical tradition but a divinely shaped destiny, a spiritual law determining its course, and which requires the total subordination of the individual to its claims. It is on the latter points that Conrad distinguishes this form of the theory of the organic state from the idea of a spiritual but humanly created community inherited from the English tradition of Burke and Coleridge. It is the religious absolutism that lies behind much Russian nationalism (Dostoevsky's, for example) that Conrad condemns as obscurantist. Indeed, Conrad's (or his persona's) term for the contradictions of the typically Russian sensibility is "cynicism":

> For that is the mark of Russian autocracy and of Russian revolt. In its pride of numbers, in its strange pretentions of sanctity, and in the secret readiness to abase itself in suffering, the spirit of Russia is the spirit of cynicism. It informs the declarations of statesmen, the theories of her revolutionists, and the mystic vaticinations of prophets to the point of making freedom look like a form of debauch, and the Christian virtues themselves appear actually indecent.[13] (P. 67)

The novel may be read, then as Conrad's critique of Russian obscurantism, and his treatment of its hold on the Russian mind extends to its religious mythologies—to its diabolism. It may well have been the diabolism in the

[13] It is noteworthy that this summary statement follows, and is a comment upon, the famous testament of Razumov, which has been taken by Conrad's critics to be an outspoken confession of faith by the author. We shall see that the testament is only a partial expression of the novel's dialectic.

work of Dostoevsky, as in *The Possessed* (*The Devils*, as it has also been translated), which provoked Conrad to demythologize the Russian infatuation with the devil. When Razumov first meets Sophia Antonovna, her eyes and facial expression impresses him as Mephistophelian, but when the English narrator meets her, Razumov's impression is given a subtler interpretation: "I was struck then by the quaint Mephistophelian character of her inquiring glance, because it was so curiously evil-less, so—I may say—undevilish" (p. 327). During the rest of the novel, this demythologizing process (to borrow a term from a contemporary theologian) continues. The peasant coachman Ziemianitch is said to have believed that his beating by Razumov was the action of the devil, and Razumov, now the skeptic rather than the naïf, says: "Ziemianitch ended by falling into mysticism. So many of our true Russian souls end in that way! Very characteristic" (p. 283).

Razumov is, however, still open to the promptings of the national superstition. When he reveals his perfidy to Natalia Haldin, he admits: "I have the greatest difficulty in saving myself from the superstitition of an active Providence. It's irresistible. . . . The alternative, of course, would be the personal Devil of our simple ancestors. . . . the old Father of Lies—our national patron— . . . whom we take with us when we go abroad" (p. 350). Razumov even comes to see the narrator himself in that light, due to an ironic misunderstanding: "every word of that friend of yours was egging me on to the unpardonable sin of stealing a soul. Could he have been the devil himself in the shape of an old Englishman? Natalia Victorovna, I was possessed!" (pp. 359–60). The last word on the subject is, however, spoken by the narrator himself, and it has a wider relevance than to the illusions of Razumov or of Russians alone:

> To the morality of a Western reader an account of these meetings [between Razumov and Mikulin] would wear perhaps the sinister character of old legendary tales where the Enemy of Mankind is represented holding subtly mendacious dialogues with some tempted soul. It is not my part to protest. Let me but remark that the Evil One, with his single passion of satanic pride for the only motive, is yet, on a larger, modern view, allowed to be not quite so black as he used to be painted. With what greater latitude, then, should we appraise the exact shade of mere mortal man, with his many passions and his miserable ingenuity in error, always dazzled by the base glitter of mixed motives, everlastingly betrayed by a short-sighted wisdom. (Pp. 304–5)

The source of this view is a humanistic, rather than a racist, anthropology and ethics. It acknowledges that the Western mind is open to the diabolic

imagination, and concludes with a warning to the West to resist the temptation of diabolic explanations in our view of Mikulin and, by implication, of
Russian politics generally.[14] Despite his temptations to characterize all
Russians using a Russian mode of thought, Conrad reasserts his Western,
skeptical, but discriminatingly sympathetic temper.

Within this sustained critique of the cardinal ideas of the Russian mentality,
Conrad has set the drama of the Russian intellectual, Razumov. It is important
to consider the content of the hero's beliefs, which are described as "liberal"
before his crisis, although they have been taken to be arch-conservative
from the outset. We shall discover that Razumov leaves his Western individualist assumptions for an exaggerated, Russian version of the doctrine of
the collective state governed by autocratic absolutism. But this belief is only
a transitional stage, brought about by a personal need for security. Razumov's
subsequent experience leads him toward a theory of community which it is
the dialectical action of the novel to propose.

Razumov is a "son of reason": that is what his name means (he recalls
Raskolnikov's foil, Razumihin, in *Crime and Punishment*). He is an intellectual,
governed by rational processes and guided by reasonable expectations—and
then the absurd breaks in upon him, the absurd being the absolute claims of
modern politics. He is an individualist who believes in his separateness from
the community, and in the value of his separateness—and then the community
claims him as its own. He is an enlightened student of Western culture and
has assimilated its ideology of political liberty and personal freedom—and
then a "conversion" leads him to assert, in a peculiarly Russian form, the
organic bonds that tie him to others.

Both in the text of the novel and in the Author's Note, written later,
Conrad insists on Razumov's alienation from family and personal connections: "The word Razumov was the mere label of a solitary individuality"
(p. 10). In consequence, the narrative identifies the hero with the nation as a
whole: "Being nobody's child he feels rather more keenly than another would
that he is Russian—or he is nothing. He is perfectly right in looking on all

---

[14] The demythologizing of political diabolism has strong parallels in a novel
that critically explores another national temperament, the German—Thomas
Mann's *Dr. Faustus*. As the close analogy between "Il Conde" and "Mario and
the Magician" indicates, the relation between these authors is not only one of
direct influence, as Mann suggested in his essay on *The Secret Agent*, but one of
profound affinity.

Russia as his heritage" (p. ix). His connection with the community is not merely an illusion; Conrad's principle is that "a man's real life is that accorded to him in the thoughts of other men by reason of respect or natural love" (p. 14). Indeed, Razumov's imagination, his constitution as a person, his identity are shaped, for better or worse, by the history of his nation; the narrative explains the difference between Razumov's response to his situation and that of a hypothetical "young Englishman" by the fact that the latter "would not have an hereditary and personal knowledge of the means by which a historical autocracy represses ideas, guards its power, and defends its existence" (p. 25).

It is thus entirely without mystical theories of race and collective mind that Razumov's existence is connected with that of Russia. In the extremity of his crisis, however, he—like the revolutionists and other Russian political actors—is led to exaggerate his identity with the group. Walking through the snow on his errand for Haldin, he experiences an almost exalted sense of oneness (the kind of experience which Freud called "oceanic," and which is familiar in mystical literature):

> Razumov received an almost physical impression of endless space and of countless millions.
> He responded to it with the readiness of a Russian who is born to an inheritance of space and numbers. Under the sumptuous immensity of the sky, the snow covered the endless forests, the frozen rivers, the plains of an immense country, obliterating the land-marks, the accidents of the ground, levelling everything under its uniform whiteness, like a monstrous blank page awaiting the record of an inconceivable history. (P. 33)

Razumov's next reflections draw the political implications from this vision: the need for a charismatic autocrat to preserve this precarious unity in multiplicity by brute force. His accession to authoritarianism is expressed as a negation of his previous liberalism:

> "Better that thousands should suffer than that a people should become a disintegrated mass, helpless like dust in the wind. Obscurantism is better than the light of incendiary torches." (P. 34)

> He was persuaded that he was sacrificing his personal longings of liberalism —rejecting the attractive error for the stern Russian truth. "That's patriotism," he observed mentally. . . . (P. 36)

In fear of the bewildering multiplicity of persons—suggested by the whirling snowflakes and expressed as "dust in the wind"—Razumov prefers the white blanket that obscures all distinctions in a monolithic unity, "a monstrous blank page," the *tabula rasa* of Russian innocence. He has been seduced by the inviting possibility of surrendering his individuality, his reason, in the collective whole, and of renouncing the difficult life of struggle and change in history for the supposed stability and peace of a nation in stasis. The narrative voice at this point makes clear what Conrad thought of these conclusions:

> In Russia, the land of spectral ideas and disembodied aspirations, many brave minds have turned away at last from the vast and endless conflict to the one great historical fact of the land. They turned to autocracy for the peace of their patriotic conscience as a weary unbeliever, touched by grace, turns to the faith of his fathers for the blessing of spiritual rest. Like other Russians before him, Razumov, in conflict with himself, felt the touch of grace upon his forehead. (P. 34)

Razumov's "conversion" is, however, only a temporary one. He immediately acts on it by selling Haldin out to the secret police, but his next formulation of his ideology must be read as an advance upon his ultramontane collectivism. The famous credo which Razumov pins to the wall above the bed where Haldin had slept (p. 66) has been taken as a confession of faith on Conrad's part. It is so, but its dialectical targets must be made clear, for it is not only an anti-revolutionary utterance but also an anti-individualistic one. The philosophy that stands behind each of its values is that of the organic state, *evolution* through *history* in the *direction* of *patriotic unity*. Its negative notes are variously distributed. "Evolution not Revolution" and "Direction not Destruction" are denials of the revolutionary creed, but "History not Theory," "Patriotism not Internationalism," and "Unity not Disruption" can be considered critiques of individualist liberal doctrines as well. Indeed, Haldin and Peter Ivanovitch, the two revolutionists whose ideologies are stated in the novel, are both committed to history, patriotism, and unity. In Russia, these were tenets of the populist revolutionary movements of the nineteenth century. It is therefore necessary for Conrad, and for his hero, to separate themselves from the excesses of both camps: from the liberal individualism of the West, which minimizes the communal life of men, and from the populist revolutionism of Russia, which pushes the theory of organism into mysticism and terrorism.

Just as Razumov's "conversion" had allowed him to justify himself in surrendering Haldin, so this *confession du foi* leads to his joining the ranks of the Ochrana. It is the classical charge against the doctrine of the organic state that the isolated individual, in search of association with a community, may be led to surrender his freedom to an oppressive state. The account given of Razumov's alienation suggests how such self-renunciation comes about:

> The unrelated organism bearing that label [Razumov], walking, breathing, wearing these clothes, was of no importance to any one, unless maybe to the landlady. The true Razumov had his being in the willed, in the determined future—in that future menaced by the lawlessness of autocracy —for autocracy knows no law—and the lawlessness of revolution. The feeling that his moral personality was at the mercy of these lawless forces was so strong that he asked himself seriously if it were worth while to go on accomplishing the mental functions of that existence which seemed no longer his own. (Pp. 77–78)

Under this threat of non-existence outside society, the individual can turn only to the state—although it is from the state itself that the threat proceeds.

Part One of *Under Western Eyes* concludes with Mikulin's immortal question (in response to Razumov's declaration of retirement), "Where to?" Part Two brings Razumov to Geneva in the service of the Ochrana, and closes as the narrator leaves him on a bridge looking down into the rushing water. The narrator remarks of the scene: "The current there is swift, extremely swift; it makes some people dizzy; I myself can never look at it for any length of time without experiencing a dread of being suddenly snatched away by its destructive force. Some brains cannot resist the suggestion of irresistible power and of headlong motion" (p. 197). Part Three opens with the same scene rendered from Razumov's point of view, and we are given an opportunity to enter one of those "brains."

> The water under the bridge ran violent and deep. Its slightly undulating rush seemed capable of scouring out a channel for itself through solid granite while you looked. But had it flowed through Razumov's breast, it could not have washed away the accumulated bitterness the wrecking of his life had deposited there.
> "What is the meaning of all this?" he thought, staring downwards at the headlong flow so smooth and clean that only the passage of a faint air-bubble, or a thin vanishing streak of foam like a white hair, disclosed its vertiginous rapidity, its terrible force. (P. 198)

The elaboration of details and their psychological suggestions indicate that we have here to do with a symbolic rather than with a picturesque Genevan landscape. The stream is like the stream of history, dizzyingly swift, destructively powerful, enigmatically lambent. "What is the meaning of all this?" Razumov may well ask. He stands at a vantage point and observes its seductive attraction; he withdraws himself from immersion in the destructive element, but his career will draw him down into it. And in the event, almost drowning, he will discover something of what lies beneath the "smooth and clean" surface.

In Geneva, a major development of Razumov's imagination takes place as his spying leads him to an enlarged awareness of revolutionaries like Sophia Antonovna. The development is concluded by a return to the river (this time to another bridge), where Razumov, despite his partial growth, seals his own destruction by writing his first spy report.

Troubled by his manifold and unwelcome commitments—to Mikulin, to the Haldins, to the revolutionaries—he determines to fulfill at least one demand, to make one of his relationships to others binding by writing his report on the radicals. But he must be alone in order to write in secret. He wishes to establish contact with others, but at the same time he seeks severance from all human relations. "I wish I were in the middle of some field miles away from everywhere" (pp. 289–90), he says, but he cannot even find a place to be alone in the midst of the city. He enters the Pont des Bergues (his movements in the novel are precise enough to follow on the map), and finds at the middle an entry into the Île Jean-Jacques Rousseau:

> On setting his foot on it Razumov became aware that, except for the woman in charge of the refreshment chalet, he would be alone on the island. There was something of naïve, odious, and inane simplicity about that unfrequented tiny crumb of earth named after Jean Jacques Rousseau. . . . He had found precisely what he needed. If solitude could ever be secured in the open air in the middle of a town, he would have it there on this absurd island, together with the faculty of watching the only approach. . . . the people crossing over in the distance seemed unwilling even to look at the islet where the exiled effigy of the author of the *Social Contract* sat enthroned above the bowed head of Razumov in the somber immobility of bronze. (Pp. 290–91)

It is possible to compare Razumov's island with Rousseau's own temporary refuge in the Lake of Bienne, the Île St. Pierre, to which he retired during his persecutions. It is equally tempting to compare the illusions of isolation and independence which both the philosopher and the fictional hero gain from their crumbs of earth. Rousseau was quickly expelled from his idyll, and

Razumov will shortly be thrust back into his double social role (indeed, his "island," like the Île St. Pierre, is connected with the mainland). The retreat does afford temporary security, but it is the indifference of the community that affords it; not only was Rousseau formerly exiled but his statue is now disregarded, his effigy "exiled"—while Razumov is in virtual exile as well.

It is not merely their parallel geographical situations and their common illusions of independence that connect Rousseau and Razumov. The presence of the statue has recently been noted by critics of *Under Western Eyes*, but, lacking an orientation toward its political-philosophical dialectic, they have not been able to give a satisfactory account of its symbolic force.[15] It is possible to do so in terms of the theory of the organic state, of which Rousseau was a major source. *The Social Contract*, which is mentioned in the passage last quoted, is one of the classical texts for this theory, and its statements bear a remarkable relevance to the concern of the novel with the hero's fate and with Russia's.

"Man is born free; and everywhere he is in chains. . . . How did this change come about? I do not know. What can make it legitimate? That question I think I can answer."[16] Once the misconceptions about Rousseau's supposed primitivism have been dissolved, these famous opening lines can be seen to broach the real problem of the treatise; what can render one state legitimate and another illegitimate? This question is dramatized in the novel's search for a genuine community—not the autocratic Russian community— and in the related search for a proper relation of the individual to that community. After reformulating the Enlightenment myth of the state of nature and the social contract, Rousseau describes the society so formed in terms that have given the cue for the later theories of the organic state:

---

[15] E.g., Tony Tanner, "Nightmare and Complacency: Razumov and the Western Eye," *Critical Quarterly*, IV (1962), 200–1, which conceives Rousseau to be the whipping boy of Conrad's attack on an optimistic conception of man. Some support is given this view by Conrad's rejection of Rousseau's autobiographical motives in *A Personal Record*: the philosopher is accused of being a "moralist," not a "novelist, whose first virtue is the exact understanding of the limits traced by the reality of his time to the play of his invention" (p. 95). But Conrad's archness toward Rousseau's egoism and idealism does not deny his own quest for the moral order of men and nations, nor does it disqualify Rousseau's works, which Conrad familiarly mentions in this passage, from his close consideration.

[16] Jean-Jacques Rousseau, *The Social Contract*, trans. G. D. H. Cole (New York and London, 1913), p. 5. Subsequent citations are from this edition and are given parenthetically.

At once, in place of the individual personality of each contracting party, this act of association creates a moral and collective body, composed of as many members as the assembly contains votes, and receiving from this act its unity, its common identity, its life and its will. This public person, so formed by the union of all other persons formerly took the name of *city*, and now takes that of *Republic* or *body politic*. . . . (Pp. 15–16)

This collective body is the source of strength to which Razumov, the alienated individual, turns, but in doing so he allies himself with a repressive autocracy, and it becomes necessary for him to free himself of this identification, to acquire an association with a genuine community or with some surrogate of it, if he is to survive. That he does so only partially is the measure of the failure of the present states to offer the alternative he seeks. The dialectic of the novel contrasts the absolutism of Russia with the democracy of Switzerland to show how close one Western nation comes toward the ideal community and to estimate the distance still to be covered.

A large part of Book III of *The Social Contract* is taken up with the types of states and their relation to the size of the nation. Indeed, Rousseau often seems to make the latter the condition of the former, although it is sometimes difficult to tell where he is being ironic. It has often been observed that this Genevese had a preference for a city-state on the model of Sparta, early Rome, or Geneva—a non-representative, direct democracy, in which all the citizens vote and administer the laws. This is possible only when the nation is small: large nations tend toward elaborate state apparatus. Rousseau is fully aware of this tendency: "The government, then, to be good, should be proportionately stronger as the people is more numerous" (p. 51). He is also fully aware of its dangers: "the larger the State, the less the liberty."

The problem suggested by *Under Western Eyes* is in part that of *The Social Contract*: what government would be superior to Russian autocracy? Would it be the small-state direct democracy of Switzerland, in which the last three parts of the novel are set—as a dramatic contrast with the opening scenes in Russia? Conrad was a frequent visitor to Switzerland after his return from the Congo, staying at a clinic near Geneva, and he returned occasionally later in life. His picture of Switzerland in general, and of Geneva in particular, contains some of the same ambivalence which Rousseau felt for the land and city of his birth. In the imagery of the novel, the major shortcoming seems to be the drabness of the bourgeois atmosphere and the banality of the landscape, but a deeper, political judgment is at work in the novel, of which the imagery is the aesthetic expression.

During an early meeting between Razumov and Natalia Haldin, the narrator surveys the scene at the Bastions, the public park at the center of the city:

> I saw these two, escaped out of four score of millions of human beings ground between the upper and nether millstone, walking under these trees, their young heads close together. . . . There was a quantity of tables and chairs displayed between the restaurant chalet and the band-stand, a whole raft of painted deals spread out under the trees. In the very middle of it I observed a solitary Swiss couple, whose fate was made secure from the cradle to the grave by the perfected mechanism of democratic institutions in a republic that could almost be held in the palm of one's hand. The man, colourlessly uncouth, was drinking beer out of a glittering glass; the woman, rustic and placid, leaning back in the rough chair, gazed idly around. (P. 175)

The language of the text emphasizes the contrast between the largeness of Russia and the smallness of Switzerland, the autocratic terror of the former and the democratic safety of the latter, the tragic possibilities of the hero and heroine of the novel and the "colourlessly uncouth," "rustic and placid" Swiss couple. What is lacking in the "cradle to grave" arrangements of the democratic state? The suggestion is deftly dropped with the remark that the couple is seen isolated among a myriad of empty tables.

Their state lacks community, which is conceived of not as a set of artificial relations among discrete individuals, but as a living culture inviting personal identification. Liberal government, it is implied, lacks the cohesive power of the emotional patriotism that binds a nation together. Conrad's collectivism must not be seen as an irrational or mystical one, like the Russian variety, but rather as a Western and modern ideal of human brotherhood. It is this kind of patriotism that Rousseau indicated when he wrote: "The better the constitution of a State is, the more do public affairs encroach on private in the minds of the citizens. . . . As soon as any man says of the affairs of the State *What does it matter to me?* the State may be given up for lost" (pp. 82–83).

Razumov begins as a man who says, what does the state matter to me? The moribund czarist state may indeed be given up for lost, but for the individual, the consequence of his indifference is almost as serious. He cannot survive without some loyalty to others; his very existence is dependent upon

others. Razumov conceives his career as a solitary effort, an application of
the Conradian work ethic outside a community of labor, an effort of the
isolated ego by dint of sheer will. The final irony of the work ethic is brought
home, however, when the hero discovers that without others he cannot even
work. The world interrupts his work, and he cannot fulfill his plans without
some others to work with or for. "And now to work," he says, three weeks
after the Haldin affair is past, and immediately thinks of Mikulin and his
silence: "What did it mean? Was he forgotten? Possibly. Then why not
remain forgotten—creep in somewhere? Hide. But where? How? With
whom? In what hole? And was it to be for ever, or what?" (p. 301). The
writing conveys Razumov's ambivalence: he fears a hiding place as much as
he fears discovery; he is more troubled at being left alone than if he were
pursued. "Was it possible that he no longer belonged to himself?" (p. 301).
There is a sense in which his existence has been mortgaged to the state, for
without the state he has no existence—unless he can find some other kind
of community.

> It was no use struggling on. Rest, work, solitude, and the frankness of
> intercourse with his kind were alike forbidden to him. Everything was
> gone. His existence was a great cold blank, something like the enormous
> plain of the whole of Russia levelled with snow and fading gradually on
> all sides into shadows and mists. (P. 303)

Razumov first turns to the state, but the state is in this case unable to
afford the individual the community he needs. He must then discover substitutes for it, and can find it only in two possible realms: class identification,
expressed in revolutionary activity, or personal relations. The class struggle is at
first rejected because it had been the source of his undoing by Haldin, and
his attempt to make an intense personal contact turns out to be with precisely
the person he is most unable to join—the sister of the man he betrayed. The
quest for an "object of loyalty" (as the American neo-Hegelian philosopher
of community, Josiah Royce, termed it), for a significant other with whom to
join the self, constitutes the plot of *Under Western Eyes*.

Razumov does "come back to us," to the autocratic state, as Mikulin
assures him he, like other intellectuals, will. It is not, however, primarily
to the state but to Mikulin himself that Razumov responds: "he could not
defend himself from fancying that Councillor Mikulin was, perhaps, the
only man in the world able to understand his conduct. To be understood
appeared extremely fascinating" (p. 297). In the practice of espionage—a
substitute vocation for his lost scholarly work—he can deal only with the

mechanical state apparatus (relaying his report through the Russian Embassy in Vienna where it is translated and coded for transmission to Mikulin). As a spy, in the secrecy which is isolation, he is effectively cut off from the human contact with the state which he had received when "the obscure, unrelated young student Razumov, in the moment of great moral loneliness, was allowed to feel that he was an object of interest to a small group of people of high position" (pp. 307–8), a group which includes his putative father. As a student he had wanted to become "a great reforming servant of the greatest of States" (p. 301), and now that he is one he finds the role untenable. He must give himself to others, to substitutes for the state, even at the cost of destroying himself. Twice he confesses, once for the sake of his class affiliation, and once for the sake of a personal attachment.

Razumov's confessions have been interpreted in peculiar ways by critics of the novel who find it comprehensible that he should confess to Natalia but not that he should do so to the revolutionists. They manage to overlook the extensive psychological study Conrad gives of Razumov's experience with Sophia Antonovna, which leads him to a more sophisticated view of revolutionaries generally than he (or Conrad) has been credited with. It is this enhanced awareness that allows the hero to come at last into their camp.

The learning process begins during Sophia Antonovna's initial interrogation of Razumov:

> her eyes rested upon him, black and impenetrable like the mental caverns where revolutionary thought should sit plotting the violent way of its dream of changes. As if anything could be changed! In this world of men nothing can be changed—neither happiness nor misery. They can only be displaced at the cost of corrupted consciences and broken lives—a futile game for arrogant philosophers and sanguinary triflers. Those thoughts darted through Razumov's head while he stood facing the old revolutionary hand. . . . (P. 261)

The occasion for these generalizations is dramatic: Razumov is being tested for veracity by one of the most experienced and mature of the revolutionaries, and he naturally regards her as an enemy.

In the course of their conversation he has an opportunity to learn more about the mentality of revolutionaries, and the audience is invited to broaden its view along with him. He begins to experience Sophia Antonovna as a personality:

> Razumov looked at her white hair: and this mark of so many uneasy years seemed nothing but a testimony to the invincible vigour of revolt. It

threw out into an astonishing relief the unwrinkled face, the brilliant black glance, the upright compact figure, the simple, brisk self-possession of the mature personality—as though in her revolutionary pilgrimage she had discovered the secret, not of everlasting youth, but of everlasting endurance. (Pp. 263–64)

With Razumov's insight into her vigor, maturity, and endurance, the audience is asked to give up one of the alternatives he had earlier posed for the classification of revolutionaries, that they are "sanguinary triflers." Whether Sophia Antonovna is, on the other hand, one of the "arrogant philosophers" may be judged from her remark on revolutionary ideology: "My dear soul, I have outlived all that nonsense" (p. 251). If she is neither one nor the other, the question is opened, what is *this* revolutionary?

Razumov continues his attempt to discover the nature of the revolutionary woman:

How un-Russian she looked, thought Razumov. Her mother might have been a Jewess or an Armenian or—devil knew what. He reflected that a revolutionist is seldom true to the settled type. All revolt is the expression of strong individualism—ran his thought vaguely. One can tell them a mile off in any society, in any surroundings. It was astonishing that the police. . . . (P. 264)

The final thought is intended to be amusing, since it calls up an image of the police in a supposedly individualistic society hunting down anyone who looks like an individualist, for these are its real enemies. Despite its banter, it marks an unsettling change in Razumov's (and, presumably, in Conrad's) estimation of the revolutionary type. Revolt can be the expression of exceptional, highly individualistic, but frustrated men and women: it is not childish folly but a perhaps vain effort to create the self in the absence of community.

A deeper insight into the nature of revolutionaries is made when the narrative shifts temporarily from Razumov's perspective to Sophia Antonovna's. She sees him in much the same terms as those in which he has just seen her:

No one is born an active revolutionist. The change comes disturbingly, with the force of a sudden vocation, bringing in its train agonizing doubts, assertive violences, an unstable state of the soul, till the final appeasement of the convert in the perfect fierceness of conviction. She had seen— often had only divined—scores of these young men and young women going through an emotional crisis. This young man looked like a moody egotist. And besides, it was a special—a unique case. She had never met an individuality which interested and puzzled her so much. (P. 269)

She is deceived, of course, about Razumov's revolutionary allegiance, but not far from the truth of his abrupt conversion to the service of the czarist state during the crisis that surrounds his betrayal of Haldin. We are invited by this complex interview to see all political actors—both revolutionary and counter-revolutionary—as real people, with all the attractiveness and dangers of human egoism, rather than as caricatures or personifications of virtues and vices.

It is Razumov's quest for a community of real people, rather than one of mystical abstractions, that leads him to choose the revolutionaries. It is this hunger for human contact that informs his words: "Not one to go to. Do you conceive the desolation of the thought—no one – to – go – to?" (p. 354). After his confession to Natalia, Razumov must confess to the revolutionists as a group because it can accept him in a way she cannot. There is a greater possibility of connection with a group than there is with a person, even one who embodies ideal love. This is not Natalia's limitation so much as it is that of personal relations generically; a person can forgive, can even love, those most estranged from him, but he cannot forget as readily as a group can do. When Razumov confesses, Natalia weeps for her own sorrow, as she must; and Razumov will always be to her the betrayer of her brother. But when he confesses to the revolutionaries, they react in confusion, some of their number injure him almost fatally, but eventually they receive him among themselves.

Without some such view of the denouement, it is impossible to explain the crowning irony by which Razumov is found at the close of the novel in the role of a patron saint of the revolutionists. They go to his retreat in southern Russia not only to make amends for their guilt (it is, moreover, not they who have deafened him but the *agent provocateur* Nikita), but also for inspiration: "He is intelligent. He has ideas. . . . He talks well, too" (p. 379). Razumov, who has been mistaken by the revolutionists as "one of *us*" (p. 208), actually becomes so in the end. The term employed in the novel is "*un des nôtres*" (p. 210); the equivalent of Marlow's term for Jim, it also recalls *nostr'omo*. Like Jim and Nostromo, the extreme individualist becomes integrated with a group at last, and it is for all of them a revolutionary movement (Jim is active in behalf of the lowliest village of the region, and Nostromo similarly aids the radical movements in the new industrial regime). They have attempted the service of the nation as a whole; finding that the latter exploits the self rather than integrating it, they turn to a class movement, at the same time developing a renewed individualism. The final irony of Razumov's union with a political community is that it occurs simultaneously with his physical isolation in deafness; his most successful communication with others is made across the barrier of a soundless self-enclosure.

That Conrad was willing to acknowledge the necessity of social change— even by the "short-cut" of revolution (as he calls it in "Autocracy and War") —may be discovered repeatedly throughout his work. That he was able to formulate his views of states and revolutions in ways more subtle than his occasional anathemas would indicate is nowhere more evident than in *Under Western Eyes*. The novel develops a dialectic between the often-quoted (but rarely interpreted) skepticism of the narrator and the serene idealism of Natalia Haldin. Their dialectic is one of Conrad's most important achievements as a political novelist, for in the act of dramatizing his theme he seems to have expanded his own horizons from a fairly narrow-minded denunciation of all things Russian to a broad, even tragic, view of human history.

Conrad's critics have not sufficiently faced up to the fact that the epigraph to *Under Western Eyes* is a testament of revolution. In an unusual procedure, Conrad quotes the words of his own character, Natalia: "I would take liberty from any hand as a hungry man would snatch [at] a piece of bread." The words are part of her response to one of the most widely quoted of the narrator's speeches in contempt of revolution:

> in a real revolution—not a simple dynastic change or a mere reform of institutions—in a real revolution the best characters do not come to the front. A violent revolution falls into the hands of narrow-minded fanatics and of tyrannical hypocrites at first. Afterwards comes the turn of all the pretentious intellectual failures of the time. Such are the chiefs and the leaders. You will notice that I have left out the mere rogues. The scrupulous and the just, the noble, humane, and devoted natures; the unselfish and the intelligent may begin a movement—but it passes away from them. They are not the leaders of a revolution. They are its victims. . . . (P. 134)

This speech is unquestionably written in Conrad's personal voice and contains refinements of thought that directly connect it with his political essays (e.g., the qualification on revolutions as distinguished from dynastic changes). The tone, it should be noted, is considerably more sympathetic to the idealists who originate revolutions than has been supposed. What is in question is the aftermath. Natalia answers with her statement of self-sacrifice: she is willing to see the idealists, including herself and her brother, swept away—even if power passes into unscrupulous hands. What would then be left of the revolution? "The true progress must begin after," she answers (p. 135).

There are, undoubtedly, strong elements of mystical populism and political naïveté in Natalia's faith, and Conrad might have considered her, at another point in his career, as one of those women who live by illusion and ought to be maintained in it. Yet her revolutionary faith is expressed too winningly for us to feel that Conrad is merely indulging her. When the narrator strikes at her faith with the question, "Are antagonistic ideas then to be reconciled more easily—can they be cemented with blood and violence into that concord which you proclaim to be so near?" and when he himself answers that it is inconceivable (pp. 105–6), Natalia replies:

> "Everything is inconceivable," she said. "The whole world is inconceivable to the strict logic of ideas. And yet the world exists to our senses, and we exist in it. There must be a necessity superior to our conceptions. . . . We Russians shall find some better form of national freedom than an artificial conflict of parties—which is wrong because it is a conflict and contemptible because it is artificial. It is left for us Russians to discover a better way." (P. 106)

The opening of this speech, too, bears the unmistakable ring of Conrad's personal tone. It is a statement of philosophical fideism, a skepticism so radical that it holds faith to be necessary in order for thought to function at all. It proposes the ironic discovery that political illusions—such as the illusion of national destiny—can be based on the evidence of the senses, on a historical sense of the realities of life in the world. This historical sense, an awareness of national tradition and a conviction of national immortality, forces Natalia and other Russians to foresee the inevitable revolution against autocracy. Further, the Russian "soul" has discovered by long experience a truth that Conrad consistently entertained: that freedom is not the liberal "artificial conflict of parties" but the reconciliation of conflicts in an organic community.

Faced with this doctrine, the narrator becomes petulant. Earlier, he had even questioned Natalia's belief in freedom: "I knew her well enough to have discovered her scorn for all the practical forms of political liberty known to the Western world. I suppose one must be a Russian to understand Russian simplicity, a terrible corroding simplicity in which mystic phrases clothe a naïve and hopeless cynicism" (p. 104). But Natalia does not scorn Western freedom; she looks for some "better way" to it than unrestrained competition. The goal lies in the organicist doctrine: "men serve always something greater than themselves—the idea" (p. 352). This is a summary statement of the dramatic burden of Conrad's tales from *Lord Jim* to *The Rover*, which see the individual fulfilling himself only in relation to social ideals. Its phrasing recalls Marlow's judgment of imperialist activity: "What redeems it is the idea only."

Natalia's vision of the future, with which the novel approaches its conclusion, is one that must be taken more seriously than visions usually are:

> "I must own to you that I shall never give up looking forward to the day when all discord shall be silenced. Try to imagine its dawn! The tempest of blows and of execrations is over; all is still; the new sun is rising, and the weary men united at last, taking count in their conscience of the ended contest, feel saddened by their victory, because so many ideas have perished for the triumph of one, so many beliefs have abandoned them without support. They feel alone on the earth and gather close together. Yes, there must be many bitter hours! But at last the anguish of hearts shall be extinguished in love." (Pp. 376–77)

The sentimental phrases of the opening of Natalia's speech mark it as in part a target of Conrad's irony, but as she develops her theme we come to see that this idealist is not blinded by the stars in her eyes—that she acknowledges the losses, intellectual and physical, which the revolution will exact. She is aware of the openness of the future, in which men exhausted by their emergence from the past will be called upon to invent their own destiny. Her faith rests ultimately on a very human, earthy fact—the power of love, of human community—in which Conrad, for all his skepticism, never stopped believing. It is with love that Conrad, like his narrator, parts from his heroine, mindful of the seductive power of her faith, "an invincible belief in the advent of loving concord springing like a heavenly flower from the soil of men's earth, soaked in blood, torn by struggles, watered with tears" (p. 377).

It is by now generally accepted that Conrad succeeded in informing his novel of Russian affairs with sympathy, though he did not entirely succeed in overcoming his prejudices or dissipating his skepticism. The result of his artistic transmutation of his political attitudes is, however, not merely to distribute sympathy to all political camps, as though making a charitable distribution. It is rather to create a political world conceived in terms of tragedy. As R. L. Mégroz, one of Conrad's earliest and best critics, observed, "what remains in the mind is the tragic nobility of people haunted by a cause too big for them."[17] Such a view shows the revolutionaries to share in the human condition: the inevitable failure in pursuit of the ideal. These ideals are the only values we have, and in pursuit of them man may achieve heroic stature—and possibly create the conditions for social progress. As Natalia Haldin and the narrator join in believing, the heroic individual passes away, having sometimes achieved self-realization in communal identity. But the social organism lives on, regenerated, it is hoped, by his sacrifice.

The prevailing critical view of Conrad's idea of history has been well summarized by Morton Dauwen Zabel in his recent edition of the political tales:

> If they may be said to convey a common or general meaning it is probably this: that though history, unlike the universe, is a creation of man, it sets into motion laws or forces that get beyond his control or outstrip his mastery and comprehension. Originating in the great ideals, ambitions, or passions of humanity, it becomes possessed by strange and irrational energies; by forces of ambition, greed, reckless or unconscious instinct; by an impersonal or abstract justice which corrupts the ideals or inspirations that animate it and so sets up a fatal enmity between human honor and brutal or inhuman circumstance.[18]

The difficulty of such a formulation is that it comes close to ascribing to Conrad a deterministic theory of history which would preclude any freedom, achievement, and heroism in his fiction. The outlook of the novels is, on the contrary, uniformly open to the future: it bears the spirit not of despair but of tragedy. There is in them no hint of a degenerative tendency in history, such as was popular at the time he was writing and is beginning to revive in our own time. There is, of course, pessimism about the fate of the individual in history, and an awareness of the dangers to the personal life in all social systems. But this is balanced by a consciousness of the desirable connection of the individual and the social organism, and an acceptance of the modifications this relationship must make in the hero's large claims on life. As for the prospects of modern revolution, Conrad had specific fears because

[17] R. L. Mégroz, *Joseph Conrad's Mind and Method: A Study of Personality in Art* (London, 1931), p. 127.

[18] Morton Dauwen Zabel, Introduction to Joseph Conrad, *Tales of Heroes and History* (Garden City, N.Y., 1960), p. xxviii.

of the nature of *Russian* history—its failure to develop a political tradition other than autocracy, which he saw as a form of nihilism. The revolution of the underdeveloped lands, like the one on the horizon in *Nostromo*, is not prejudged: it may ultimately create the organic community which Western imperialism has failed to create (although it is this same economic imperialism which is the precondition for the revolution).

Conrad's skepticism, which has been held to be pessimistic, is much more radical than that: it does not venture to predict the form of the future, though it indicates the forces in the past and present that are driving toward change. Man is not the helpless victim of the world of history he has created; all efforts to show him as such are attempts to reduce him to the condition of the natural forces out of which he makes his history. Professor Zabel does acknowledge this tragic sense of openness and freedom in Conrad and suggests that, though the "pure of heart" may be defeated, they may in the midst of disillusionment yet become " 'open-eyed, conscious,' and if possible 'informed by love.' We are left with little more than this as a solution to the riddles of intrigue, confusion, and defeat which Conrad traced in Costaguana, Russia, Europe, or the East; this and one other thing—the 'undying hope.' . . ."[19] It is enough to be left with the ideal of love, of hope for human community, however difficult it is to imagine its development out of modern states. The vision acts as an encouragement to change, and Conrad's is the most potent secular hope for the future to be found in modern literature.

It is a tragic hope, which puts the burden of creating the future on the men of the doomed present. "So foul a sky clears not without a storm": the Shakespearean epigraph of *Nostromo* reminds us of Conrad's aesthetic—shall we say, prophetic—tradition; it is the mode of tragedy. The sacrifice of its choicest spirits may lead to the failure (or success, followed by stagnation) of progressive politics. But it may also lead to liberation through the tragic experience of learning through suffering, purgation through empathy, and inspiration through symbolic myths of social fulfillment. Conrad stands in much the same relation to our times as Sophocles did to post-Periclean Athens, for his final vision of the hero's simultaneous defeat and redemption leads us to a response that transcends our historical debacle. Ours is a tragic awe of the hero's—and the novelist's—healing powers for a sick society.

[19] *Ibid.*, p. xiii.

Sir Stamford Raffles

APPENDIX TO CHAPTER IV

Conrad's position on East Indian colonial administration may be deduced from his fiction to run somewhat as follows: in checking native wars and exploitation of minorities, that government was best which governed. The Dutch were reprehensible in the *Buitengewesten* (islands outside Java) for their infrequent visits and commercial favoritism, for upholding rapacious native chiefs, and for anti-English prejudices. Free trade would be, desirable and a switch to British administration might produce a better native and commercial policy. To the extent that Conrad was an admirer of James Brooke, he might also be supposed to have been sympathetic toward Brooke's principles of domestic rule in Sarawak, as cited in this chapter. How relevant are Conrad's ideas to the history of the archipelago, and where do they stand in the spectrum of political opinion?

English policy in the East Indies goes back to Sir Stamford Raffles, who, while Lieutenant Governor during the 1811–16 British occupation of the Dutch colonies (during Napoleon's hegemony in The Netherlands), proposed and began a series of energetic reforms. He permitted free trade in place of the Dutch East India Company's monopoly (actually, the administration of the islands had passed from the Company to the state just prior to British entry), held that unworked lands belonged to the Crown, and opened them for leasing by citizens of all nations. He abolished forced labor, tried to abolish slavery, acquired government revenues by a system of land taxation, and exercised vigorous control over native warfare, but otherwise left the rajahs free to maintain their customary rights over their subjects.

A most praiseworthy system, it would seem, but its inherent injustices and potential for abuse are manifest even though Raffles was not long enough in office to apply it thoroughly. (He failed to convince his government to retain the Indies after the Napoleonic wars, but went on to become the founder of Singapore.) Free trade would have meant the gradual acquisition of a monopoly by English traders, since they had greater experience and better-coordinated activities (traditional Liberals upheld the justice of monopolies gained by victory in competition). The new land taxes could not be paid by the peasants, and they were led to substitute their labor, with the same result as the previous *corvée* system. The opening of plantation leases to foreign speculators exposed the natives to the worst evils of European exploitation, so that later the exceptionally humane Dutch Governor Van der Capellen departed from his Liberal economic principles in order to protect them. Raffles' policy with the rajahs has also been accused of combining the worst features of both alternatives: it undermined traditional native culture by interfering with native customs (such was the argument of the influential Dutch anthropologist Snouck Hurgronje), while otherwise allowing the native rulers to tyrannize over their people.[1]

After Van der Capellen's humanitarian attempt to restrict unbridled competition had led to the Java War of 1826 against the native rulers (who were deprived of the profits of leasing their lands to foreign speculators), and after a short period in which pure Liberal theory was applied and failed roundly in an economy without the supposedly rational motives and open market of capitalist countries, the famous (or infamous) culture system of van den Bosch was introduced in 1830. The culture system (*Kultuurstelsel*) established tax assessments heavy enough not only to defray the costs of the colonial administration but to provide a handsome profit for the home country. It called for payment of either a certain percentage of the native's crops or one-fifth of his working time. The collections were made through the native chiefs, now called "regents" of the Dutch authority, who were free to apply their own methods of exaction. *Corvée* was employed on government or concessionary plantations, which produced export crops and received all the proceeds.

What is most noteworthy about van den Bosch's policy, in the present context, is that it differs very little from Raffles' supposedly advanced and humane program. Raffles was more outspoken in behalf of free trade, but his decrees tended toward monopoly; he wanted to break the power of the native rulers, but his schemes left direct power in their hands; and his efforts to collect land taxes resulted in deliveries of produce and in forced labor, just as under the culture system.

It was only in the 1860's that a wave of humanitarian revulsion against their country's imperialism grew among Dutchmen, provoked by the publication of a muckraking novel, *Max Havelaar*, by "Multatuli" (E. D. Dekker) in 1860. By 1870 a new turn was taken as the culture system declined: a Land Law was passed guaranteeing the natives the lands they traditionally cultivated, while reserving uncultivated lands for the state and opening them to settlement by colonists. Dutch emigration to the Indies increased, the *Buitengewesten* began to be colonized, and by 1890 a system of income and

---

[1] This summary has been compiled from works representing a spectrum of viewpoints on Dutch and British policies: Clive Day, *The Policy and Administration of the Dutch in Java*, pro-Raffles, anti-van den Bosch; Jean Bruhat, *Histoire de l'Indonésie*, Marxist; D. W. Van Welderen Rengers, *The Failure of a Liberal Colonial Policy: Netherlands East Indies, 1816–1830* (The Hague, 1947), critical of both British and Dutch; Bernard H. M. Vlekke, *Nusantara: A History of the East Indian Archipelago* (Cambridge, Mass., 1943), apparently objective; E. S. DeKlerck, *History of the Netherlands East Indies* (Rotterdam, 1938), vigorously imperialist; and B. Schrieke (ed.), *The Effect of Western Influence on Native Civilizations in the Malay Archipelago* (Batavia, 1929), a collection of anthropological accounts.

land taxes had been instituted. Beginning in the very period when Conrad was trading in the archipelago, and increasingly in the decade in which he was writing his early tales of his experiences there, the reforms were being instituted that would bring Dutch imperialism closer to his own desires.[2]

There are several ways to explain Conrad's failure to respond to the developments we have been tracing: he may not have seen the effects of policy changes in The Hague at a small river in northeast Borneo—although the minimal Dutch policy of securing order by suppressing piracy, headhunting, and tribal wars was already coming into effect. He may have felt the economic changes and disliked the way they were administered. He may have resented any Dutch authority, whether oppressive or liberal, preferring any British administration, even one with the same principles. It may be impossible finally to decide this question, but it is significant that he chose to begin making his reputation as a novelist in England by writing novels which assumed the perfidy of the Dutch. Despite his later exposures of jingoist shams, it seems that the temptation to appeal to a jingoist audience was sufficiently powerful to compel his slighting references to England's competitors in the imperialist race.

---

[2] Authorities are, however, divided on the extent of the change at that time: e.g., "the non-active policy again became the leading principle and continued to be so up to the close of the last century" (De Klerck, *History of the Netherlands East Indies*, II, 374); "the period between 1870 and 1900 is clearly one of transition in which a new Indonesian world took shape" (Vlekke, *Nusantara*, p. 293).

APPENDIX TO CHAPTER VI

One character of *Nostromo* stands outside the class structure of Costaguana, and almost outside the dramatic structure of the novel itself. It is appropriate on the former account that this character be a Jew, Señor Hirsch; on the other hand, his apparently gratuitous presence provokes us to speculate on Conrad's attitudes toward Jews within the scope of his political and social thought.

Conrad has been found guilty of unpleasant remarks about Jews in his personal life, e.g., the ascription to Jews in general of disreputable business practices and unpleasant personal habits (*LL*, I, 178, August 24, 1895). The only Jew besides Hirsch in his fiction (or are we to take Stein to be Jewish as well?), the innkeeper in "Prince Roman" who helps the hero join the nationalist revolution, is, however, presented in a quite different light: he identifies himself with the Polish cause at great personal risk.[1] Anti-Semitism is later used by Conrad as an indicator of the disturbed emotions of the alienated man, as when Razumov mistakes one of the revolutionists for a Jew and sprinkles his speech with disparaging remarks against Jews (*UWE*, pp. 208, 287).

Given this mixed evidence on Conrad's attitudes toward Jews, there is bound to be some uncertainty about Hirsch's role in the novel. It is nevertheless unaccountable that the central dramatic fact in Hirsch's career should be so widely misinterpreted. It has been said that Hirsch is an example of contemptible fear, that his dying act of spitting in his torturer Sotillo's face is an involuntary spasm, and that his last appearance—hanging from a beam—reduces him to the grotesque. One can maintain that Conrad's attitude toward Hirsch is not one of contempt but of ironic sympathy, and that his account of Hirsch's final moments demands of us something more than sympathy—perhaps tragic awe. It is important to make this adjustment of critical perspective because to a large degree Hirsch is evaluated through Nostromo's eyes. Insofar as the latter represents the people, the relationship of these characters is an imaginative portrayal of the position of the Jews in modern society, particularly in relation to the revolutionary class.

Hirsch begins in isolation from the community and stands apart from its political struggles. When Gould refuses his business propositions (because he is a Jew, it has been suggested), "He enveloped in a swift mental malediction the whole country, with all its inhabitants, partisans of Ribiera and Montero alike" (p. 203). But his attempt to escape political commitment and save his

---

[1] It does not alter the point to note that Conrad took the portrait of the innkeeper from the Polish classic, *Pan Tadeuz*, by Adam Mickiewicz (see Krzyżanowski, *Joseph Conrad*, p. 54).

own neck only lands him at the heart of the action, concealed in the boat in which Nostromo and Decoud transport the silver. Eventually he falls into the hands of one of the military chiefs who are invading Sulaco, and the anti-Semitic propensities of military dictators are given a chance to show themselves.

The significance of Hirsch's suffering under torture is defined by the difference between Monygham's reaction to it and Nostromo's. Monygham has been held by F. R. Leavis to be a figure of "ideal purpose" (in contrast to Decoud, who lacks "ideal purpose"), but whatever we may call the Doctor's devotion to Mrs. Gould, it leads him to general contempt for and immoral use of others. (Conrad explains it as based on Monygham's sense of degradation after betraying others under torture.) Nostromo is especially aware of this contempt in Monygham's indifference to the presumed loss of the silver, in his mocking suggestion that Nostromo steal the treasure, and in his final use of the hero to carry the call for help to Barrios' army. Toward Hirsch, Monygham acts similarly, suggesting to Sotillo that the treasure has been hidden and that Hirsch knows its whereabouts, thus instigating the torture. For Monygham, the Jew is expendable: "I confess I did not give a thought to Hirsch," he says in answer to Nostromo's accusations (p. 439).

Nostromo, on the contrary, is deeply moved by Hirsch's death and swears: "You man of fear! . . . you shall be avenged by me—Nostromo" (p. 461). It is difficult to accept this identification of the man of courage with his opposite, the coward, unless we also interpret Hirsch's final act of spitting in his tormentor's face as an act of heroic defiance born of despair. The social implication of Nostromo's resolve to avenge Hirsch is that the people, whom he represents, may ultimately accept the Jew as part of the community—that the Jew may one day overcome his alienation.

Bibliography

I. WORKS BY CONRAD

The Collected Edition of the Works of Joseph Conrad. London, 1946 ff.

CONRAD, JOSEPH.   *The Secret Agent: Drama in Four Acts.* London, 1923.

————. *The Secret Agent,* in *Ridgeway's: A Militant Weekly for God and Country,* I (1906–7).

CONRAD, JOSEPH, and HUEFFER, FORD MADOX.   *The Inheritors.* Garden City, N.Y., 1914.

————. *The Nature of a Crime.* Garden City, N.Y., 1924.

Conrad to a Friend: 150 Selected Letters from Joseph Conrad to Richard Curle. Edited by Richard Curle. New York, 1928.

Conrad's Polish Background: Letters to and from Polish Friends. Edited by Zdzisław Najder, translated by Halina Carroll. London, New York, and Toronto, 1964.

Joseph Conrad: Letters to William Blackwood and David S. Meldrum. Edited by William Blackburn. Durham, N.C., 1958.

Joseph Conrad: Life and Letters. Edited by Gérard Jean-Aubry. 2 vols. London, 1927.

Joseph Conrad's Letters to His Wife. Preface by Jessie Conrad. London, 1927.

Letter to Ramsay MacDonald, May 27, 1924. Henry W. and Albert A. Berg Collection, New York Public Library.

Letters from Joseph Conrad, 1895–1924. Edited by Edward Garnett. London, 1928.

Letters of Joseph Conrad to Marguerite Poradowska, 1890–1920. Translated and edited by John A. Gee and Paul J. Sturm. New Haven, 1940.

Lettres françaises. Edited by Georges Jean-Aubry. Paris, 1930.

WINAWER, BRUNO.   *The Book of Job: A Satirical Comedy.* Translated by Joseph Conrad. London and Toronto, 1931.

II. WORKS ON CONRAD *(selected for relevance to his politics)*

ALLEN, JERRY.   *The Sea Years of Joseph Conrad.* Garden City, N.Y., 1965.

BAINES, JOCELYN.   *Joseph Conrad: A Critical Biography.* London, 1960.

BROTMAN, JORDAN L.   "Joseph Conrad: Social Critic." Unpublished Ph.D. dissertation, University of California (Berkeley), 1955.

CONRAD, JESSIE.   *Joseph Conrad and His Circle.* London, 1935.

————. *Joseph Conrad As I Knew Him.* New York, 1926.

CONRAD, JOSEPH.   *Tales of Heroes and History.* Edited by Morton Dauwen Zabel. Garden City, N.Y., 1960.

DEAN, LEONARD F. (ed.).   *Joseph Conrad's Heart of Darkness: Backgrounds and Criticisms.* Englewood Cliffs, N.J., 1960.

FORD, FORD MADOX [Hueffer].   *Joseph Conrad: A Personal Remembrance.* London, 1924.

————. *Portraits from Life.* New York and Boston, 1937.

————. *Return to Yesterday.* New York, 1932.

GORDAN, JOHN D.   *Joseph Conrad: The Making of a Novelist.* Cambridge, Mass., 1940.

GUERARD, ALBERT J.   *Conrad the Novelist.* Cambridge, Mass., 1958.

GURKO, LEO.   *Joseph Conrad: Giant in Exile.* New York, 1962.

HAGAN, JOHN H., JR.   "The Design of Conrad's *The Secret Agent,*" *ELH–A Journal of English Literary History,* XXII (1955), 148–64.

HAUGH, ROBERT F.   *Joseph Conrad: Discovery in Design.* Norman, Okla., 1957.

HAUSERMANN, HANS W.   *The Genevese Background: Studies of Shelley, Francis Danby, Maria Edgeworth, Ruskin, Meredith, and Joseph Conrad in Geneva.* London, 1952.

HAY, ELOISE KNAPP.   *The Political Novels of Joseph Conrad: A Critical Study.* Chicago and London, 1963.

HEWITT, DOUGLAS.   *Joseph Conrad: A Reassessment.* Philadelphia, 1952.

HOWE, IRVING.   *Politics and the Novel.* New York, 1960.

JEAN-AUBRY, GÉRARD.   *The Sea Dreamer: A Definitive Biography of Joseph Conrad.* Translated by Helen Sebba. London, 1957.

Joseph Conrad Korzeniowski: Essays and Studies. (*The Neophilological Quarterly* [*Kwartalnik Neofilologiczny*], Special Number.) Warsaw, 1958.

KARL, FREDERICK R.   *A Reader's Guide to Joseph Conrad.* New York, 1960.

KRZYŻANOWSKI, LUDWIK (ed.).   *Joseph Conrad: Centennial Essays.* New York, 1960.

LEAVIS, F. R.   *The Great Tradition.* New York, 1948.

LEE, RICHARD E.   "The Political and Social Ideas of Joseph Conrad." Unpublished Ph.D. dissertation, New York University, 1954.

LOHF, KENNETH A., and SHEEHY, EUGENE P. (eds.).   *Joseph Conrad at Mid-Century: Editions and Studies, 1895–1955.* Minneapolis, 1957.

MÉGROZ, R. L.   *Joseph Conrad's Mind and Method: A Study of Personality in Art.* London, 1931.

MORF, GUSTAV.   *The Polish Heritage of Joseph Conrad.* London, n.d. [1930].

PETERKIEWICZ, JERZY.   "Patriotic Irritability: Conrad and Poland: For the Centenary," *Twentieth Century*, CLXII (1957), 545–57.

RETINGER, JOSEPH H.   *Conrad and His Contemporaries: Souvenirs.* London, 1941.

SAID, EDWARD W.   *Joseph Conrad and the Fiction of Autobiography.* Cambridge, Mass., 1966.

SHERRY, NORMAN.   *Conrad's Eastern World.* Cambridge, 1966.

STALLMAN, ROBERT W. (ed.).   *The Art of Joseph Conrad: A Critical Symposium.* East Lansing, Mich., 1960.

TANNER, TONY.   *Conrad: Lord Jim.* ("Barron's Educational Series.") Woodbury, N.Y. [and London], 1963.

————.   "Nightmare and Complacency: Razumov and the Western Eye," *Critical Quarterly*, IV (1962), 197–215.

TILLYARD, E. M. W.   *The Epic Strain in the English Novel.* London, 1958.

TRILLING, LIONEL.   "On the Modern Element in Modern Literature," *Partisan Review*, XXVIII (1961), 9–36.

UJEJSKI, JÓZEF.   *Joseph Conrad.* Translated by Pierre Duméril. Paris, 1939.

VAN GHENT, DOROTHY.   *The English Novel: Form and Function.* New York, 1961.

WARREN, ROBERT PENN.   Introduction to *Nostromo.* New York, 1951.

WOHLFARTH. PAUL.   "Joseph Conrad and Germany," *German Life and Letters*, XVI, n.s. (1963), 81–88.

III. POLITICAL REFERENCES

AFRICA

CROWE, S. E.   *The Berlin West Africa Conference: 1884–1885.* London, New York, and Toronto, 1942.

DELCOMMUNE, ALEXANDRE.   *L'Avenir du Congo Belge Menacé.* Brussels, 1919.

GIDE, ANDRÉ.   "Voyage au Congo Belge: Carnets de Route," *Journal: 1939–1949: Souvenirs.* Pléiade edition, Paris, 1954. Pp. 679–864.

MILLE, PIERRE.   "L'Enfer du Congo Léopoldien," *Cahiers de la Quinzaine,* 7th ser., No. 6.

MOREL, E. D.   *Red Rubber.* London, 1907.

PYRAH, G. B.   *Imperial Policy and South Africa: 1902–10.* Oxford, 1955.

ROBINSON, RONALD, and GALLAGHER, JOHN.   *Africa and the Victorians: The Climax of Imperialism in the Dark Continent.* New York and London, 1961. (Later editions are subtitled *The Official Mind of Imperialism.*)

TWAIN, MARK [Samuel L. Clemens].   *King Leopold's Soliloquy: A Defense of His Congo Rule.* Boston, 1905.

EAST INDIES

BARING-GOULD, S., and BAMPFYLDE, C. A.   *A History of Sarawak under Its Two White Rajahs: 1839–1908.* 2 vols. London, 1909.

BRUHAT, JEAN.   *Histoire de l'Indonésie.* Paris, 1958.

CLIFFORD, SIR HUGH.   *A Prince of Malaya.* New York, 1926.

DAY, CLIVE.   *The Policy and Administration of the Dutch in Java.* New York and London, 1904.

DEKLERCK, E. W.   *History of the Netherlands East Indies.* 2 vols. Rotterdam, 1938.

KEPPEL, HENRY.   *The Expedition to Borneo of H.M.S. Dido for the Suppression of Piracy: With Extracts from the Journal of James Brooke, Esq.* 2 vols. London, 1846.

MUNDY, RODNEY.   *Narrative of Events in Borneo and Celebes, Down to the Occupation of Labuan: From the Journals of James Brooke, Esq.* 2 vols. London, 1848.

PAYNE, ROBERT.   *The White Rajahs of Sarawak.* New York, 1960.

RENGERS, D. W. VAN WELDEREN.   *The Failure of a Liberal Colonial Policy: Netherlands East Indies. 1816–1830.* The Hague, 1947.

RUNCIMAN, STEVEN.   *The White Rajahs: A History of Sarawak from 1841 to 1946.* Cambridge, 1960.

SCHRIEKE, B. (ed.).   *The Effect of Western Influence on Native Civilizations in the Malay Archipelago.* Batavia, 1929.

VLEKKE, BERNARD H. M.   *Nusantara: A History of the East Indian Archipelago.* Cambridge, Mass., 1943.

WALLACE, ALFRED RUSSEL.   *The Malay Archipelago.* London and New York, 1894.

———.   *The Revolt of Democracy.* London and New York, 1913.

IMPERIALISM

BENNETT, GEORGE (ed.). *The Concept of Empire: Burke to Attlee, 1774–1947.* London, 1953.

Cambridge Modern History, The. Edited by A. W. Ward, G. W. Prothero, and Stanley Leathes. Vols. XI and XII. Cambridge, 1909.

HOBSON, J. A. *Imperialism: A Study.* London, 1905.

HOWE, SUSANNE. *Novels of Empire.* New York, 1949.

JAMES, ROBERT R. *Lord Randolph Churchill.* London, 1959.

SCHUMPETER, JOSEPH. *Imperialism and Social Classes.* Translated by Heinz Norden. New York, 1960.

THORNTON, A. P. *The Imperial Idea and Its Enemies: A Study in British Power.* New York and London, 1959.

LATIN AMERICA

EASTWICK, E. B. *Venezuela: Or, Sketches of Life in a South American Republic.* 2d ed. London, 1868.

MASTERMAN, GEORGE FREDERICK. *Seven Eventful Years in Paraguay: A Narrative of Personal Experience amongst the Paraguayans.* London, 1870.

MUNRO, DANA GARDNER. *The Latin American Republics: A History.* New York, 1960.

RIPPY, J. FRED. *The Capitalists and Colombia.* New York, 1931.

ORGANICISM

ARNOLD, MATTHEW. *Culture and Anarchy.* Edited by J. Dover Wilson. Cambridge, 1952.

BAKER, JOSEPH E. (ed.). *The Reinterpretation of Victorian Literature.* Princeton, 1950.

BOSANQUET, BERNARD. *Aspects of the Social Problem.* London and New York, 1895.

———. *The Philosophical Theory of the State.* London and New York, 1899.

BRADLEY, F. H. *Ethical Studies.* 2d ed. rev. Oxford, 1927.

BRINTON, CRANE. *English Political Thought in the Nineteenth Century.* Cambridge, Mass., 1949.

———. *The Political Ideas of the English Romanticists.* Oxford, 1926.

BURKE, EDMUND. *Reflections on the French Revolution.* Everyman's Library. London and New York, 1910.

COBBAN, ALFRED. *Edmund Burke and the Revolt against the Eighteenth Century.* 2d ed. New York, 1960.

———. *Rousseau and the Modern State.* 2d ed. Hamden, Conn., 1961.

COLERIDGE, SAMUEL TAYLOR. *Aids to Reflection and the Confessions of an Inquiring Spirit. To Which Are Added His Essays on Faith and the Book of Common Prayer, etc.* London and New York, 1893.

DAVIE, DONALD. *The Heyday of Sir Walter Scott.* London, 1961.

DeLAURA, DAVID J. "Arnold and Carlyle," *Publications of the Modern Language Association of America,* LXXIX (1964), 104–29.

ELIOT, GEORGE. *Essays of George Eliot.* Edited by Thomas Pinney. New York and London, 1963.

FORBES, DUNCAN.   *The Liberal Anglican Idea of History.* Cambridge, 1952.
HOLLOWAY, JOHN.   *The Victorian Sage: Studies in Argument.* New York, 1965.
JONES, W. T.   *The Romantic Syndrome: Toward a New Method in Cultural Anthropology and History of Ideas.* The Hague, 1961.
MILNE, A. J. M.   *The Social Philosophy of English Idealism.* London, 1962.
MUELLER, IRIS W.   *John Stuart Mill and French Thought.* Urbana, Ill., 1956.
MUIRHEAD, J. H. (ed.).   *Bernard Bosanquet and His Friends.* London, 1935.
————.   *Coleridge as Philosopher.* London and New York, 1930.
————.   *The Service of the State: Four Lectures on the Political Teaching of T. H. Green.* London, 1908.
PARIS, BERNARD J.   *Experiments in Life: George Eliot's Quest for Values.* Detroit, Mich., 1965.
PFANNENSTILL, BERTIL.   *Bernard Bosanquet's Philosophy of the State: A Historical and Systematical Study.* Lund, 1936.
PREYER, ROBERT.   *Bentham, Coleridge and the Science of History.* ("Beiträge zur Englischen Philologie," Vol. XII.) Bochum-Langendreer, 1958.
RICHTER, MELVIN.   *The Politics of Conscience: T. H. Green and His Age.* London, 1964.
ROUSSEAU, JEAN-JACQUES.   *The Social Contract.* Translated by G. D. H. Cole. London, 1913.
RUGGIERO, GUIDO DE.   *The History of European Liberalism.* Translated by R. G. Collingwood. London, 1927.
STRAUSS, LEO.   *Natural Right and History.* Chicago, 1953.
TRILLING, LIONEL.   *Matthew Arnold.* New York, 1955.
WELSH, ALEXANDER.   *The Hero of the Waverly Novels.* New Haven and London, 1963.
WHITE, R. J. (ed.).   *Political Tracts of Wordsworth, Coleridge, and Shelley.* Cambridge, 1953.
————.   *The Conservative Tradition.* London, 1950.
WILLIAMS, RAYMOND.   *Culture and Society: 1780–1950.* New York, 1960.
WOLLHEIM, RICHARD.   *F. H. Bradley.* Harmondsworth, 1959.
WOODRING, CARL R.   *Politics in the Poetry of Coleridge.* Madison, Wisc., 1961.

POLAND

Cambridge History of Poland, The. Edited by W. F. Reddaway *et al.* 2 vols. Cambridge, 1950–51.
COATES, W. P., and COATES, ZELDA K.   *Six Centuries of Russo-Polish Relations.* London, 1948.
HAYES, CARLTON J. H.   *The Historical Evolution of Modern Nationalism.* New York, 1931.
HERMAN, MAXIME.   *Histoire de la Littérature Polonaise (dès Origines à 1961).* Paris, 1963.
KOHN, HANS.   *Pan-Slavism: Its History and Ideology.* Rev. ed. New York, 1960.
KRIDL, MANFRED (ed.).   *An Anthology of Polish Literature.* New York and London, 1964.
LEWINSKI-CORWIN, EDWARD H.   *The Political History of Poland.* New York, 1917.

REVOLUTION

ANDERSON, ROBERT.   *Sidelights on the Home Rule Movement.* London, 1906.
BERDYAEV, NICOLAS.   *The Origins of Russian Communism.* London, 1955.
BROGAN, D. W.   *The Price of Revolution.* London, 1951.
CARR, E. H.   *Michael Bakunin.* London, 1937.
CASSELL, RICHARD A.   *Ford Madox Ford: A Study of His Novels.* Baltimore, 1961.
COLE, G. D. H.   *A History of Socialist Thought.* 5 vols. London and New York, 1956.
English Review, The. Vol. I (1908–9).
FORD [HUEFFER], FORD MADOX.   *England and the English: An Interpretation.* New York, 1907.
GARDINER, A. G.   *The Life of Sir William Harcourt.* 2 vols. New York, n.d.
GOLDRING, DOUGLAS.   *Trained for Genius: The Life and Writings of Ford Madox Ford.* New York, 1949. [Title of British edition: *The Last Pre-Rafaelite.*]
HALÉVY, ELIE.   *A History of the English People in the Nineteenth Century.* Translated by E. I. Watkin and D. A. Barker. 6 vols. New York, 1961.
Marx and Engels: Basic Writings on Politics and Philosophy. Edited by Lewis S. Feuer. Garden City, N.Y., 1959.
SCHWITZGUÉBEL, A.   *La police politique fédérale. Collection de brochures populaires à un sou.* Geneva, 1879.
THOMANN, CHARLES.   *Le mouvement anarchiste dans les montagnes neuchâteloises et le Jura bernois.* La Chaux-de-Fonds, 1947.
VASSILYEV, A. T.   *The Ochrana: The Russian Secret Police.* Edited by René Fülöp-Miller. Philadelphia, 1930.
VENTURI, FRANCO.   *Roots of Revolution: A History of the Populist and Socialist Movements in Nineteenth Century Russia.* Translated by Francis Haskell. New York, 1960.
WELLS, H. G.   *A Modern Utopia.* London, n.d. [1905].
———.   *The Outline of History.* New York, 1929.

Index

Avrom Fleishman, *Conrad's Politics: Community and Anarchy in the Fiction of Joseph Conrad*

Designed by Gerard A. Valerio

Composed in American Garamond by Baltimore Type and Composition Corporation

Printed offset by Universal Lithographers, Inc., on 60 lb. Perkins and Squier

Bound by The Maple Press Company in G.S.B., S/535